B·L·O·O·D
M·O·N·E·Y

B·L·O·O·D
M·O·N·E·Y

*The Story of the Baroness
de Stempel Scandal*

KATE WHARTON

ILLINGWORTH·REMEMBERS

EBURY PRESS
London

First published by Ebury Press
an imprint of the Random Century Group
Random Century House
20 Vauxhall Bridge Road
London SW1V 2SA

British Library Cataloguing in Publication Data
Wharton, Kate
Blood money : the story of the Baroness de Stempel
scandal.
1. Fraud – Biographies – Collections
I. Title
364.1630922

ISBN 0-85223-975-0

Typeset in Sabon by Tek Art Limited, Croydon, Surrey

Printed and bound in Great Britain by
Mackays of Chatham Plc, Kent

C·O·N·T·E·N·T·S

Acknowledgements

Many people have helped with this book. First, let me thank those kind people in Herefordshire and Shropshire who gave unstintingly of their time: Veronica and Geoffrey Bowater, Jane and Ken Davison, Susan Savery, William Ripley, Brigadier and Susan Sole, Lady Ransome, Marie Louise Osborne, Avis Ades, Mary Jo Corfield, Susan Evans, Ben Scott, along with many others.

Similarly, I would like to thank the villagers of Markington who spoke so movingly of Lady Illingworth and Mr 'Bill'. My thanks, too, to Albert Oslar, Lady Illingworth's ex-chauffeur.

My journalistic colleagues, such as Jon Griffin, Craig Seton, Nick Hobdell and David Graves, were always ready to discuss aspects of the story with enthusiasm and generosity that greatly helped both during the trials and afterwards. The West Mercia Fraud Squad and members of the West Mercia CID were always courteous and as co-operative as they could be within the strict confines of their position.

I am most grateful, too, to Rowena Webb, my editor at Ebury Press, who put up with panics and varying emotions always with sense and sensibility. Last, and as far from least as it is possible to get, I would like to especially thank Kate Clarke, herself the author of two classic crime books, *Murder at the Priory* (with Bernard Grafton) and *The Pimlico Murder*, for her unfailing assistance and interest throughout the writing of this book.

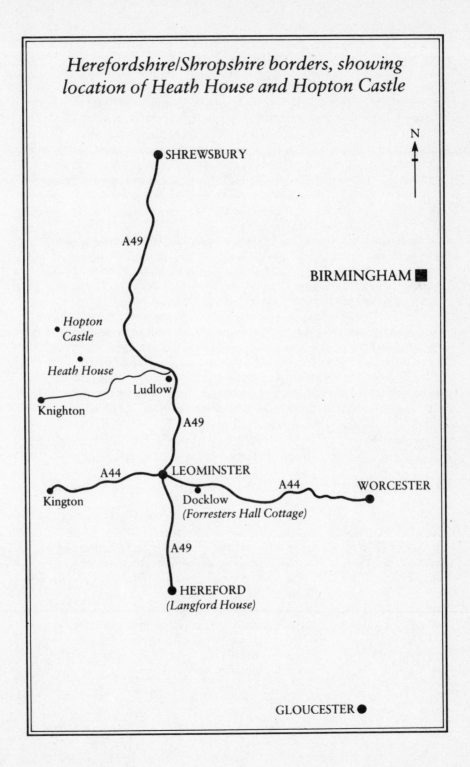

Herefordshire/Shropshire borders, showing location of Heath House and Hopton Castle

Diary of Events

1900	Margaret Wilberforce born
1931	Margaret Wilberforce marries Lord Illingworth
1934	Susan Wilberforce born
1957	Susan Wilberforce marries Simon Dale
1959	Susan Dale buys Heath House
1972	Susan Dale petitions for divorce
1973	Divorce granted. Susan Dale leaves Heath House for mother's house at Weobley
1977	Susan Dale (now Wilberforce) moves to Forresters Hall, Docklow
29 February 1984	Lady Illingworth visits Docklow for 'holiday'
17 June 1984	Lady Illingworth's will forged at Docklow
11 September 1984	Susan Wilberforce marries Baron de Stempel in Jersey
6 December 1984	Lady Illingworth moves to Hereford General Hospital
6 November 1986	Lady Illingworth dies in Langford House, Hereford
December 1986	Baron and Baroness de Stempel divorce
11 September 1987	Simon Dale murdered at Heath House
7 December 1987	Baroness de Stempel, Marcus and Sophia Wilberforce arrested
14 December 1987	Baron and Baroness de Stempel, Marcus and Sophia charged with fraud
6 January 1988	Baroness, Marcus and Sophia charged with murder
27 January 1988	Murder charges against Marcus and Sophia dropped
4 January 1989	Committal proceedings at Bromyard Magistrates Court
18 July 1989	Murder trial commences at Worcester Crown Court
1 August 1989	Baroness acquitted of murder and manslaughter
6 December 1989	Baroness pleads guilty to forgery and theft
19 February 1990	Fraud trial commences at Birmingham Crown Court
19 April 1990	Baron found guilty
21 April 1990	Marcus and Sophia found guilty. Sentencing.
12 May 1990	Writs issued on behalf of Illingworth estate
19 May 1990	Memorial service for Simon Dale at St Edward's Church, Hopton Castle

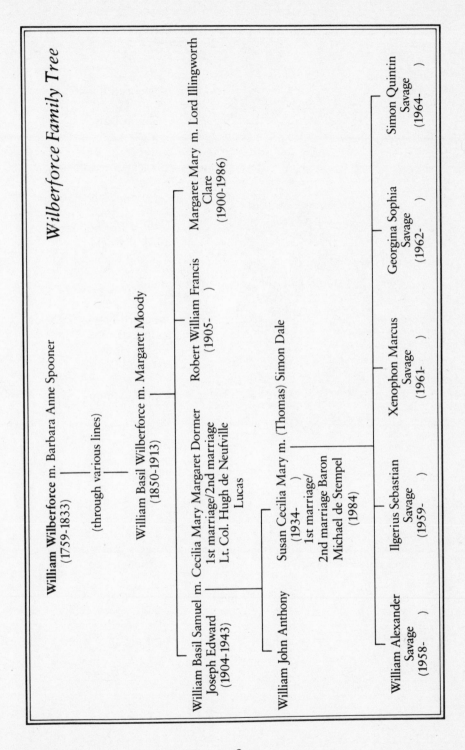

Wilberforce Family Tree

William Wilberforce m. Barbara Anne Spooner
(1759-1833)

(through various lines)

William Basil Wilberforce m. Margaret Moody
(1850-1913)

Robert William Francis
(1905-   )

Margaret Mary m. Lord Illingworth
Clare
(1900-1986)

William Basil Samuel m. Cecilia Mary Margaret Dormer
Joseph Edward   1st marriage/2nd marriage
(1904-1943)   Lt. Col. Hugh de Neufville
                                    Lucas

William John Anthony

Susan Cecilia Mary m. (Thomas) Simon Dale
(1934-   )
1st marriage/
2nd marriage Baron
Michael de Stempel
(1984)

William Alexander
Savage
(1958-   )

Ilgerius Sebastian
Savage
(1959-   )

Xenophon Marcus
Savage
(1961-   )

Georgina Sophia
Savage
(1962-   )

Simon Quintin
Savage
(1964-   )

S·O·M·E O·N·E

Some one came knocking
   At my wee, small door;
Some one came knocking,
   I'm sure – sure – sure;
I listened, I opened,
   I looked to left and right,
But nought there was a-stirring
   In the still dark night;
Only the busy beetle
   Tap-tapping in the wall,
Only from the forest
   The screech-owl's call,
Only the cricket whistling
   While the dewdrops fall,
So I know not who came knocking,
   At all, at all, at all.

              Walter de la Mare

I·N·T·R·O·D·U·C·T·I·O·N

Against the harsh, intimidating architecture of Risley Remand Centre, with its high perimeter wall of solid yellow concrete and its stained interiors, Susan de Stempel looks paper-thin. After more than eight hundred days in custody her complexion presents the pale, parchmenty texture common to most prison inmates. Only the eyes are as carefully made-up as ever with shadow, liner and mascara, and the mouth lipsticked. Her hair is as black as a raven's wing. There is something curiously old-fashioned about the grand remnants of her beauty. Here is a face that thinks of its appearance in terms that were current thirty, forty years ago, even longer. She is sadly conscious, she makes a point of saying, that 'the face is gone', 'the neck is gone'. She talks of herself as belonging to an era when a woman's looks were the greatest sum of what she possessed.

Waiting to see her in the little room next to the visiting hall – a room heaped high with large, ugly stuffed toys, reminding one that this is where children visit their mothers – I look up and there she is, escorted by one of the prison staff to a line of tables flanked by simple wooden chairs. We sit opposite each other, sometimes in the middle of a row, sometimes at the end, but always within earshot of a staffer or 'screw', as she unhesitatingly calls them. We talk in deliberately low voices, which heightens the dramatic effect if making it very difficult to hear. Her voice is a 'small' one anyway, which at the murder trial became at times impossible to distinguish in the grand confines but bad acoustics of Worcester County Court. Frequently I am reminded of the muttered whispers of after-dark talking at school.

Ruefully, she apologizes for always wearing the same outfit: a beige tweed skirt, brown shoes and stockings, a blue and white patterned blouse with a little round collar, a bright blue sailcloth top – the kind you get at 'arty' shops – and a white woollen scarf which she time and time again rearranges round her neck. Pale she may be and the eyes, despite the careful lining, slightly too sunken for a

11

woman of her age, but prison life has not daunted her spirit. Rather, one feels in a curious way that she enjoys the endless though quiet confrontation between herself and the prison staff. There is an attitude of silent contempt on her side. There is something too of the stubborn, rebellious child still in her and it shows in the cool, deliberately off-hand manner with which she greets any remarks from the 'screws'. She has the ability, one senses, to distance herself from the bare, ugly walls around her and, one thinks, the bare, ugly facts about her.

An ex-prisoner who shared the confines of Pucklechurch Remand Centre, near Bristol, for two months with her while she was on remand for murder described her as weird. 'She just sat there sewing, never speaking. She called herself Cecilia even though the name on her cell was Susan. She would stay in her room all the time like a recluse. She looked sad and miserable and wore tatty old clothes, a shirt or a blouse and a dirty old jacket. The most you got out of her was "Nice day". That's as far as any conversation went.' To this same prisoner Susan de Stempel appeared 'a bit of snob. I think she looked on herself as not like a real criminal. I think she was a very unhappy woman. She was very withdrawn. I never once saw her smile. No one heard her talk about her background. She never boasted that she had been well-to-do. You would have thought she was an ordinary person.'

Some might think that, many would not. Few who attended either the murder trial or the fraud trial came away with the impression that Susan de Stempel was ordinary. I did not myself. Far from it. The more I saw her, the more curious and enigmatic she became. Easy to see why she called herself by her second name, Cecilia – Susan belonged somewhere else, outside, the real world; easy to understand why she should distance herself from the loud pop music, the lesbian fights and dope-taking she said she witnessed all round her. Other facts about her were rather harder to comprehend.

Only once did she refer to the future, when I asked her what she would do when the time came for parole. She laughed in a slightly sarcastic, rather low-voltage way: 'I don't think I'll take parole. It's not really freedom in my view. I'd rather have all or nothing at all. I think that's a Wilberforce feeling coming out in me.' For a moment the boldness left her face as she added, 'I do worry slightly about the hate mail I might get. Also, my cottage at Docklow has twice been vandalized. Only a few weeks ago someone broke in and stole stuff and scratched graffiti over the walls. I don't want to go back to that.'

*

For nearly two weeks in 1989, at the height of a blazing English summer, and subsequently the following February for a protracted nine-week hearing, Britain was enthralled by the dark revelations of the de Stempel scandal, reminiscent of the worst excesses of Jacobean tragedy. Murder, anger, envy, sexual perversion, corruption – every aspect of human betrayal was highlighted as the circumstances of the murder of Simon Dale and the defrauding and 'dumping' of Lady Illingworth were disclosed before a fascinated public.

I was present at both the murder and the fraud trials and became intrigued. I had to find the link between the woman I had met before the trials commenced and the self-confessed liar and forger who emerged at the end of them. For they were not the same. I had first met Susan de Stempel nearly a year before the murder trial, when she was already remanded in custody at Pucklechurch. I read the first accounts of her arrest with avid interest and went to spend a few days in Shropshire and Herefordshire to find out more of her background. Those few days were enough to hook me. So, in June 1988, after obtaining through her solicitor exclusive rights to the story, I drove to Pucklechurch to see her.

We had already exchanged smiles and nods at some of the interim court hearings when the Crown Prosecution Service asked for extra time in preparing its case, but this was the first time I was to experience the 'quiet voice' and that secretive smile that seemed directed more against the world than to the person sharing her conversation. Her youngest son, Simon, was also present. We talked of flying and the special flying maps she was not allowed to have – presumably, she laughed, because *they* thought she might be planning a break-out. We did not discuss the case – I had promised not to do so until it was over. She had a sort of gallantry and a sense of the grotesque that I enjoyed. She had charm. And she had the ability to enlist sympathy.

As the weeks and months rolled by, however, and the full facts of the cases emerged a very different portrait of Susan de Stempel appeared. Cunning replaced charm, evil replaced enigma, deviousness replaced defiance. It was as if, given the same canvas, another artist had painted a totally different portrait on it: a portrait of a woman obsessed with money and possessions, driven with envy of half her family, driven to madness by sexual jealousy. A woman whose scheming involved all who touched her, whose convolutions of lies and deception amazed even worldly barristers. A woman who is hated, it is now said, by the two children she corrupted.

Her story has been compared to an Agatha Christie novel, but is in fact far more redolent of the novels of such subtle purveyors of evil as Georges Simenon or Ruth Rendell. It is their exposés of greed and destruction which characterize this story, rather than Christie's simple tales of bodies and butlers. It is an ironic fact, however, that Susan de Stempel gave as part of her alibi for the night her husband was murdered that she had been in bed watching a television adaptation of *Murder at the Vicarage*.

1

T·H·E M·U·R·D·E·R

HEATH House is beautiful despite its bloody history, a house that in a peculiar anthropomorphic way is as much a character in the following events as the human personalities that inhabited it and were so profoundly affected by it, dominated by it – and who continue to be dominated by it. Each time I have come to see it its beauty has held me as strongly as it held others. Right now it sits gracefully in the deep green of midsummer. As the afternoon gives way to evening, rabbits duck and weave and play in the uncut grass on the north side. A laburnum tree in full suburban flower stands incongruously behind a pink-petalled rhododendron. The lawn is thick with buttercups and daisies. The drive off the main road that runs between Leintwardine and Bucknell on the border land of Herefordshire and Shropshire, is, however, dark and forbidding. I have abandoned my car at the roadside with trepidation and dislike the walk down through tall trees. First to come in sight is the cottage next to the house: it looks dismal despite a thick coat of bright blue paint that has been lavished on doors and window frames. It's the wrong blue for a country cottage and does nothing to camouflage its dilapidation.

Out on the south side of the house the Queen Anne front glows gracefully as it was meant to do, looking out over the far Welsh hills with patrician affection. The topiaried hedge that bounds the garden does not look too ragged, while the glorious copper beeches that block the view on the south-west are in magnificent leaf. A cursory view from the south side might give the impression that the house was well and good. Even the shuttered windows would not dispel that thought. After all, people go away for a time, don't they?

It is on the north side that the atmosphere clouds and gives rise to feelings of melancholy and neglect. Here is a house that is forlorn, its pride vanquished. Here one knows that something is wrong, that the house is locked and empty for bad reasons. A line of tall, unkempt

15

potted geraniums left carelessly along a wall suggests long-term human absence. The ground-floor windows are shuttered and locked. Even the bright red of the famous kitchen door does nothing to alleviate the brooding, malevolent presence that still hangs in the air, three years after the events of this story occurred.

This time, peculiarly, I feel it is not a time to stand and stare at the house, trying to feel my way back. Perhaps it is too near the anniversary of the murder. My dog growls and whines in an uncharacteristic way. Does she, too, feel ghosts walking near her?

Yet the last time I was here I felt nothing like this. It was wintertime, and thousands of snowdrops bobbed their little white heads in the cold breeze. The trees were stripped, the drive less dank and dark. It was not frightening. Rather, one felt the winter had purified everything. All seemed forgotten, even forgiven. And spring lay ahead.

Light came reluctantly to start the day on Friday, 11 September 1987. It crept gradually first through the tallest trees showing up the dark copper hues of the beeches on the south-west side of the sleeping, shuttered house. It meandered through the fruit trees in the orchard on the south-east, revealing the beehives set amongst them, descending finally to the dark green of the yew hedge that had been carefully cut within the last few weeks. Inside the house, room after room picked up the light without reaction. Nothing moved. No one stirred and turned in their beds, muttered and went back to sleep again. The light grew, revealing rooms for what they were: attic rooms designed for servants but now empty save for a few beds and bits of furniture, bathrooms empty of even toothbrushes, face flannels and towels. It crept down the great staircase to the grand rooms of the house – the library, the drawing room, a vast master bedroom with a huge four-poster bed tucked under an even larger canopy in the Egyptian style. Nobody stirred in the huge bed. It had not been slept in for over fourteen years.

But in a smaller bedroom, in a single-size four-poster, the man of the house turned and turned again and woke up. He raised his head from the pillow and sniffed the air. The scent of the day, the feel of the light upon his face told him it was gone eight o'clock. It was time to get up, time for breakfast. And breakfast, like all his other meals, had become an important part of his day. Sometimes he worried slightly about the importance they were taking on. After all, gluttony was not simply overeating – it was the passion people brought to their food that was as much the sin as the overindulgence. Or so he

16

had been told. He laughed slightly. Overindulgence was not likely to be part of his days, not now, not in the foreseeable future. The bread of life – literally speaking – was the mainstay of his diet. Though supper last night had been a different thing. Good meat and vegetables, pudding, decent cheese and a highly drinkable wine. Because it was not his everyday sustenance, it had tasted all the better. The company, too, had been good, the conversation lively. Thinking it over was a good start to the day.

Down in the blue-tiled kitchen, where the large refectory table took up so much space, he felt his way over the shutters on the east wall, releasing the catches as he came to them. More of the day's grey light filtered through. He could not see, but he knew from past memories what it would be like; neither the end of summer nor the gold of autumn, but a grey, grey day which is really the hallmark of the English climate, he thought. Still, not a bad light for seeing stones the colour they were, or English architecture the way it was. He had the imprint of the house so strongly in his brain that he didn't need eyes to see it again. All he had to do was pull the switch in his mind marked 'house' and the lovely sweet Queen Anne façade would pop up just as if he were running a lantern slide.

Back to food again. Was it cold enough to make porridge? Or would that signify that it was autumn, winter already. No, no, he had had a good dinner the night before – toast and marmalade would suffice. He turned on the wireless to hear the news, and the deliberately modulated voice of Radio 4's newsreader was ending the weather forecast. He caught the words 'light rain, drizzle, an area of low pressure' as he cut himself two slices of bread for toast. The coffee was already in the blue and white jug, waiting for the kettle to boil. He swung with ease from cupboard to table to cooker. Almost blind he might be, but a man knew his own house. He put butter and marmalade on the table, along with a knife and plate.

He made the coffee. It smelt good. Leave it two minutes before straining. Ah yes, there was nothing like it – that first cup of the day. Behind him the wireless continued to chatter and inform. He had heard it before and he would, he thought to himself, hear it again. His concerns were deeper, more fundamental. Besides, it was going to be a busy day, unusually busy for him. He thought of the day's programme and smiled. Such a lot to do. He snapped off the wireless and gulped the last mouthful of coffee, noticing that there was enough left in the pot for after lunch.

At the working end of the table there were a lot of papers he must put into order before Geoffrey arrived. He must check with Mary Jo what books needed to go back to the library. He must put his thoughts into order before he saw the osteopath. Really, far too little research had been done on the link between the brain and eyes and spinal cord. Far too little on robotic intelligence. He knew there was some interesting work going on in Edinburgh but as he couldn't get there, he'd have to wait and read whatever papers they published on the subject. He collected together his tall stick with the smooth place for his thumb, a thick coat – it was colder than he thought – and patted the back pocket of his trousers where his wallet was. Over the contact lenses already in place, he wore thick pebble spectacles. With these aids he could see a vague blur, a pinprick immediately in front of him – nothing else. But he had found it possible, just possible, with the additional help of a magnifying glass, to read a little. However, that might not be necessary in a few years' time.

What he had particularly enjoyed the previous evening was talking to the man from the Radar Establishment at Malvern, who had not pooh-poohed his theories that it might be possible to bypass the eyes altogether and imprint an image on the brain without them. This, of course, was leading to all sorts of other ideas about the brain itself. And now he had been told that this Mr Holding, the osteopath at Leominster, believed that he could help a patient's eyesight. Could it be by manipulation? Could that reinvigorate the optic nerve? It would be fascinating to hear his theories. Could there be hope that sight might return? It was a subject he had deliberately stopped himself thinking about. Better to get on with life as it was. Outside, Geoffrey gave the mildest of hoots to indicate he was there. The man put his coat on and carefully checked the lobby door and the front door. Outside he paused, and knew from his own instincts that she – that they – were not there. Not yet.

Conversation with Geoffrey was easy. They chatted about the previous evening, when both had been present. In fact, it had been Geoffrey and Veronica Bowater's idea for Simon Dale to meet 'the man from Malvern', as he was coming to be known. The big man thanked his friend. He was well aware of their many kindnesses, which would never be taken for granted. As they drove towards Leominster, Geoffrey worried audibly about the car. 'There's something the matter with it,' he said. 'I can't trace it exactly, but it's been going in fits and starts for the last few days. I had a look at the carburettor but couldn't find anything. It could be the petrol pump playing up. If so, let's hope it gets us to Leominster and back.'

Simon nodded and momentarily felt vulnerable, impotent. The wish to see the osteopath and concern at the same time for his friend vied in his mind. 'Don't worry,' said Geoffrey, sensing his thoughts. 'The old boot will get us there.'

The traffic in Leominster was bad – everybody, it seemed, had come to town that day. But then Friday was always a busy day. After all, it was the second largest town in the county and, as the locals were never tired of telling strangers, it was the place where the Mercian Earl Leofric founded a nunnery – him that was husband of the lady Godiva who had stripped and streaked through Nottingham mounted on a white horse. The first streaker in English history. At the Royal Oak they never stopped laughing at the story. It was enough to make you wince.

Simon liked Leominster. He had liked it in the days when he could see. It was not as grand as Ludlow, of course, but it was as good as Ledbury. He had spent a lot of time studying the priory church of St Peter, which was supposed to be sited on the spot where Leofric had built his nunnery. He had found the church stimulating from an architectural point of view: it was possible to trace from it the styles as they evolved from Norman to Perpendicular. And although it had been almost destroyed by fire in the last year of the seventeenth century they had had the sense to start rebuilding it almost immediately afterwards. And a long time they took over it, he chuckled to himself – over two hundred years. It had been completed by Gilbert Scott as short a time ago as the late nineteenth century.

But his favourite part of the church, one he did not tell the others, was a ducking stool which was used for 'disciplining scolds and tradesmen giving short measure'. The last time it had been used was in 1809, for a couple of bad-tempered nags called Jenny Pipes and Sarah Secke. He wondered if either had looked like his ex-wife, Susan, now the grandly titled Baroness de Stempel. Heath House could have done with a ducking stool, he thought. The trouble was that she was just as likely to have got *him* into it. He sighed, remembering how sour their marriage had become. It was long over now, but the anger in her could still frighten him.

'I'll wait for you and bring you back,' said Geoffrey. 'I'll probably nip into the Royal Oak at some point, but otherwise I'll be in the waiting room. It won't take that long, will it?'

Simon grunted. 'Not too long, I hope.'

He disappeared into a room furnished with what looked like modern instruments of torture, while Geoffrey settled himself with the *Daily Telegraph* he'd brought with him. More trouble in the Middle East, another case of IRA terrorism . . . he sank deeper in his chair.

They were on the way back, on the road between Leominster and Leintwardine, when the car got worse than ever – almost stopping, surging forward for a bit, then almost stopping again. Simon sat silently, aware that there was nothing he could do to help except get out and walk. 'I don't know how long this is going to last,' said Geoffrey. 'It could pack up at any moment. While you were seeing Holding I took the precaution of telephoning Mrs Corfield. She'll take you on to Heath House. I think I'm going to have to get this to my garage for them to deal with.' Simon thanked him with his usual rather old-world courtesy. It was, his friends agreed, one of the nice things about him that his disabilities had not soured his relationships with other people. He could and did thank very gracefully.

The big man knew more about Leintwardine, the nearest village of any size to Heath House, in Roman times than he did of it today. Oh yes, he had friends in the place whom he saw regularly, but his readings took him way back in time. Leintwardine they might call it, but *he* called it Bravonium, the name of the Roman fort that had once existed there. The church was built on Roman foundations, too. But then it was typical of the Romans to choose a site that was sheltered by the hills and watered by two rivers – the Clun and the Temme. The more he knew of the Romans, the more he respected them. But then the more he knew of previous settlers in this area, the more he respected them, too. It was the present century, he was inclined to think, that had fouled things up. History was a vital, living force – he had plans in that direction. Who knows what might lead from the people coming to see him later in the day?

Standing with his thumb stick outside Griffiths the butcher, Simon Dale was a familiar sight in the cheerful, bustly morning atmosphere of the village. He could hear the voices inside the shop exchanging pleasantries with Griffiths himself. A fine butcher, everyone agreed, best meat in the area. He didn't see Mary Jo Corfield as she approached; and nor, such were his thoughts, did he hear her say hello. Not until she took him by the arm and said 'Good morning' did he realize she was there.

'Ah, good morning,' he replied in that deep, loud voice of his, 'Geoffrey got in touch with you.'

'I've got to drop two local election forms off at the lodge and farm on the way back,' she said. 'That won't worry you, will it?'

He shook his head. Taking him by the arm, she led him off to her car which she had left standing by the garage next to the butcher. It was 12.45.

He always had the same food for lunch, day in, day out. It had been good enough for medieval England, he used to say, setting out the bread and cheese; it was good enough for him. He offered Mary Jo some but she declined; she had eaten already. He also offered her a glass of wine, which she accepted. He was in rattling good form, she noted. The company of the last day or two had given him fresh vim and vigour. So much so that he appeared completely oblivious of the people working outside the house – even the girl who had climbed up the scaffolding outside the big hall and was painting the window above it.

The afternoon had settled into a dark, dreary day, more November than September. They needed all the lights on in the kitchen. Simon and Mary Jo had their coffee and then settled to work at one end of the huge table.

'There are some papers from an archaeological magazine I'd like you to read. Stop when I tell you, and we'll mark that passage up so that I can come back to it more easily. There's a red marker somewhere around.'

She didn't mind reading to him. Simon made it easy, sitting next to her at the table. He was so used to it by now that she no longer felt self-conscious, as she had at the beginning. Really, it was easier than reading to the children. Simon had taken his glasses off and left them on the table between them. He was wearing a dark sweater, much darned, and a pair of brown trousers. The collar of his shirt was just visible under the neck of the jumper. The darns in that jumper were a local joke. As he bent his head towards her, a white frill of rough hair puffed out over both ears and emphasised the high dome of his forehead. He had never been a good-looking man, and old age suited him as well as any. The telephone rang and he went to answer it in the big hall. He had a brief word, said he was looking forward to seeing them and replaced the receiver. Then he had a few words with the girl on the scaffolding and went back to the kitchen.

Simon was well known for his disciplined attitude to work. He might be blind, he might be alone, he might be poor, but work went on. It had become not only the saviour of his life but the main impulse behind it. The two of them worked till teatime. He was more than usually conscious of time that day, what with people coming to see him and food still to be bought. Mary Jo stopped reading at 4.45 and tidied up the papers at the end of the table. She suggested giving him a lift to the heath but he liked to walk, he said. And indeed he was a well-known sight in the lanes around Heath House, walking confidently in the middle of the road, thumb stick hitting the ground before him. 'It never occurred to him that he might be run over,' a neighbour told me. 'He'd stride along for miles. You wouldn't have known he was a certified blind man.'

At five o'clock he again said a few words to the girl on the scaffolding before striking off in the gloom up the drive. Then he turned right and along the road to the little black and white cottage that marks the bend where the road turns towards Leintwardine or goes straight on up to Hopton Heath. He knew his way. At the bend he never faltered but went straight on past the garage on the left until, at the top of the road, he came to where it swings round to the little railway station over the bridge or round to the right to Clungunford.

There is a small island here with three or four houses grouped together, and it was the white-painted house on the extreme end that he wanted. George Hills, nurseryman and gardener, lived here: a round-faced, cheerful man with wide bowed legs and a slow way of talking but with the greenest hands in the county. It was George who had made him his two thorn sticks with the thumb pieces, George who sold him good vegetables and fruit very cheaply when in season. He believed in following the seasons; that way you got the best food. George's lettuces had more flavour than any shop stuff. He stopped off for some runner beans and a handful of courgettes; he'd had some tomatoes off him earlier in the week and didn't need any more for the time being. Blind as he was, he always remembered to duck under the rose arch as he made his way back up the path.

His visitors were coming from thirty miles away. Some time about six. He hurried. He knew *she* was outside, and God knows what might happen if he weren't there before them. Be sent away with a flea in their ear in no uncertain terms. Susan Evans, who used to work for him as Mary Jo Corfield now did, had said she was travelling over with a friend who was interested in the Arthurian presence in Herefordshire. She'd bring her two boys and they could play about while her friend discussed King Arthur. She'd added that Ben knew a lot about Arthur. It could be revealing for both of them.

He was back in time, thank goodness. He left his coat in the lobby, first locking the outside door behind him. He did not want to be interrupted. He knew there was a nearly full bottle of sherry in the big hall for when it was appropriate. In the meantime there was supper to prepare. He'd have to get on with it: toad in the hole with potatoes and some of George's runner beans. A few courgettes, too – vegetables eked out a meal splendidly. He had made the batter that morning. All he had to do was arrange the sausages in a dish and pour it over them and then into the oven. Soon over. He wiped his hands on the tea towel and thought he heard them by the front door. He went to see if it was them. . . .

Ben Scott was driving his new white caravanette towards Heath House. Susan Evans was beside him and the two boys, Matthew and Dominic, in the back. It was a dark, drizzly sort of evening as they swung off the road and started down the drive towards the house.

Susan, who hadn't seen the house for two years, was immediately struck by the difference in its appearance. Then the house had looked drab, falling to pieces almost, but now with all the brand-new white paint everywhere it positively shone. The drive was back, where before it had been so overrun you could scarcely see it. Suddenly, they spotted the water butt. Bang, there it was, under the arch and right in the middle of the drive – there was no way round it to get to the front of the house.

'We'll have to walk,' Susan said to Ben.

At that moment the Baroness, Simon's ex-wife, appeared at the window. No one had heard her approach, but now her angry eyes stared in.

Susan Evans gulped, then asked, 'Are you Susan?'

'Are you the famous visitors?' she replied. 'I'm the mad former wife – or that's what he thinks. Only he's mad, too. Anyway, what's the point of seeing him? The upstairs is full of fleas and the downstairs is filthy. He's slumming it in the kitchen.' She paused, then repeated, 'What's the point of seeing him? He'll be out in a month.' And with that she strode away.

The whole incident upset Ben a great deal, and he decided there and then to lock the car and put on the alarm. There was no knowing what could happen.

They walked across the back of the house and round to the so-called 'kitchen door', which was, in fact, the door to a little lobby running between the kitchen and the grounds. It was locked. There was no sign of Simon. Susan led Ben round to the front of the house, where they were just about to knock on the door when the handle turned and there was Simon, smiling, and as pleased as punch to see them.

Simon shook Ben Scott by the hand while Susan Evans made the necessary introductions. He had been looking forward to seeing him, he said, ever since Susan had telephoned him last week. Come in and sit down in the big hall. No, no, let's not have a cup of tea. Let's have a glass of sherry before a cup of tea. Let them follow the same old-fashioned custom. Susan knew her way round – she found a bottle of sherry and glasses in the drinks cupboard. They sat sipping. It was good sherry, Ben noticed – better than he expected having been told of the big man's finances. And big he certainly was. All of six foot three, and heavy without being fat with it. And he had this very deep voice, rather loud. He was touched when Susan said she expected the men would like to talk, so with Simon's permission she and the boys would roam around the house.

'Could the boys use the rocking-horse room?' she asked.

'Certainly, certainly,' he replied.

Ben eased them both into a conversation about King Arthur. He was aware, he said, that Simon had written a book on the subject. In fact, Susan had typed some of it. What had happened to it? Simon explained, with bitterness, that every publisher he had sent it to had turned it down.

'They don't want to know. At least, they don't want to know any new theories about Arthur. I've put years of work into it. I know I'm right, this – this particular place, right round this house – is Arthur's true domain. I'm sick and tired of all this modern rubbish about Camelot being in Somerset – Cadbury Castle, to be exact. I tell you I've just had two papers printed in the *British Archaeological Monthly* disproving the connection completely.' He leaned back in his chair and laughed as he added, 'I said to pluck this name out of all the murk and mists of Arthurian romance and link it to Cadbury just because the river there is called the Camelot is like identifying chalk in terms of varieties of cheese!'

The talk progressed as the two enthusiasts delved deep into the subject. Ben was invited to come down to the cellars and see the foundations of a pagan temple. They discussed the influence of paganism on Christianity and the unifying effect that Druidism had had on the Welsh and English divisions. They were looking at marks in the cellar when suddenly the window was pushed open and the Baroness peered in. 'You're letting rain get into the cellars,' she said. 'You're ruining the house.'

The big man turned his back to ignore her. She went away and he apologised to Scott. 'She's always angry whenever I have guests. Take no notice of it. And I'm afraid the children have been taught to think in her way. She's turned them against me. There's nothing I can do about it.' For a second he seemed subdued and sad, an aging man locked away in dreams and thoughts, living in history because the present was too painful. Then, remembering his guest, he smiled and suggested they find Susan and the boys. Any embarrassment was over.

It was Susan's turn, however, to be embarrassed. One of the boys had unwittingly pulled out the tail of one of the rocking horses. They had managed to put it back – it wasn't really their fault, it was actually broken. Simon laughed and said that didn't matter a bit. The mood lightened even more as Susan chided him about the Arthurian novel he had written. The ending was far too sad, she said; it must have a happier one. 'In that case, *you* can write it,' he answered. 'I haven't sent it yet to Mills and Boon!'

They laughed and began protesting that it was late – look how dark it was, they must be going home. Simon knew it was dark, and the boys had to get to bed. He did not seem unhappy – in fact rather elated. His plans for turning the house into a college of historical learning had not been abandoned, he informed them; there were people interested in the idea. His voice boomed before them as he escorted them through the passageway to the western door they called the milk door. Outside, it had begun to drizzle fast. A wet, beastly night, they all agreed. 'Come back and see me again,' he invited Scott. 'There's so much to talk about. There are plenty of people who think like us. We're not alone.'

They wished him luck with his venture and walked over to the car. Afterwards they were to remember that the ex-wife was 'lurking' by the archway near the milk door. She would have heard their conversation. Indeed that, in their opinion, was what she was there for. They said their final goodbyes. Ben Scott unlocked the car, turned off the alarm, started the engine and drove away. It was now about 8.30.

In the kitchen Simon Dale turned on the electric cooker for his toad in the hole. He sipped a second glass of sherry, then slipped off his wristwatch in order to peel the potatoes. The runner beans and courgettes were on the table. Susan Evans had left the dirty glasses on the draining board. He'd told her not to bother about washing them up – he would do it the next day. The house was very quiet, though the wind was getting up; it would be a squally night. But in the kitchen it was bright and cheerful. He turned on a ring for the potatoes – they took longer than the other vegetables.

It was then that he heard a noise at the door nearest the kitchen. He listened – yes, there it was, someone was knocking at the door. He took his keys, opened the door between the lobby and the kitchen, skirted the deckchair that was propped up against the wall and opened the outer door. . . .

The arm that went up high above the person's head held a long steel weapon. It came crashing down to hit him on the top part of the forehead. His skin split and blood spurted. He fell back, stunned, colliding with the deckchair which fell to the floor as he backed into the kitchen. He could not see, only feel. His arms flailed wildly, trying to hold off his assailant. Again up went the arm and the weapon came crashing down on his head. He fell back further, shifting the heavy table with his weight. The arm went up and came down twice more. As he lay slumped, with his head resting against the table, the arm went up for the final time. The blow hit him viciously across the larynx, breaking it. His body fell across the floor, jamming the lobby door partly open. The blood rushed from his nose and mouth as he choked to death. His hands gripped the sweater below his throat, and then slackened. Simon Dale, ex-architect, amateur archaeologist and father of five, was dead – murdered. The time was approximately 8.45.

2

T·H·E   A·R·R·E·S·T

THE cooker ring was red-hot, the Pyrex dish in the oven burnt to a cinder. On the table still lay the runner beans and courgettes. Near them were the stems of two tomatoes – the existence of which was to be of some importance over the following days. Five sherry glasses, one cracked, one half full, stood on the draining board. The pieces from a broken china dish littered the floor. The body lay as it had collapsed the night before, and with the hands now raised as if in supplication. The electric light burned overhead, the shutters were closed. Outside the wind howled and the rain fell. It was the sort of day on which people commiserated with each other. Nothing stirred in the beautiful house, nothing at all. At eleven o'clock the telephone rang. Its sudden noise shattered the dreadful silence. It rang once, twice, up to five times and then was silent. The house returned to its awful brooding self.

At 10.30 two vehicles had come swishing down the drive – a white Mercedes van and a grey Peugeot. A tall young man got out of the car and a woman from the van. They were the Baroness and her youngest son, Simon. Together they unloaded a chainsaw and bench and placed them near the cottage. The young man nodded to his mother, got in his car and drove away. She walked across the back of the house, the north side, to the kitchen garden and orchard that lay on the east side near the kitchen door. She was worried, she had said, about the wind lifting up the lids on some of the beehives there. She put a brick on one and returned to the cottage. She did not notice the kitchen light on. She had work to do – cutting up logs. She was to say in court later on that she had that same day looked in at various windows and seen nothing wrong. She was, she added, more concerned with the guttering of the house, which might not cope if the weather worsened. After a while she left.

In the afternoon she returned with the same son. They brought ladders and steps for further work on the house: they were painting the outside, cleaning it up prior to putting it on the market. If they could not do much about the interior, at least they could make the exterior look as smart as possible.

Again, the ex-wife was later to claim she did not notice anything at all amiss. Nor did she feel frightened at being near the house on her own. Previously she had always felt it necessary to carry on her arm a long, jemmy-like weapon because of her ex-husband's violence. Why had she not felt frightened this day? she was asked in court. 'You feel safe with a chainsaw in your hands,' she coolly replied. Later that day, on her return to her cottage in the village of Docklow, twenty-seven miles away, she had washed all the clothes she had worn that day and Friday. It was, she assured the court, her normal custom.

The following day, Sunday, the winds had blown the bad weather away. As if in reparation the skies were bluer than usual, the sun as sweet as summer. Inside the kitchen, where the cooker was still on, it was sickeningly, disgustingly hot and decomposition had begun its dreadful work. In Docklow, where the Baroness lived with three of her children, it was, as for most of the nation, a late morning. It was later for Marcus, Sophia and Simon Wilberforce than for their mother, who got up and drove into Leominster for the Sunday papers. That morning she and the elder of the two boys swept the chimney. It was decided that in the afternoon they would visit a local garden that was open to the public – Spetchley Gardens, some twenty-five miles away. Nothing was said about Heath House. Work on that could relax for one day.

Sunday advanced through the sunny morning hours. At Heath House the beautiful Queen Anne front looked breathtaking seen from the road to Bedstone. It seemed serene, confident, a proud example of the best in English domestic architecture, enough to make tourists reach for their cameras. Nothing showed externally of the awful scene within.

Giselle Wall, a small, dark woman in her early forties, had worked for Simon Dale since July. She had listened to his obsessions, read his manuscripts and been entrusted with typing out his vast history of England covering the three-hundred-year period from AD 300 to 600. She had promised to bring over the manuscript as soon as it was ready. She had finished that week and had telephoned him to say that she would deliver it at the weekend – probably on Sunday. That afternoon she rang to tell him she would be over, if that was all right with him, about teatime. Along with other assistants and local friends, she knew without always consciously acknowledging it how much he depended on these small visits. They broke the solitude of his life and gave him back a little of the gregariousness that was his by nature.

Accordingly, when she received no reply she decided to ring again. And ring again she did repeatedly. At 2.10, at 2.30, at 3.00 and at 3.30 the bell rang in the dusty, silent house, disturbing nobody. By the third call she sensed something was wrong; it was most unusual for him not to reply. He might miss one call, but not several. Finally, when the last call – at four o'clock – went unanswered, she decided to drive over and see for herself. He could have had a slight accident, she reasoned, fallen over a chair or a log, some obstruction. He was blinder than he thought, and it was a wonder that something like this had not happened in the past.

She lived six miles away in a small village. Even at the slowest – and she had not driven that slowly, with the worry in her mind – it was reckoned that she must have arrived at Heath House about 4.20. As she left her car, some supersense alerted her that all was not as it should be. Even though the sun was blazing outside there was a light on in the kitchen and lobby. More disturbing still was the fact that the kitchen shutters were closed. Normally they were never closed during the day.

Swiftly she moved up the three concrete steps to the bright red door that marked the kitchen end of the house. Purely out of a sense of good manners, she knocked before trying the handle. To her surprise, it opened. It was then that she first became aware of the terrible heat emanating from the kitchen. It was then, too, that she saw a deckchair lying on the ground, broken. And it was then, too, that the awful smell within the heat got to her. Holding her breath, she went through the half-open kitchen door and saw the body on the floor – saw the blood around its head, saw the red-hot ring still burning bright on the cooker.

She turned and fled from the scene, raced down the steps and into her car and drove to the nearest house, Heath Lodge, where Mike Hollis, an antique dealer, lived. When he came to answer her bangs on the door she told him of the dreadful scene she had discovered. They must, she told him, get an ambulance, a doctor. Had he had a heart attack? But surely there wouldn't be so much blood, would there? Surely there wouldn't be any blood at all? What *had* happened? Hollis tried to soothe her. He'd ring 999 and get an ambulance over immediately.

He rang through, was connected to the ambulance service and described what he had been told. They'd get one over at once, came the reassuring, authoritative voice of the operator. Mike Hollis put down the telephone and turned to Giselle Wall.

'I don't want to go back there,' she said. 'I don't ever want to go back – it's ghastly. Absolutely ghastly.'

Nor should she, Hollis told her. Together they would wait for the ambulance. After all, who knew what had happened? The person who had done it could still be there around the house somewhere. It might be the work of a dangerous lunatic. Every day you read cases of it happening, even in remote rural areas. Comforted, she stayed with him.

Craven Arms ambulance service prides itself on quick reactions to call-outs. Within fifteen minutes of Mike Hollis's emergency call an ambulance descended the drive to Heath House. John Abbotts, the ambulanceman, went straight into the kitchen. The heat was appalling, the worst he had ever encountered. The smell was bad, and he could tell that decomposition had started. The electric stove was so hot it was a wonder it hadn't started a fire. The first thing he did was to turn it off. Then he took another look at the body. The body and hands were stiff and there was congealed blood lying in a circle round the head. He noticed that there was blood, too, on the table and broken china on the floor, and decided to ring the police immediately.

As quickly as the ambulancemen had turned up, so too did the police. At the committal stage of the murder case it was stated that a mobile sergeant, a highways man, called at the house and, realizing that the scene had all the appearance of a murder, contacted Leominster CID. Meanwhile a doctor, Margaret Davies, arrived and confirmed that Simon Dale was dead. The 'full majesty of the law' swung into action. From now on and for weeks to come, the house would not be empty.

Detective Constable Geoffrey Daniels arrived from Leominster. He was followed by a camera team photographing the body, lobby and kitchen in close detail. As is common in modern crime investigations they also made a short video of the scene including shots of Simon Dale's battered head in close-up, which were to cause a small furore later in court.

The drive was cordoned off. For the immediate future nobody except the police and those with police permission would be allowed down it. Within an hour Detective Inspector Derek Matthews and his sergeant arrived. He was to lead the murder inquiry, which would be under the overall control of Detective Superintendent David Cole. Matthews told Daniels to have the body taken away to Hereford

County Hospital for immediate examination by the police pathologist, Dr Peter Acland.

On cursory investigation, borne out by more careful checking, it was obvious that this was no ordinary robbery with violence. There were no signs of a break-in anywhere along the extensive length of the house on either side. Nor was there any sign of furniture or goods having been stolen. There was no evidence, apart from the kitchen and lobby, of any disturbance in the many rooms that confronted them. Most revealing of all was the fact that the dead man's pockets had not been rifled; a wallet still containing £25 in notes was discovered in his back trouser pocket. As Matthews admits, it was a puzzling case from the beginning in the sense that the terrain was not a usual one; not often are detectives faced with a large house and extensive grounds to probe, analyse and determine what is or isn't relevant evidence.

He and his colleague remained at the house for several hours, measuring, checking, examining papers and letters, and working out the complicated pattern of the house. After talking gently to Giselle Wall they allowed her to go home. They took a statement from Mike Hollis, then left the murder scene in the hands of the other police officers and made their way back the twenty-four miles to Leominster Police Station.

From here it was decided, after consultation with David Cole, to call on the dead man's ex-wife and acquaint her with the news. The time was now nearly 12.30 a.m., well over, as was later to be determined, twenty-four hours since Simon Dale had been bludgeoned to death.

Docklow is an anonymous sort of village. There is no village green with houses round it, no village shop in which people might meet and exchange pleasantries, the time of day, the terrible state of the weather. Admittedly there are a church and a pub, but oddly enough they do not a village make. Perhaps it is because, except for a few houses, Docklow seems to consist of nothing but a section of the road that lies between Leominster and Worcester. The road signs indicating Docklow at either end seem almost an unnecessary bit of signposting.

Forresters Hall Cottages are a pair of small semi-detached houses, probably Edwardian, situated at the western end of the stretch of A44 that dubs itself Docklow. Both lie behind high, thick hedges on the side of the road directly opposite the church. Both have front lawns, divided from each other by another high hedge, and both rear gardens are similarly concealed from each other. At the front a pathway connects the two cottages, so that in order to approach the more westerly one the visitor has to walk in front of its neighbour. No. 2, in which Dale's three children and their mother had lived since 1977, has a large gravelled area for cars and a double garage. The house is not spacious – three bedrooms plus bathroom upstairs, two rooms and a kitchen downstairs. The number of people who had resided there three years previously was to astound the police in their subsequent investigations.

At half past midnight, just into the morning of Monday, 14 September, Detective Inspector Matthews, accompanied by his sergeant, knocked on the door of No. 2. After some time Marcus Wilberforce opened the door. For seconds the policemen stood in the doorway adjusting their reactions, for this was no plain workman's cottage. Nothing could have been more misleading than the plain, shabby exterior of No. 2 Forresters Hall Cottages. While they gazed in amazement the Baroness came downstairs, fully dressed, and invited them inside, where they were even more surprised – 'staggered' was the word they used in court – at what they could now see in greater detail. This was an Aladdin's Cave, not a cottage. The whole house was crowded with antiques and paintings: there was hardly room to stand, so overcrowded was it. Two glass chandeliers hung from the beams, thick Oriental carpets were piled on top of each other on the floor, grand paintings covered the walls. As they moved to seat themselves on the sofa, they noticed a letter addressed to a Lady Illingworth lying on the floor. Matthews picked it up and, as he handed it to the older of the two boys in the room, asked, 'Who is Lady Illingworth?'

Marcus replied, 'Aunt Puss.' Matthews and his team were to learn much about Aunt Puss in the days to come.

Detective Inspector Matthews explained that there was a problem at Heath House. The Baroness asked if Dale had burnt the place down, adding by way of explanation that her ex-husband had not agreed to its sale. Giving evidence later, Matthews said:

Neither the Baroness nor Marcus asked us why we were there. Eventually I explained that Dale was dead. There was little or no reaction to the news. No specific details were requested about the death. On at least two occasions, and possibly a third, the Baroness asked if the house had been broken into. I said there was no evidence of forced entry. Later I took possession of the poker from the car. The Baroness, wearing a two-piece suit, was the spokesperson. She was calm and collected. Marcus was nervous and belligerent. Sophia was bubbly and talkative. Simon was quiet and disinterested.

Responding to criticisms that she displayed no emotion at the time, the Baroness explained in the same court: 'I was brought up strictly and you do not show emotion. When I was small I used to be sat on a chair for ten minutes and not allowed to bat an eyelid. I had to keep absolutely still.' She also gave her family's view of the police visit that night. She said that they had arrived and hammered noisily on the door – so much so that they were all woken up and thought from the disturbance that thieves were trying to break in. She told her son Marcus to ring the police, at which point the people outside said they *were* the police. Commenting on them, she said in a dismissive tone but with underlying relish that 'they looked incredibly furtive and had such an impertinent manner about them'.

By now an Incident Room had been set up by the police in the nearby village of Bedstone. A forensic team, led by Dr Norman Weston, was meticulously examining Heath House and its adjacent cottage, used for housing gardening equipment, room by room. They took samples of hair and fibres from the kitchen, checked for blood in the cottage and took swabs from the drains. Nothing that might lead to the identification of the murderer was ignored. Murder inquiries are a long, hard slog and this was to be no exception.

The pathologist, Dr Peter Acland, had by now concluded that Dale had suffered five head blows, but the one that had killed him was the blow across the larynx which had caused him to inhale his own blood and die from respiratory failure. 'It probably took him three to five minutes to die,' he said. The forensic experts, too, had established the approximate time of death. The heat in the kitchen had made it a difficult task, but after many experiments with cooking toad in the hole they concluded that it was between 8.30 and 9 p.m.

The entire surrounding area had been sealed off. Police officers were combing the four-acre grounds – literally on hands and knees – while others were conducting house-to-house inquiries within a five-mile radius. At this time it was estimated that more than a hundred officers were working round the clock in the hunt for the killer. As Matthews said afterwards, 'There wasn't a hedge for miles around that we didn't search.' Meanwhile, at the Bedstone Incident Room, the telephone calls flooded in – calls from locals, calls from eccentrics, even calls from the mentally deranged. As one officer commented, 'You'd be surprised at the weird things we're told on the telephone – everything from strangers with mad staring eyes to flying saucers and visitors from outer space! Sifting through it is one hell of a job!'

But two months later the police still had no strong evidence pointing in any one direction. They had combed the hedgerows, they had searched the fields, they had conducted hundreds of interviews – but nothing was leading them anywhere other than to the inhabitants of Heath House itself. And that is the conclusion they came to again and again in their discussions. Was this not a family affair? They decided to bide their time and, in the meantime, spread the net further.

They appealed to the public for help in tracing a red Cavalier-type car which had been seen on a bend of the road on the Bucknell side of Heath House at 10.30 p.m. on Friday, 11 September. They also wanted to interview a male hitchhiker in his late twenties, who had been wearing a fawn three-quarter-length jacket and a red headband round his long, shaggy hair. Various witnesses had seen him walking along the main road from Hopton Heath to Bucknell between 11 p.m. and midnight that evening. He had again been sighted on the Sunday near Bucknell railway station, attempting to hitchhike in the direction of Knighton to the west of the area. A light-coloured estate car with a dark grille had also been seen on Saturday morning – between 8.30 and 8.45 – parked two hundred yards on the Bucknell side of Heath House. A woman had been noticed getting out of the car and walking to the gateway of a field overlooking the house. A girl stayed behind in the car, sitting in the front passenger seat. Yet more witnesses had seen an elderly, grey-haired man walking in the fields to the west of Heath House on the Saturday morning, about 9.40. Who was he? Would he please come forward and help the police with their inquiries? The last note on a list of unchecked facts concerned an elderly man seen on the footpath from Jay Lane to Buckton at about 4 p.m. on the same day. A complete list was published in the local press, but to no avail. Nothing emerged to change the circular nature of those discussions at the police headquarters in Hereford where the murder inquiry was now based.

At this stage the police had, they admitted, still not been able to establish a motive for the murder, and neither had they found a murder weapon. The head of one team, Detective Chief Inspector Parry, said at a press conference: 'The difficulties have been that we are dealing with very large premises in a rural, isolated area, and that Mr Dale himself was something of a recluse.'

*

But unknown to the public the police were pursuing an aspect of their investigations that was to lead them to yet another astonishing crime: the major defrauding of Margaret, Lady Illingworth, or Aunt Puss as she came to be known to everyone. Under the direction of the head of the West Mercia Fraud Squad, Detective Inspector Mike Cowley, the police began investigations into the financial status of Simon Dale's family. It is a common enough occurrence – one, in fact, that operates in every murder inquiry and for obvious reasons: money is often the motive for any number of crimes, not the least murder. In this case it was Susan de Stempel's financial status that they examined. They had already received a startling impression of the dichotomy that existed between her public persona and her private life: the shock of her opulently furnished home had not gone unrecorded. Furthermore, why did a simply, even drably dressed woman, who complained frequently of how frugal an existence she and her children had been forced to live, have brand-new cars parked alongside her semi-detached cottage? The Peugeot estate, the Mercedes van and the ordinary Peugeot saloon together added up to many thousand pounds' worth of car – it did not fit the picture of penny-pinching poverty that she claimed.

Five days after the murder of Simon Dale, on 16 September, the Fraud Squad questioned her. She told them that she had two bank accounts only, and both were in her sole name. Solemnly they noted this fact. It naturally added to their suspicions, therefore, when in the course of a search of No. 2 Forresters Hall Cottages they chanced upon a letter from a bank in the Channel Islands revealing the existence of a joint bank account in the name of Susan de Stempel and Lady Illingworth. What they found was even more startling than the Aladdin's Cave of furniture and possessions. Lady Illingworth, Susan's aunt, although by all records a very rich woman, had died a pauper in receipt of state supplementary benefit at a council-run old people's home, Langford House in Hereford.

By now the police could see that all was most definitely not as it should be, and the grounds for their suspicions were confirmed in subsequent inquiries. Detailed examination of various bank accounts revealed a will dated 17 June 1984; further bank accounts; and the sale of Lady Illingworth's property, including furniture, stocks and shares, Premium Bonds and National Savings certificates. Inquiries to bank managers in the Channel Islands disclosed jewellery sales, the proposed purchase of a house in Alderney, professional advice given on various matters by a firm of accountants in Guernsey called Spicer and Pegler, and the purchase of a flat in Spain in Sophia

Wilberforce's name. There was still more to come. In fact, at the fraud trial in Birmingham the police advanced eleven hundred pages of evidence accompanied by fifteen boxes of photographs and other exhibits. The involvement of Michael de Stempel, the Baroness's second husband, was discovered; so, via bank accounts in the Channel Islands, was the collusion of Sophia and Marcus Wilberforce.

Discussions with the medical staff at Langford House and Hereford General Hospital concerning Lady Illingworth's stay with them also disclosed the poor mental state she was in on admittance and her death in 1986 from Alzheimer's disease. As Detective Inspector Mike Cowley put it:

> Because of the circumstances of Lady Illingworth's last few months of life being so at variance with her previous existence, and the odd details of her cremation – she was cremated as a pauper – with no members of her family present and no announcement till some months later of her death, we decided to send the 1984 will and a sample of documents in the name of Lady Illingworth transferring her assets to Susan for forensic examination. They revealed a total of sixty-seven forgeries. Clearly a case of fraud on a massive scale existed.

At the same time the murder inquiry, despite hundreds of interviews with people in London, Gloucestershire, Worcestershire and the Shropshire–Herefordshire border country, had come up with nothing to link the murder of Simon Dale with anyone except, in the police's view, members of his own family. A special reconstruction of the crime had been shown on BBC television's *Crimewatch* in November, two months after it happened, but nothing resulted from this or other appeals. But what they did have by now was a possible murder weapon – a jemmy that Susan de Stempel was known to use had been found hanging on the back of a cupboard in the cottage next to Heath House, and could have inflicted the injuries that killed Simon Dale. The police also had, in their opinion, evidence of a strong motive.

Together the murder and fraud teams discussed their findings with David Cole, head of the whole operation. It was decided to initiate proceedings not only against the family, but also against Susan's ex-husband, Baron Michael de Stempel, who had been present at Docklow during the crucial months of the alleged fraud. Accordingly on Monday, 7 December 1987 Susan de Stempel and two of her children, Marcus and Sophia, were arrested on suspicion of fraud and murder. A laconic announcement in the *Hereford Times* of 10 December, under the heading 'Man's death: Arrests', merely reported: 'Detectives investigating the death of 68-year-old Simon Dale whose body was found at his home at Heath House, Hopton Heath, on Sunday, 13 September, arrested three people on Monday. They are being held at Hereford Central Police Station, where they are helping with inquiries.'

The names of the suspects were not revealed until a week later, on Monday, 14 December at Hereford City Magistrates Court, when Baroness Susan de Stempel, fifty-three, her children Xenophon Marcus Wilberforce, twenty-six, and Georgina Sophia Wilberforce, twenty-five, together with Baron Michael Victor Joseph Walter de Stempel, were charged with conspiring to defraud Margaret Clare, Lady Illingworth and her estate at Docklow between 1 January 1983 and 8 December 1987. At the end of a seventy-five-minute hearing the Baroness, the Baron, her son and daughter were refused bail and remanded in custody.

Four weeks later, the murder team felt they had a case to answer. Investigations into the Baroness and her family were well under way.

3

R·E·B·E·L W·I·T·H·O·U·T
A F·O·R·T·U·N·E

SUSAN de Stempel was born, on 16 May 1934, a Wilberforce. Margaret Illingworth is also a Wilberforce. A vast tribe that bears a name famous in English history, membership appears to impart a pride, an hauteur to all who share it. And although Susan Wilberforce, as she was born, only once referred to it when dismissing the idea of parole – 'I don't think I'll take parole. I'm too much of a Wilberforce for that' – her family background is obviously not insignificant.

Its fame springs from one man, William Wilberforce, the anti-slaver. He was born in Hull in 1759, the only son of a rich merchant, Robert Wilberforce. The family takes its name from the village of Wilberfoss, situated midway between York and Pocklington on the outskirts of the ancient forest of Galtres. In medieval times these woods were inhabited by herds of wild boar, after which the area was named Wild-Boar-Foss, later contracted to Wilberfoss. According to *Burke's Landed Gentry*, the lordship of Wilberfoss was held by the de Kyme family of Linc and passed by marriage to the direct ancestors of the present families of Wilberfoss and Wilberforce.

William, the anti-slaver, was exceptional from the beginning. At the age of seven he was sent to Hull Grammar School, where he was stood on a table to read aloud as an example to the other boys. His father died two years later and the boy was sent to live with an uncle, also William, in Wimbledon, South of London; but subsequently he was removed on the grounds that his aunt was perverting him to Methodism.

At Cambridge, now heir to a considerable fortune, he was well known for his kindness, charm and hospitality. As the *Dictionary of National Biography* records, there was always a great Yorkshire pie in his rooms for all his friends to share. At this stage he was already acquainted with the future Prime Minister William Pitt the Younger, and this acquaintance was to become a strong friendship when he joined the House of Commons as Member for Hull. In 1788, supported by Thomas Clarkson and leading members of the Quaker sect, he began his nineteen years' struggle for the abolition of the slave trade, seeing victory in March 1807 when the Abolition of Slavery Bill was passed in Parliament. He continued to press for the abolition of slavery abroad, and the total abolition of slavery itself, but failing health forced him to retire in 1825.

Although not himself a Catholic, he also argued in Parliament for the emancipation of Catholics and their admission to the House of Commons – an argument that was to have considerable influence on two of his sons. When Wilberforce died in 1833, such was the nation's respect and love for him that he was buried with full honours in Westminster Abbey. Throughout his life he was known not just for his moralistic fervour but for his vivacity, playfulness and unaffectedness. He was an excellent mimic and sang well: even the Prince of Wales was moved to congratulate him on his voice.

Three of William's sons became well known – Henry William, Robert Isaac and Samuel. It was during their lifetime that this burgeoning family was to split down the middle, with two of the three converting to Roman Catholicism while the third, Samuel, rose high in the Anglican Church, becoming Bishop of Oxford and then Winchester. Both Henry William and Robert became Catholics under the influence of Cardinal Newman, whose mid-nineteenth-century Oxford Movement had changed the religious convictions of so many undergraduates. Their conversion was the more extraordinary in that both had previously taken Anglican orders. Henry William was to become a journalist, editing and owning the *Catholic Standard* and fathering nine children, while Robert joined the Roman Catholic Church in Paris in order to avert the possibility of harmful publicity for his brother, Samuel, who was by then Bishop of Oxford. Sadly, Robert three years after his conversion died on his way to Rome, where he had been accepted as a student at the Academia Ecclesiastica; it was said that the Pope had offered to pay his expenses. He left two sons, one a vicar in Yorkshire, the other a successful lawyer.

It was Samuel, 'Soapy Sam' as he was dubbed by Lord Westbury, the Lord Chancellor, who increased the family's social standing and, importantly, its coffers. When his wife died she left him her father's extensive acreage at Lavington in Sussex. But before this he had made a name for himself as he moved swiftly up the Anglican ladder from rector of Brightstone in the Isle of Wight at the age of twenty-five to becoming, ten years later, rector of Alverstoke, Hampshire, canon of Winchester and chaplain to the Prince Consort. In 1845 he was installed as Dean of Westminster and described as 'a very quick, lively and agreeable man, who is in favour at court'.

Subsequently, as chaplain to the House of Lords, he had the freedom of that establishment and was said greatly to enjoy debate, speaking frequently on subjects as diverse as education, cruelty to women and children, and the treatment of prisoners. It does not take a very fanciful mind to wonder what he might have thought of Susan de Stempel who also said, after some weeks in Pucklechurch Remand Centre, that when 'all this is over' she would speak her mind on prison reform and the changes necessary within certain places of confinement.

According to *Chambers Biographical Dictionary*, 'The charm of [Samuel Wilberforce's] many-sided personality, his administrative capacity, his social and oratorical gifts, were apt to be forgotten in the versatile, ecclesiastic nickname Soapy Sam.' But there were also many who thought Lord Westbury's sobriquet well earned, and heartily applauded his description of Samuel's *Essays and Reviews* as 'a well-lubricated set of words' containing 'a sentence so oily and saponaceous that no one can grasp it'. In fact, 'Soapy Sam' was dismissed by many who thought his capacity for evasion on theological matters, allied to the fact that two of his brothers had converted to Roman Catholicism, left him open to the accusation of duplicity. Lord Westbury found him singularly charmless, and commented briskly on his behaviour: 'Though often in hot water he always came out with clean hands.'

Appointed Bishop of Winchester in 1869, he was killed by a fall from his horse four years later while out riding in Hampshire. Only days beforehand he had told the House of Lords: 'I hate and abhor the attempt to Romanize the Church of England.' At his funeral Wilberforce Catholics and Anglicans sat rigidly on opposite sides of the church. Of Samuel's two younger sons, Ernest Roland became first Bishop of Newcastle and then Bishop of Chichester, while Albert Basil Orme became Archdeacon of Westminster, chaplain to the Speaker and 'an eloquent advocate of temperance'. Thus we have a great and important English family neatly split down the middle in terms of adherence to the Anglican or Roman Church.

Susan Wilberforce descended via the Catholic side. The family house, Markington Hall near Ripon in North Yorkshire, had its own chapel, where mass was celebrated by a visiting priest, and her education took place at Catholic convents. What lay in her childhood that was to shape her adult life and lead to the ignominy of her standing trial for murder and being convicted of serious fraud?

Markington Hall, which had come into the Wilberforce family through marriage in 1750 and where she grew up, is a moderately large though far from imposing country house built of local stone and set bang in the middle of the village. Markington is a pleasant place consisting of a number of grey stone houses, two pubs and a village shop, all set in rolling sheep country divided by low grey stone walls and not far from such tourist places as Fountains Abbey and the cathedral city of Ripon.

Although Markington Hall is the most important house in the area, it does not dominate: the atmosphere, far from that created by another Yorkshire house, Castle Howard, in TV's *Brideshead Revisited*, is of good solid northern sense – quite contrary to what was popularly supposed in the more flamboyant press. It was not the custom in the North Riding for worthy village folk to doff their caps in a servile manner to those up at the manor, yet there was an underlying acceptance that the Wilberforces inhabited a rather different world from that of ordinary people. It was this difference that sustained Susan when, as it seemed, the world turned against her.

She herself was much amused by the *Brideshead* comparisons and remarked to me at one point, 'I don't recall anyone in Brideshead ending up in prison!'

Here were born and grew up Susan's father, uncle and aunt. 'Mr Bill', as her father, William Basil Samuel Joseph Anthony Edward Wilberforce, was affectionately called, was much liked: an elderly farm worker, Tom Atkinson, recalled him as a very friendly figure in the village. 'There was nothing grand about the Wilberforces,' he said. 'They talked to everybody. He played cricket for the village team. He was a tall six-footer, so was his brother Robert, but he were thicker built. Quieter, too. Then there was Miss Margaret – sister to them. She was named Margaret but we all called her Miss Puss. She was a lovely lady, as friendly as you could have. I've even danced with her at village dances. There was no side to the family at all. They didn't give many snooty parties. There was one I recall which they called living whist. Everybody had to be dressed like a playing card. There was a caller who called out the moves and whoever it was had to move. There was a lot of laughing that summer day. It was good fun.

'They had an airstrip, I seem to recall. I know there was an aeroplane they had. And a big shed they kept it in.' And then he laughed, as he added with a hint of wickedness in his voice, 'I know one thing they didn't have – they didn't have money.'

Much as the villagers admired and even liked the Wilberforce family, one thing they realized was how financially strapped they were. The Hall might be old and the furniture antique, but when it came to ready cash the locals noted how careful the squire was. The truth is that the family's ancestor, the great anti-slaver William Wilberforce, had never been a very rich man: he had houses and he had furniture, but he did not have great income. And as his health faltered in later years he was forced to use his capital to maintain the household. Susan de Stempel was well aware of this. 'People like us don't have money,' she would say, 'we have things.' By things she meant, for example, furniture and pictures.

Against this background of high estate but low income it was not difficult to see why Margaret Wilberforce should marry a rich husband. Life in 1930s' Yorkshire was not so very different from the eighteenth century of Jane Austen. Tom Atkinson was in no doubt: 'Money was the reason Miss Puss married that lord. She had set her heart on marrying some Catholic gentleman – name of Dormer – but he didn't have any money. Well, not enough it was said. So she looked around for someone else. Perhaps it wouldn't be the same today, but in those days it mattered more. She found this Lord Illingworth to marry – a big, heavy man, a lot older than her. Still, he had a purse full of money.' He paused and then said: 'The funny thing is that Mr Bill married a Dormer – same family.' Bill Wilberforce had married a Cecilia Dormer. What he did not add was that the two women – Margaret Illingworth and Cecilia Wilberforce, as she became – would never be entirely happy in each other's company. Perhaps the enmity was the result of jealousy on Margaret's part that her brother could have the bride of his choice while she had to settle for money before romance. Or perhaps it was simply incompatibility.

Cecilia Wilberforce, née Dormer, came from a family much longer in the Catholic faith than relative newcomers like the Wilberforces: she could trace her Catholicism back to the early seventeenth century. In a rare moment of enthusiasm *Burke's Peerage and Baronetcy* describes the family of Dormer as of the 'greatest antiquity' in the county of Buckinghamshire. They were settled there at a very early period, it records, and quotes one of the first as Richard de Doremere, who held lands at West Wycombe in 1244. The first baronet was created on 10 June 1615, becoming a baron precisely twenty days later. On the female side Cecilia Dormer was a Borwick, her mother being the daughter of the first Baron Borwick of Hawkshead in Lancashire. Altogether she could boast a pedigree rather grander than the Wilberforces.

Cecilia does not, however, seem to have made much impression on the villagers. The few who remember her describe her simply as 'a quiet woman'. She was not given to smiling easily and certainly had no strong rapport with the village's inhabitants. Only one recalled her, in unusual terms, as a 'rabid Catholic'. Not even Tom Atkinson with his good powers of recall remembered Cecilia Wilberforce: 'Her and Mr Bill weren't around much after his wedding – his army life took him away.' All he could bring to mind was that she was 'a very serious woman, very Catholic. She was a tall woman, too, but I never saw her laughing or smiling, not like Miss Puss.' He sighed, as if to say 'Poor Miss Puss.'

Nor did Robert William Francis Wilberforce, the second son, figure much in the villagers' recollections. 'He went to London, something to do with the law,' one said rather dismissively. It is 'Mr Bill' whom they salute, and not altogether because of his death in the Second World War. He was killed in action in Tunisia in 1943, on his daughter Susan's ninth birthday.

What of Susan's upbringing? In her early childhood she was to see more of her aunt than of her own mother. Army duties took the young captain of the King's Own Yorkshire Light Infantry (a fittingly local regiment) and his wife abroad, with the result that Susan and her brother John, four years her senior, were largely looked after by nannies.

Home was still Markington Hall, but instead of their parents being in charge, the young Wilberforce children referred to their Aunt Margaret and her husband, Lord Illingworth, who had married the pretty young 'Miss Puss' in 1931. They had rented the house from the Wilberforces to use as a country home during the squire's absence abroad. Lord Illingworth was thirty-five years his wife's senior, and divorced. The family disliked the age difference and the fact that he was a non-Catholic – and, even worse, divorced. But one thing they could not fault him on – he was by any standards a very rich man, who had made himself a fortune as a Bradford wool merchant.

From 1935 for almost ten years Aunt Puss and her husband, and to some extent, her brother Robert, the children's uncle, acted as their guardians. Lord Illingworth may have been older than his Wilberforce bride and he may have been divorced, but what he could do – and did do – was spend money. He did so without restraint.

In their time as tenants at Markington the Illingworths spent generously on the house, adding another wing and converting a barn into a second chapel; the existing chapel within the house had become too small for the number of visiting Catholics from the area who worshipped there as a local chapel of rest. Today it is still used in the same way, with a visiting priest from Bishops Thornton arriving to say weekly mass on Sunday afternoon.

In 1939, at the age of five, Susan Wilberforce was sent to St Mary's Convent in Ascot. It is not unusual for convent schools to have very young girls in their care, particularly if the parents are working abroad or, as is often the case, foreigners. One of the top Catholic girls' schools in the country, St Mary's is run by nuns of the Institute of the Blessed Virgin Mary which was founded in the early seventeenth century with the precise intention of 'educating girls in the Christian faith'. The large red-brick building is surrounded by the usual playing fields, tennis courts and gardens. It is conveniently near London, less than forty-five minutes by car, and boasts a number of well-known, even famous ex-pupils such as Lady Antonia Fraser and Nell Dunn, both writers.

In the light of what happened, it is interesting to note what its present prospectus lists as being the aims of the school:

The process of education involves a joint effort between the school, the parents and the girl herself. Children cannot be forced to learn any more than they can be forced to become committed Christians, but they can be encouraged and motivated by example. We believe wholeheartedly that the way to both scholastic success and spiritual maturity lies in stimulating each child's natural inquisitiveness and, as she matures, giving her appropriate instruction, security and support that will enable her to grow in confidence, ability and Christian commitment. The school is a place for learning in many senses. At St Mary's girls discover what it means to be a member of a community where harmony depends on unselfishness and tolerance. Discipline is necessary but we aim to teach girls the value of self-discipline, and that their needs and desires must be balanced against those of their fellows. The emphasis, therefore, is always on respect and consideration for others. From the presence of the Religious Community and the integral nature of religion in school life, girls learn what stability their faith offers and what a challenge it gives them in facing up to the problems in today's world. From excellent teaching and facilities they acquire competence in a wide range of academic, artistic, social and practical skills. . . . Girls here find themselves in a small, warm and caring community with a happy atmosphere. . . .

Did the five-year-old Susan Wilberforce find it a happy atmosphere? Others did. A contemporary recalls what it was like in those early war years:

My parents thought it was completely hideous as a building but I rather liked it. I remember there were loads of pipes going down the back from the lavatories and long passages with teak floors. There were big grounds and, though it was really part of outlying suburbia, you had the feeling it was quite secluded. There was a marvellous kitchen garden where a few of us would slip out after prayers in the evening and fill our knickers with gooseberries. There were pine trees around, greyish sand if I remember rightly, and azaleas. We used to run through the pine trees to get to the swimming pool. We slept in dormitories but we each had our own little bedside locker and curtains round our beds. We wore a navy blue gym tunic, navy cardigan and a terrible tie. In the summer we wore cotton dresses. I don't remember much about the food – pretty bad, I think, but then it was wartime. We had bread and dripping for elevenses and that was super.

We had mass every morning and benediction every evening. On the good side, I think it opened up for me an exciting spiritual world – it was where I learned to have a private self. I'd come from rather a disordered background and I liked the order of the place. But there was a bad, bleak side to it – I suppose there is at all boarding schools unless you happen to be the type that revels in them. Being a Catholic school I had a bad time when my parents got divorced. I was told it was not to be discussed with anybody. And another time when I asked what adultery was I was sent to Reverend Mother! Another time I had brought back a book from home – we were allowed to read to each other in the dormitory at night – and I started on this book about Jesus which had a description of Mary Magdalen with her bosoms hanging out. I went merrily reading on until I was caught. Shock. Horror. How could I? Where had the book come from? I suppose it was some sort of satire about Jesus which in my innocence I hadn't realized. Anyway, the upshot of that was I nearly got sent home.

There was, really, looking back, a lot of repression. Nobody would have dreamt of talking to us about life and sex. Nobody explained to us about bosoms and periods. When these happened it was frightening. I can remember to this day staring down at my chest and wondering what was happening to me, but I didn't discuss it with anyone. You just did not talk about *those sort of things*. Everything was hidden. Isolation was the great punishment. If you were naughty, you were made to feel beyond redemption. They threw hell at you very easily. My fear of not being respectable stems from my days at Ascot. And yet it wasn't a snobbish school. The girls on the whole did not come from grand backgrounds, rather middle-class. I had a friend who lived in Wimbledon whose father had a leather factory. That was the level. Nobody was expected to go on to university. In the whole of my time only one person went on to Oxford or Cambridge. I expect it's different now. But by modern standards you certainly weren't educated.

There was a brilliant nun called Mother Bridget who taught us English and had us reading Jane Austen by the time we were twelve and loving it. There was a lovely fat nun, too, called Mother Alfie – not that exactly, but something like that – who taught us sewing and made us enjoy it. And there was a very soft, kind-hearted nun called Mother Barbara who used to sing lullabies to us at night and kiss us goodnight, but that was stopped.

There were a fair amount of crushes amongst the girls, with little love notes flying about and quite a lot of ganging up. That I detested. Also the cold. We were always so cold – we had a lot of coughs and colds as a result, I think. The biggest prize of all was to be taken to the station to meet whatever visiting priest was coming to see us. Oh, the excitement.

Susan Wilberforce wasn't in the same year as me, but I dimly remember her as tall and dark with a long black pigtail. She was a shadowy sort of person, didn't make that much impression. She had very round cheeks in those days, so we called her 'Chubby' Wilberforce.

'Chubby' Wilberforce did not fit in at Ascot. By all accounts she was already unhappy there by the time her father died when she was nine, and it is interesting to conjecture what effect his death might have had on her. She was secretive to a degree unusual in her age, and family members talk about this as something of a wonder. Yet might it not have concealed a hurt, sensitive, proud child unable to express her feelings in a happy, outward manner? Might she not have found a deeply disturbing symbolism in the death of her father on her birthday? There is nothing to show that she had a warm, affectionate relationship with her mother; if anything, it is suggested that she did not. She looked more on Lady Illingworth as a mother, it was stated in the fraud trial. It was an admission which inevitably added to the repugnance with which the illegal appropriation of her funds was received by the jury.

Who knows what role her father might have played in her later life? He was, after all, the well-loved hero of the village, and some of the affection in which he was held might have been extended to her. Susan is on record as having said that she did not want to be reminded of Markington. To visit the sturdy, compact Yorkshire village is at once to be made aware of its past squire, where his name is carved with pride. A cricket field and pavilion have been named after him, and there is a commemorative window in the nearby Catholic church at Bishops Thornton.

Whatever the effect of his death on her may have been, at the age of twelve Susan Wilberforce was expelled from St Mary's after a long period of unco-operative behaviour. Every convent has its quota of girls who kick against the rules, who find the combination of religion and discipline too much for them, and it was symptomatic of the rebelliousness in Susan's nature which was to show itself many times later.

Along with her nonconformity, there also seems on first acquaintance a lack of affection. She does not strike one as a woman who expresses warmth in an easy physical manner. She is not given to embracing her friends. She is cool and hard and undemonstrative – except about her expulsion from school, on which she is most ready to express her feelings. During one of our conversations at Pucklechurch, while she was on remand between the two trials, she laughed quite gleefully at it. Despite the years that had ensued, over forty years, in fact – this expulsion obviously gave her an extra cachet, marked her out from the rest. A female rebel without a cause. It was a trait that was to colour or disolour the rest of her life.

From Ascot Susan was sent to another Catholic boarding school, at Oxford. Not a convent, Rye St Anthony was founded in 1930 by two spinsters, Elizabeth Rendall and Ivy King. It consists of a large Victorian merchant's house with modern extensions, situated just off the London road and very near the city centre.

As a lay Catholic community Rye St Anthony attaches, it says, 'great importance to the transmission and development of our faith'. Again, like Ascot, its aims sound ironic in view of the later history of one of its pupils. They are to 'provide a good Christian education which would enable each individual girl to develop her talents to the full, and to produce the qualities of character which would lead her naturally into responsible adult life'. The cynic might wonder – unfairly, admittedly – where the talents for forgery and a quite exceptional deviousness figure in that description!

According to her own story, Susan Wilberforce was then sent to a finishing school – again a convent – just outside Paris to study music and domestic economy. This is a shadowy part of her life. What is typical is the little knowledge even old friends have of such early periods in her life. She was always to keep her companions in different compartments, only allowing one set an insight into what happened at any one time or, more realistically, what she *said* had happened. 'Too much knowledge is a dangerous thing' was the rule of the game she played with people all through life. She set out to create a maze about herself in which certain friends could wander a little but in which only she knew the secret of their route. And she always took care to see that friends did not meet each other in the same area of the maze.

At seventeen Susan returned to Errolston – the senior section of Ascot – to concentrate further on 'domestic economy'. It is not a fact she releases in her biographical notes. Possibly her mother or even Lady Illingworth interceded with the authorities at Ascot to have her back. Both would have held considerable sway with the nuns, who would dearly love an old Catholic family and, even more, a title. Susan, however much she may have desired a more rigorous intellectual education, was clearly following the traditional pattern of upper-class girls, who were not expected to have careers or academic qualifications. 'I am educated but without a single O-level,' she said of herself in an interview with the Fraud Squad.

Gillian Bence Jones, a lifelong friend from that time, said the Errolston days were happy. 'Errolston was great fun. It was not at all strict. I didn't go to the main school – Errolston was regarded very much as a finishing school – but I didn't get the impression the discipline was the same. We took very easy subjects – cookery, cleaning, embroidery – the sort of nonsense that was supposed to fit you for running your own house. Not that it did. Susan was great fun in those days. She was very witty and very open. She was very headstrong but outwardly very controlled. I don't recall her being devious and I don't recall her being at all snobbish – rather the reverse. She played the piano beautifully. A lot of men were mad about her – Lord Bute, for one.'

Cosseted by Lady Illingworth she had the whole of London society to choose from. But there was one problem she had to resolve. As Susan Wilberforce moved towards adulthood, what was this witty yet rather defiant girl going to do for money? Her confidantes at Errolston were all comfortably set up; was the same true for her?

Her mother had returned to live at Markington some time after her husband had been killed at El Alamein; but a few years later she married again, to Lieutenant-Colonel Hugh de Neufville Lucas of the Indian Cavalry, and went to live in Scotland. There were family murmurings of disapproval at the young widow remarrying and removing herself from Markington to Perthshire, and new eruptions of discord between herself and her former sister-in-law, Lady Illingworth. Old Markington inhabitants grin cheerfully when they mention the 'lack of love' that existed between the two women. Obviously the whole village was fully aware of the tension in the 'Big Hall'. But, on reflection, is it surprising that two rather grand women, both with a claim to be chatelaine of the same house, should fall out? John Wilberforce himself has testified that his mother and Lady Illingworth did not get on. 'There was a degree of mutual dislike and jealousy between them,' he said. More discord erupted because, the Illingworths thought, they had received little thanks for all the restoration work done to the Hall at their behest, not to mention the money spent on it.

At any rate, Susan now 'lost' her mother again; the children stayed behind at Markington. By this time John was about to go up to Oxford, while his sister was being 'finished' at Errolston. One of her stories – which cannot be substantiated – is that she was training as a concert pianist when an attack of polio forced her to abandon it. Neither the Royal College of Music nor the Royal Academy, however, can trace her name as a student. Nor does the arduous training it requires seem likely to fit in with schooling at a Paris convent or domestic economy at Errolston. It is not the first time that someone has glamorized their past; but, if it is a lie, it is significant in the light of others, more grandiose, told later on.

On her second marriage their mother relinquished her life interest in the Markington estate, which under the terms of their father's Will went equally to the two children. But it was not until Susan reached her majority in 1955 that she had recourse to her share, which consisted of 600 acres of the estate while John retained the Hall and 400 acres. There had been a previous amicable, and informal, division between them of the furniture at Markington.

The year 1953 saw Susan blossom as a young debutante. It was not, however, her mother who 'brought her out' but her aunt, Lady Illingworth – evidence, once again, of their special relationship. The odd fact is the age at which she came out – nineteen is 'advanced' in debutante terms: most girls come out in their seventeenth or eighteenth year. It suggests that there might have been a disinclination on the new Mrs Lucas's side – or even Susan's – to follow this traditional path. If the problem was money, then once again the familiar generosity of the Illingworth coffers came to the rescue.

In the same year, John had finished at Oxford brilliantly, getting a First in Greats and a Second in Mods. Within a few months of obtaining his degree he had married in New York, with Susan present, and started his career in the Foreign Office. Since he was unable to afford the upkeep, Markington was to be let until 1967.

The focus of their lives now shifted to London and the benign influence of their aunt, Margaret Illingworth, who after the death of her husband had now taken up sole residence in Grosvenor Square.

Albert Illingworth had died in 1942. His background had been good solid Northern business. He was a past president of the Bradford Chamber of Commerce, and ten years before his marriage to Margaret, in 1921, he had been created a Baron for his work as Postmaster General.

The *Daily Mail* of 19 November 1931 contained this description of the wedding:

> Tenants from both the Wilberforce estates and from Lord Illingworth's estates in Yorkshire were present at the wedding, and the two villages joined in the festivity. There were flags at the windows of the little cottages in Bishops Thornton and they stretched all the way down the main street of Markington two miles away, where the bride's home, Markington Hall, a fine old Elizabethan house, stands. The little church was full, and in spite of the rain, villagers stood outside waiting to scatter their rose petals. . . . Later all the tenants had lunch in the village hall here and the bride and bridegroom made two visits from the Hall to meet them. . . .

The report also contains a touching little story about a Mr T. Gregg who, despite bad rheumatics, waited in the pouring rain to see them. 'I've known her all her life ever since she was a baby. Do you know who cycled five miles for the doctor then, all the way to Ripon? Me.' While the rain fell and his rheumatism treated him sorely he recounted how, when he was gardener at the Hall and Miss Wilberforce was a little girl, she mischievously used to hide his gardening tools from him. 'But now I'm just waiting here to give her a wave of my hand, and if she sees me she will smile at me.' She did, the report is glad to record.

Was the marriage a happy one? Close family members aver that it was; only Susan Wilberforce alleges that it was not. She claims that Lord Illingworth was a great womanizer who forced his wife to join him in perverted sexual practices and took photographs of her in various indecent postures. She herself told me that, while sifting through a box of Lady Illingworth's possessions after her death, she came across a number of obscene photographs not just of Lady Illingworth but of young boys engaged in unnatural acts. 'They were her husband's,' she whispered. 'I burnt them all. I didn't want the children to see them.'

Whatever the truth of her allegations, life on the exterior, at least, was for Margaret Illingworth a happy one. Her husband was extremely rich, they possessed a beautiful home in Grosvenor Square and enjoyed a splendid social calendar that had them wining and dining in the best places, with frequent trips to Switzerland and Monte Carlo. Nor did her life change much after Lord Illingworth died in 1942. He left her the magnificently furnished house in Grosvenor Square, two Rolls-Royces and a large quantity of jewellery, plus nearly £50,000 a year from investments on trust for her lifetime. The trust would terminate, he stipulated in an odd twist to his Will, if Lady Illingworth were to become a nun and enter a convent. It was said afterwards that his reason for this was a virulent dislike of Catholicism which he had repressed during his marriage to a devout Catholic.

No. 44 Grosvenor Square, opposite the American Embassy, was a very grand house indeed which, in the Illingworth heyday, took twelve servants to run. It had forty rooms, a large courtyard garden and extensive wine cellars. Built in 1725 by Sir Richard Grosvenor, it was famous for being the house at which the first despatches of the victory at Waterloo arrived. On the evening of 21 June 1815 Lord Liverpool, the Prime Minister, was due to dine with the Foreign Secretary, who then resided at No. 44. In the excitement of victory dinner was cancelled, whereupon the French chef, it was said, in high dudgeon, threw all the food on the fire! In later years Lady Illingworth used to give an annual party to celebrate the event.

That she was a tireless, indefatigable hostess is in no doubt. Regularly, twice a week, dinner parties for twenty-six people would be given, the long Regency table in the dining room carefully set with antique silver. After her husband's death she still entertained lavishly, her guests eating off silver plates 'to save the crested china'. Another party which the press revelled in was given for the descendants of William the Conqueror; they included an astonishing gathering of celebrities as diverse as Paul Getty, the Duchess of Leeds and the Duke and Duchess of St Albans.

On another occasion she was in bed with tonsillitis in the upper part of the house while the servants were having their tea in the basement. She thought she heard a noise, she later told a reporter from the *News of the World*, but ignored it and went on with her own tea. Suddenly the doors between her bedroom and dressing room 'opened very slowly and the pale dark face of a strange woman peered through! I was terrified and screamed and rang and rang my bell ... and the face at the door disappeared in a flash.' Not, however, before a certain amount of jewellery and trinkets had been taken from her ladyship's dressing case. The entire dressing room had been ransacked, but as she joyfully told the reporter, 'The thief was evidently out to get big things: fortunately for me, however, my diamonds were locked up elsewhere, and I was wearing my pearls in bed.' She had the wit to see the humorous side of this, explaining that she knew it was absurd to wear pearls in bed but that some instinct had told her to keep them on. They were, after all, worth £4000.

What is interesting about the story – headlined 'Sick-Bed Drama' in the *News of the World* – is a plea she made for the return of a special gold coin which she explained had been given to her by her husband on their marriage. Does it sound like the request of a woman who had been unhappily married and forced into degrading sexual acts?

Albert Oslar, who was her chauffeur for twenty years, says that everyone in Grosvenor Square knew and loved her. 'Doormen would doff their hats when they saw her, everyone and anyone would pay their respects, she was the central figure in that community.' To this community came Susan Wilberforce. What could be more natural than that a rich, gregarious party-lover like Lady Illingworth should take over her niece's coming-out ball? Which is what she did, even lending Susan her house and the necessary jewellery for the occasion. The *Tatler* called the dance, at which three hundred guests whirled and twirled and dined beneath glittering chandeliers while champagne poured endlessly in the awning-covered courtyard, 'one of the most memorable dances' of the 1953 season. It was held on 23 June, two days after the famous Battle of Waterloo anniversary.

The Russian emigré aristocrat, Baron Michael de Stempel, was a guest at the ball. It was the second time Susan had met him, the first being at a party at Oxford the previous year when her brother John had introduced them. 'He took one look at me and thought I was the girl for him. I took one look at him and thought he was the most extraordinary man I had ever met in my life . . . and hated him on sight.' In fact, he became the most important man in her life and their twisted love-hate relationship ('dependent aggressive' as psychologists call it) was to influence her powerfully for nearly forty years.

Meanwhile Uncle Robert, her father's brother, had set Susan up in a small flat in Earls Court. It was a typical gesture of generosity from a man who would continue to help her and her children financially when they experienced difficult times later on – not that he ever got much thanks for it. Most reluctantly did she attend his funeral in 1984, refusing to return to Markington Hall afterwards for refreshment. But then, as the fraud case revealed, she had much on her mind at the time.

Life for a deb in 1953 was pleasant enough. Although Britain was only just beginning to emerge from hardships like rationing, and many goods were still in short supply, enough existed to guarantee a satisfyingly hedonistic life for the glittering classes. 'You couldn't keep your head up for the buns flying through the air,' recounts a deb of the time. Restaurants might be few and far between compared with today's number, but then people did not eat out as commonly as they do now. 'We went to people's houses a lot, or their flats in some cases.'

The two popular nightclubs of the period were the 400 in Leicester Square and the Milroy in Hamilton Place. Princess Margaret was a devotee of the Milroy, where Paul Adam was the bandleader who affectionately watched the young cavort in front of him. 'Every other deb was in love with Paul or alternatively sighing over Hutch who used to play the piano at Quaglino's or the Allegro. He used to do three-week stints at both places. We'd arrive at 10.30 for dinner and Hutch used to come on about midnight. He was marvellous, a superb cabaret star, as smooth as silk.'

When they weren't dancing and giggling and throwing bread rolls at the 400 or the Milroy, they were giving repeat performances at Kettners or Hatchetts and sighing over Tommy Kinsman and his band. 'If he thought you were pretty enough he'd ask you to sign his drum and you'd be in seventh heaven,' remembers the same deb. Lance Percival was just launching out in cabaret at the Condor Club in Soho, which was known for its 'cheap nosh', and the young Marquess of Milford Haven, best man to Prince Philip at his wedding to the Queen, was thought to be the best-looking man in town.

The five years of socialism that had existed immediately after the war might almost never have been, Suez and its ramifications were looming on the horizon, the Cold War diving below zero – but the deb class of 1953 had a pretty jolly time. 'The most extraordinary aspect I now recall,' said another deb of that vintage, 'is that we never bothered to ask our partners how they paid for it. I cannot remember ever looking at a bill, let alone asking the poor man if he'd like a sub. Very different from today. They hadn't invented "going Dutch". There was one would-be beau who took me out every night for three weeks on the trot and I never once asked him if he could afford it. I suppose we were the last of the Bright Young Things.'

How did Susan Wilberforce fit into this milieu? Her background was suitable enough on both sides of her family: solid Yorkshire squirarchy on her father's side, long-established Catholic aristocracy on her mother's, but the signs are that she did not find it that congenial. Gillian Bence Jones, also a deb of that era, says, 'Susan was rather lazy. There might be thirty to forty dances to go to but Susan would condescend to go to ten. She certainly was not an indefatigable party-goer. She really only did the season in a perfunctory way. I think she liked sailing and she played the piano very well – she had a good piano in her flat – but on the whole she was more intelligent than the general run of girls. She had a good brain. She was rather witty. She could be very sarcastic.'

The years between 1953 and her marriage in 1957 are a vague period. More accurately, they present another example of her famous secrecy. From all accounts it appears that, like many others of her class, she took odd jobs here and there, interspersed with long holidays. Curiously, amongst several interviewed not one debutante of that era, apart from Gillian Bence Jones, recalls Susan Wilberforce. Did she deliberately keep a low profile? It would seem so. What little she earned was augmented by family trust funds and the sale of part of her share of the Markington contents.

In London, Susan has said that she became 'an interior designer' working for David Hicks. If so, today he has no memory of her working for him – but then why should he? Certainly not if she were just an odd upper-class girl working in his office or showroom. The small-time job which many debs enjoyed cannot be dignified by a professional title. It could be one of the sadnesses of Susan Wilberforce's life that she had an active mind yet little scope to exercise it. For someone who did not adore parties, life in London with its predictable social circles could be incredibly tedious. Is it then so surprising that this aristocratic 'rebel without a cause' should suddenly plunge into marriage with an outsider?

'She was heartily tired of the nonsense of her London life,' says a friend from that time. 'She was ripe for something new, only not having a career what could she do but marry – marry someone as totally unlike her family as she could find.' The man who occasioned this dramatic reaction, the man she set her eyes on, was Simon Dale.

·4·

T·H·E B·A·T·T·L·E O·F
H·E·A·T·H H·O·U·S·E

SUSAN Wilberforce met Simon Dale at a party. She was by then twenty-three and growing tired of the debutante round; he was thirty-eight, very tall – six foot three – wearing thick pebble glasses, already more than half bald and with a deep booming voice. Yet she fell for him hook, line and sinker. Or so everyone was led to believe.

A debby friend recalls Susan emotionally exulting at having fallen in love at first sight with the man she was going to marry. 'I saw him across a room, taller than anyone else, and knew that was the man I was going to marry.' It all sounds like the words of the hit of the moment, 'Some Enchanted Evening', from the American musical *South Pacific*. And it also sounds suspiciously like her remarks on first meeting Michael de Stempel. Underneath, the rebel was obviously a passionate romantic. She was to marry him within a few weeks of their meeting.

Who was Simon Dale? It was fashionable at the time of the murder and fraud trials to dismiss him as a half-mad, half-blind ex-architect crawling along a lower-class floor hopelessly out of his depth with his aristocratic wife and the rest of the Wilberforce family. It is far from the truth, however.

When the Wilberforces heard of the impending marriage they were deeply shocked. Both Lady Illingworth and Susan's mother were for once united in their disapproval. Her mother went so far as to describe her daughter's behaviour as like that of 'a pregnant parlourmaid'. The whole family disapproved. 'My uncle Robert was very worried about Dale's apparently limited means and prospects as an architect who was already half-blind,' recalls John Wilberforce. Uncle Robert and, no doubt, other members of the family, including Lady Illingworth, made strenuous efforts to stop the marriage. Robert Wilberforce, a solicitor, urged them to agree to some form of trust or marriage settlement that would protect Susan's assets from the Markington estate, but to no avail. Emotions ran high; John supported his uncle, while Susan and Simon together pooh-poohed the need for a settlement. They resented and resisted these concerns and said so in no uncertain fashion. From this time, John reveals, 'Susan increasingly distanced herself from myself and other members of the family.'

Simon Dale's background was good, honest, professional middle class. His father, Tom, was an Oxford-based architect who became diocesan architect to the Bishop. Simon, who had a brother and two sisters, was born on 17 June 1919. He went to the famous Dragon School in the city as a day boy and afterwards to a very minor public school, St Bees, set on the Cumberland coast. He began to read architecture at Cambridge, but the war intervened before he could finish his studies. On grounds of bad eyesight he could have claimed exemption, but chose not to. A rather touching and highly indicative story in the light of later events has him, according to his sister, Alison, deliberately learning the sight chart off by heart so that he could pass his army medical. A strength revealed itself there that would emerge again in the years of estrangement from his wife.

Simon served in the Royal Engineers in India, among the hill tribes of North India, and later in the Seychelles. After the war he completed his architectural studies and worked with his father in Oxford before moving to London. Robert Clifford, best man at their wedding, was much incensed at the portrait of Simon painted by Susan during the murder trial. 'He was a delightful man, cheerful, good-tempered, very like his father Tom in the sense that he too was a cheery individual. They had a house in north Oxford that Tom Dale had designed and built. The funny thing was that Tom was a small man while Simon was so large.'

It was Robert Clifford's now deceased brother Hugh who had first made friends with Simon Dale at Cambridge during the early years of the war. 'I first met him', says Robert, 'at our parents' house in Devon where he visited several times, including a memorable day when he helped me land a record salmon of 26 lb.' In 1949 Hugh Clifford married and subsequently, as a vet in the Colonial Service, was posted to Uganda. Simon was godfather to their daughter, christened in Devon. After his own marriage, Robert Clifford again saw Simon Dale and his sister Alison. The other Dale daughter became a nun, and the other son died. But Simon and to a lesser extent Alison became friends of the family, visiting the Cliffords in Gloucestershire and, for a time in the fifties, at Banbury in

Oxfordshire where they then lived: 'Our guest book shows in 1953 the name in capitals S. DALE and two inked thumb prints.' It was a typical Simon Dale joke.

With Hugh abroad in Uganda, it came as only a minor shock when Robert was asked, at two days' notice, to be Simon's best man. The wedding was at a Catholic church in north London, 'in apparent secrecy'. Only five people were present – the bride and groom, Alison Dale, Robert Clifford and the priest conducting the service. When the question arose of who should give the bride away, there was no one else available but the best man. As Clifford reminisces affectionately, 'There cannot be many who have been called on for both duties at a wedding!'

Simon Dale wore a dark 'formalish' suit, the bride something 'summery'. The date was 27 August 1957. Afterwards there was no reception. 'We just went, nobody was asked back to celebrate or anything like that. They wanted it very quiet because of such family disapproval.' What did he think of Susan Wilberforce, whom he had not met before? 'She was rather striking – pale, slender, very shy, rather cold somehow.'

The Dales took a flat in the Old Brompton Road in South Kensington, where life seemed happy enough. Simon, although handicapped with worsening sight, still had enough work, and three months after their marriage Susan found herself pregnant. When their first son, Alexander, was born on the last day of July the following year, they wrote to Robert Clifford to ask him to be his guardian if anything happened to them. 'She didn't want the Wilberforces to take over. I got the impression that she had severed herself completely from them. In fact, I think one of the reasons Simon married her was because she seemed so isolated, so alone – even if it might be of her own choosing. I don't think she married him under great pressure – if anything it was the other way about. She wanted him more than he wanted her. Here was this erudite, amusing man with a deep booming voice and a tremendous capacity for enjoyment. What a change from her stuffy formal relatives!' Photographs in the Clifford family album support his view. Those of Simon show a cheerful, extrovert man, laughing or smiling and very like Alexander in appearance. Clifford agrees. 'He was very like his first son in looks – the boy has inherited the same receding hairline!'

It must have been just after their wedding that Simon and Susan planned the move to Heath House. For, as a friend from those times, Christopher Hurst, recalled, they both seemed very happy when he called on them in their flat. London was not for them; they had seen this beautiful house in Herefordshire and had obviously decided what a magnificent task it would be to save it. 'He was not unsnobby himself,' said Hurst. 'Simon liked getting on with the gentry. The idea of being lord of the manor quite appealed to him. I remember that on the news of his wedding his father said, "I see Simon has married into the landed gentry." ' Cheerfully, Susan broke a family trust to find the £2000 with which to buy the property.

Heath House, on the borders of Hereford and Shropshire but technically in the former, was built in 1625. In his *Buildings of Herefordshire* Pevsner affords it little space other than to say:

> Heath House. Probably c.1650–60. Brick, English bond, with two projecting wings to the N. Hipped roof with dormers. The S side is flat, of eight bays and two storeys. Doorway (re-set?) in the third bay, with tapering pilasters, beaded up the edges. What remains of original windows is of the wooden cross type. The staircase with turned balusters is either imported or re-used, i.e. original in its parts but not in their assembly. On the first floor a room with fine, strong mid-C17 panelling.

A cursory examination. Obviously Pevsner did not fall for Heath House. William Ripley, a descendant of the family that once owned it, was far more informative, though he stressed that his dates might be slightly out, albeit not seriously. He had many historical papers and even pictures of the house in former times. What he said was fascinating, particularly in the light of later events: 'Heath House was built by a Mr Hethe in 1625 in Jacobean times. He was described by the local gentry as "not quite a gentleman". I don't know why. Perhaps it was because he was a Roman Catholic. Anyway, the house was sold about 1660 to the Beale family who lived there for nearly three hundred years. They altered its shape and added the Queen Anne front.' The Beales, he added, were a local grand family who had first acquired the Hopton Castle estate. The castle itself plays a part in the history of Heath House, for they are linked, it is rumoured, by an underground tunnel. It is also probable that the fine, heavy staircase of Heath House was saved from the castle when it was sacked in the Civil War.

According to W. T. Barber's *Exploring the Marches and Border-lands of Wales*, Hopton Castle was given by Henry II to one of his supporters in 1165. 'The very sight', he writes, 'of this square keep must have enraged the Welsh, but the 10 feet thick walls were strong enough to withstand and abort any attack.' But then he adds compellingly, 'If any Marcher border fortress is haunted this grim, ruined Norman castle must surely be, for in 1644, after resisting for three weeks, its mounds became slippery with the blood spilling from the thirty-three Roundheads who, after surrender, were massacred by Royalist soldiers.'

In her delightful reminiscence of life in the region in the 1930s, *An Idler on the Shropshire Borders*, the Sunday afternoon writer Ida Gandy, who lived at Clunbury, recounts a visit she made one springtime, and her meeting with a local shepherd: ' "Best be off to see it now before it grows dark," he said. "When I was a lad the old folk would tell of how the ghosts of the poor soldiers murdered there often wandered round at nightfall. Not that I believe it myself. Still, best to go in daylight." ' 'I knew enough local history', recounts Mrs Gandy, 'to understand what he referred to.'

During the Civil War the castle, which belonged to a fervent Republican named Wallop, held out with a garrison of only thirty-three men for nearly three weeks under Colonel More of Linley against a far stronger Royalist force, led by Sir Lewis Kirke of Ludlow. When finally hunger forced their surrender, every man was put to death except their leader.

A local historian and writer, Veronica Bowater, whose cottage faces out over the ruined castle, offers a slightly more detailed version:

> They were local men and two maidservants collected by Colonel More. Altogether they killed over a hundred Royalists trying to scale the walls. After repeatedly asking them to surrender the Royalists started to dig under the castle in order to mine it. Colonel More then requested that his men have full honours if they surrendered. This was refused. He asked for quarter for his men. Whether this was signified or not it is known that the garrison did surrender, whereupon the maidservants were beaten and sent about their business while the men, save for Colonel More, had their hands and genitals cut off before being tied back to back and drowned in the lake behind the castle. They were battened down to die. Colonel More was sent to nearby Brampton Bryan and not heard of again. The castle has the reputation of being the most haunted along the Welsh border.

A ghost in the form of a Cromwellian soldier is still supposed to haunt the upper rooms at Heath House. In recent years a local psychic, Avis Addis, paid a visit to Heath House at Simon Dale's invitation. Afterwards she commented, 'It's one solid haunt. I felt a presence up there in the attic and one in the dining room. It was a very unhappy house.'

It is not surprising, since the region round about is popularly supposed to be amongst the most haunted in Britain. The Welsh

Marches – the border country between England and Wales – delights the eye with its blend of hill, valley, woodland and thickly hedged meadows dotted with sheep, but its history is one long bloody war, beginning long before the Roman conquest and continuing until Henry Tudor's victory over Richard III at Bosworth Field in 1485.

Fortunately the days of the Beale family at Heath House seem to have passed happily, without incident. At the sweet little church of St Edward, set in the middle of a field at Hopton Castle and virtually acting as home chapel, there is a brass plaque placed in the west wall commemorating the seventy-year life of Thomas Beale, from 16 June 1816 to 22 May 1886. The east window is of stained glass mundanely depicting the four Evangelists, though with a charming inscription along the bottom that reads: 'To the memory of Lt. Col. Henry Yelverton Beale who died April 5, 1869 aged 44, this window was erected by her who owed the happiness of her life to his love.' In this account of the hatred and anger that existed between one man and a woman in later years at Heath House, it is refreshing to come back at times to that tender dedication.

The Beales seemed to have disappeared without record, even to the extent of having family portraits sold off by the next owners of Heath House, Sir Henry Ripley's son. One did linger on in the neighbourhood; William Ripley recalls his father being friendly with Arty Beale, who lived at Leintwardine.

Six years before buying Heath House in 1886, Sir Henry Ripley, first baronet, MP for Bradford and a rich wool merchant, had acquired the Bedstone estate and built Bedstone Court – now a public school, Bedstone College. Over the next few years lots of Ripley cousins, according to William, moved in including Setons, Sunderlands and Garnetts. 'The place was like a rabbit warren,' he adds cheerfully. One of the more famous was the Pre-Raphaelite painter Charles Compton Seton.

But by 1920 the cousins had gone and the second baronet's widow, Eugenie, Lady Ripley, lived there in grand style. Heath House came into its own. There was a large staff and sufficient gardeners to keep the place looking immaculate. The gardens were a dream. Eugenie herself was, by all accounts, a pretty, elegant woman who liked entertaining, enjoyed a quarter of a bottle of champagne mid-morning and kept a pet parrot. Sadly her reign came to an end probably some time in the thirties and during the Second World War the house became a secretarial college.

William Ripley's father, Sir Hugh Ripley, was then given the house as a wedding present. It was queried at the time whether this was actually a kindness, since the house had come to be regarded as something of a white elephant. 'My father wanted to lop off one of the wings to make the place more tenable – it was far too big as it was, and in a bad state. But Lord Euston, together with the rest of the council of the Historic Monuments Commission, refused on the grounds that it was a listed building. So my father decided to demolish the whole thing. Ironically, that was allowable. Part of the contents were sold off and some of the downstairs panelling stripped and sold, too. There's supposed to be a pub in Leominster that has it, but I don't know which one. At this time, also, my father was trying to run the walled garden as a market garden. I remember in the fifties an old gardener called Mr Crewe helped him. And there was a gamekeeper who lived in the grounds and had two goats that used to graze on the front lawn. Before he went my father took out the overmantel in the library depicting Perseus rescuing Andromeda. It was dated 1720 and is now established in my own cottage. He also removed a little old painting of the Virgin Mary that had replaced the crucifix torn down by the Cromwellians. There are still the marks on the staircase wall where the Roundhead swords hacked it out.'

A demolition order lay over Heath House. The happiness of Eugenie, as owner, had long since retreated. It seemed that another proud house, queen of all it surveyed, would vanish – victim, as so many were, of changing economic fortunes. The bulldozers arrived. And then along came the Dales. . . . The year was 1959.

How Simon Dale came to find Heath House is not specifically recorded. It is known that he was helping to restore houses in Shropshire about this time, so it seems likely that on his travels he came across this one. His sister Alison remembers being taken to see it even before he married Susan Wilberforce in 1957, so its attractions must have remained with him for a number of years. Their friend Christopher Hurst was shown a photograph in 1958. 'My heart absolutely sank', he said, 'on looking at this picture of a crumbly old house which they had decided to buy and restore. But they were mad about it. Not only would they restore it to its original grandeur, they would people this exotic place with children. Nine children was the number they mentioned.'

Susan bought Heath House from Sir Hugh Ripley in her name – a fact that Simon was bitterly to regret in subsequent years. They moved in just seven days before Christmas, with one son aged seventeen months and another aged just seven days. Only three rooms were habitable. They had set themselves a truly awesome task and one in which the dreams could so easily turn to nightmares. At that stage, however, all they knew was love and optimism.

Displaying considerable architectural skill, Simon Dale rebuilt the famous staircase bit by bit. Robert Clifford says that Dale first reinstalled the top right part of the staircase, which led to the attic rooms. Here they had a flat while restoration work continued. Eventually he would re-establish the left-hand branch of the staircase, leading to the drawing room and downstairs to what is now the kitchen and great hall. 'He really did brilliant work to make that house livable in. In their spare time the two of them went searching for the appropriate furniture at sales around the county.' Judging by the number of four-poster beds in the house, it must have been a fruitful search. Not all the contents were Susan's. She herself admitted in the run-up to the murder trial that a quarter of the furniture belonged to her ex-husband.

Friends who visited them in their early days at Heath House commented on how happy they seemed. Ann Devey-Smith saw them there in the early sixties: 'The house was surrounded by scaffolding, there was this tall, rather "peering" man – Susan's husband. Alexander, the first child, was crawling around while Sebastian, the second son, was in a pram. Susan', she recalls, 'seemed happy and content.' So thought the Cliffords about the same period. 'We arrived with a whole carload of children – three of our own and two others. The Dales had three – Alexander, Sebastian and Marcus, who was in a carry-cot. We all had tea on the lawn and played games. Susan was quietly efficient, bringing down all the tea things from upstairs – they hadn't moved downstairs in those days – without any fuss. She was a striking-looking woman, I thought, and very efficient. They both appeared happy and relaxed. Simon was talking about the Cromwellian ghost and was already interested in the ancient history of the house. He was a very jovial character in those days. A big laughing man whom I never heard complain.'

Looking back over their lives at this period, did Susan, as has been supposed, see in their purchase of Heath House a return to the landed houses of her childhood and youth? Did she secretly envisage becoming the lady of the manor dispensing largesse to a grateful peasantry? Did he, already suffering a crippling, untreatable eye condition that would inevitably end in virtual blindness, regard this as his one great architectural achievement, which would bring him fame and fortune?

Robert Clifford says Simon was always working on notions such as an unsupported stressed roof designed along the lines of a bent bow for buildings like aircraft hangars that he could patent and sell. 'He was a great man of ideas,' he said of his friend. Another idea of Dale's had been a prefabricated, module-based neo-Georgian house that could be erected swiftly. Again, he expected with an optimism that appears to have been one of his strongest traits to patent the idea and then sit back and watch the money roll in. It didn't.

It was quite normal for him to sit quietly at a table by the window for hours at a time, pencil in hand, dreaming up inventions, adaptations, restorations. It was a characteristic that was possibly delightful at first but would become increasingly irksome as their financial pressures mounted. So too was his growing obsession with the history and mythology of the land around him. It is as if, restricted by failing sight from being involved in the greater world, and becoming less and less able to perform ordinary architectural functions such as the work on stone houses in Scotland that he had been engaged in when they first moved to Heath House, he dug deep – literally as well as intellectually – into the very foundations of Heath House. It did not endear him to a wife who was overstretched with the exacting work of bringing up several young children and worried about the dark financial clouds that were massing on the horizon. The laughter went on, the delight in restoring the old house continued, the purchasing of furniture increased, but the marriage was beginning to crack.

'We didn't think they were quite the thing, somehow,' recalls a member of the local landed gentry, 'so we didn't have much to do with them. There was something fly-by-night about them. Something rather desperate about her, particularly. In fact, my mother told me she had met Susan's mother down on a visit, who had told her that Susan was a bad hat. Well, after that we certainly didn't have much truck with them. Nor, I think, did many people. Poor things, I assume they led rather an isolated life. I hope our attitude didn't contribute to what happened. . . .'

A professional musician himself, Robert Clifford recalls from visiting Heath House in the early days that there was an ancient French harp without any strings in one room and a piano in another, but interestingly he never had any musical conversations with Susan or saw any evidence of the would-be concert pianist she had claimed to be. But then it can be argued that, with so many children to look after, she would have had little time to display such talent, or even to express an interest.

Their next child, a girl, Sophia, was born in 1962, one year after

Marcus, and two years later, in 1964, their final child, Simon, arrived. By the following year the marriage was failing badly. The reasons were abundant: money was running out, the big house was inordinately demanding in terms of energy and resources, as were the five children born within six years, plus an increasingly handicapped husband. What had been laughter and humour and love turned to bitterness, anger and tedium. Susan claimed that her husband 'shut himself away for weeks at a time, only emerging to have meals and insisting they be rigidly on time'. They had no social life, she added, because they had no money and Simon was such a bore as well as mean. According to Susan he took no notice of Christmas or birthdays – hers or the children's – and was moody and violent. She had used up her own money and had had to borrow from friends. She told Ann Devey-Smith that one Christmas she had been forced to rifle the children's money boxes in order to buy food.

Francesca Tesi, Italian-born second wife of Susan's future husband Michael de Stempel, visited the Dales late in 1969 when their relationship was obviously very bad. She recalled, 'She was a snob. Typical English. Mousey, not elegant, not well dressed. A county type in a boring cold house. No heating, bad food and all the time giving the impression I was a bloody foreigner. Simon, he hardly appeared, and when he did, he didn't speak.'

According to Susan, in statements made to the police following the murder, Simon was also violent and abusive, hitting her repeatedly on the base of her spine, which later caused back trouble, and attempting to beat the children. 'He never hit Sophia,' she said, 'but he tried to beat the boys on several occasions.' Defending them had led her to throw coal at him, and on one occasion 'I tried to kick him in the balls when he was going for Marcus but I only got him in the groin.'

But the real revelations concerned their sex life. What had been a fine, rewarding and playful sexual tension between them had soured immeasurably. All love had gone from the marriage, she insisted, as early as 1962, but that did not stop her husband from being 'very sexually active. He was very aggressive about it. It was certainly not love. He simply wanted to satisfy himself.' Furthermore, she informed the police in a statement that shocked the judge in the murder trial, Simon Dale was sexually perverted. He tried to insist on anal sex but she refused. He also bought face cream and wanted her to rub it into him. He accused her of being sexually inhibited. And, as if that were not all, she added, he also liked parading in women's clothing, wearing high heels and lipstick! Although, as was observed cynically at the trial, where does a man with size 12 shoes get high heels?

Against such a background of active hatred his continuing research into the history of King Arthur, his curious notions on the link between the eyes and the brain, his theories, too, about the remains of an Armenian settlement from the year AD 400 struck her not as frivolous, tangential and time-consuming but as deliberate, downright cruelty. What did it matter to him if she and the children starved? She was now estranged from all those at Markington, although still the recipient of her uncle's charity, which paid the children's school fees. She had always been secretive and reclusive, so what damage to her pride must the failure of her marriage have produced? Should she run weeping back to Markington with her tail between her legs, bringing her children with her? Never. She had only to envisage the smug satisfaction of John's wife, Laura, whom she disliked, the 'we told you' feelings of the rest of the family, to reject such a solution.

At this time she was in constant touch with Michael de Stempel, the bizarre figure who features prominently in the rest of this story, and with whom she had remained in occasional contact since their first meeting in the early fifties. Though not overtly sexual it was nevertheless a strong and binding friendship. He maintains that he was lending Susan money at this time to pay for food and heating. Simon earned no money at all, or so she pleaded to friends; what money he had he kept to himself. Michael de Stempel claims that 'Simon never bought a pair of socks, or a handkerchief. And never paid the milk bills.'

In 1972 Susan began divorce proceedings on grounds of cruelty. She was advised to change her plea to one of 'unreasonable behaviour', and it was on these grounds that she was awarded a decree nisi in July 1973. She remained in the house, however, for a further two months. Hindsight argues that it was the summer holidays – the children, who were all by now at boarding school, would have been home – and it would have been a difficult time to move. Whatever her reasons, the fact is that she stayed for a short while but in September of that year walked out. The physical violence was too much for her. Later she painted a dreadful picture of two isolated creatures trapped together with insufficient funds or outlets to ameliorate the anger, distrust and fear they endured. As once the marriage had blown hot, so now it blew icy with contempt and rage.

'One day,' she said, 'I just picked up my handbag, got in my car and went.'

She went to her mother's house in Weobley, less than twenty miles away. With the death of her second husband in 1970, Cecilia Lucas had settled in Herefordshire. The village she chose is a well-known one, famous for its wealth of black and white half-timbered houses. It is a place much frequented by tourists, with the inevitable craft shops, art galleries and restaurants. Susan Dale went from one beautiful home to another because Mellington House, situated halfway up the main street, is as handsome an example of English architecture as Heath House. Curiously enough, it also boasts a glorious Queen Anne façade, though the back of the building reveals its medieval origins. There is a fine one-acre garden.

Villagers have little recollection of Cecilia Lucas who, by the time Susan arrived, was an old woman, half-blind, devoted to her little dog but understandably taking little or no part in village life. A part-time gardener remembers her as a very quiet woman. Another villager considered her 'very retiring. She wouldn't even answer the door when someone came. She had a high wall – fencing actually – put all round her garden so the little dog couldn't get out.' Eventually she moved to a nursing home before her death in 1974. But Susan remained with her children at the house.

Susan's secrecy and reclusiveness were by now exhibiting extreme characteristics. Her five children, now aged between nine and fifteen, were not allowed to mix with any other children – village or otherwise. The front windows of Mellington House were permanently screened from the road by heavy net curtains. No one knew what went on inside that house. But gossip abounded when one day it was noticed that some ivy that had been creeping up part of the front wall – possibly causing damage – had been removed during the night. Why could she not have performed this simple task during the day? A village shopkeeper revealed that she would leave her shopping until last thing and then dart across the road just before closing time. 'And then she'd buy the oddest stuff – six large packets of Daz at a time.' Another shopkeeper laughed as he recalled what little foxes the two eldest boys had been. 'Not above a bit of shoplifting, now and again. They were right little devils.'

It is Grace Slade, however – a pleasant, friendly woman – who knew the strange family at Mellington better than most, simply by virtue of living next door. 'We at that time used our house as a holiday house – for weekends, Christmases and the long summer holidays.' He was an architect in Leamington, and, since they had children the same age as some of the Dale family, they thought it might be nice to let the children mix. But, Grace Slade recounts, 'They just weren't allowed to mix and that was that. They weren't even allowed to speak a single word to anybody. On the hottest days if our children were out in the garden hers had to come in. We had a son the same age as Sebastian but the two boys weren't allowed to go off together. He was a nice boy, Sebastian, though rather rigid and shut in for his age. Sometimes when he was cutting the front lawn we would talk to him, but as soon as his mother saw him doing this she would call him in and he wouldn't come out again. She spent a lot of time gardening. There was this big lawn which she would cut with a push mower – it took a lot of energy. I can't fault her on that. But she was abnormally secretive. She was a cruel mother when you consider it. Keeping those children so terribly isolated. . . . But she was a good-looking woman, nobody could deny that.'

During her time at Weobley Susan Dale abandoned her married name and reverted to her maiden name, Wilberforce. When they could – at eighteen and probably under pressure from their mother – the children followed suit. A friend of Simon's was aware how much this last act of aggression hurt him. 'Despite the divorce Simon got on well with Sebastian, who frequently stayed with his father even after Susan left. One day there was a small party somewhere which both went to. Sebastian was a little distance from his father, but as he was being introduced to another guest the room went silent in the way they do and the name Sebastian Wilberforce rang out. I could see Simon had heard. He didn't say anything at the time, but it shook him and it hurt him. She had really taken his children away. Rarely did Simon show any bitterness about his ex-wife but very occasionally he did, and I'm sure the change of name was one of the reasons.'

At Weobley Grace Slade recalls how litigious Susan Wilberforce could be. 'One day lying on the mat with all the other letters was one from a firm of solicitors in London telling us our chimney was in a dangerous state and liable to fall in on Mellington House. Would we do something about it? Well, it was absurd. My husband was a practising architect, and he could see there was nothing the matter with the chimney. He wrote back on his headed paper and told the solicitor the chimney was in excellent condition. When I did talk to her about it she just said coldly, "That's what solicitors are for." It obviously never occurred to her to have an informal word with us. Weird. I bet her solicitor's bills were enormous.' They were. Both she and Simon used solicitors like winged messengers. While she had the benefit of legal aid for the murder and fraud trials, it was revealed at the end of the fraud trial that for her private affairs she owed her solicitors over £11,000.

Little as she mixed with the village, it did become known that she had left a violent husband of whom she was afraid. How she conveyed this when practising such seclusion is not clear. Funnily enough, odd job man Bert Preece has pleasant memories of her: 'She was a nice woman to me. Perfectly friendly in a stiff sort of way. Good on the teas, too. You didn't lack for a cup of tea there. I liked her. All this wicked woman stuff – wasn't on as far as I'm concerned.'

During the first year at Weobley her brother John visited her on two occasions. He was home on leave from his diplomatic post in Washington and needed to sort out the details of their mother's will and the disposal of her furniture, which was quite valuable. It was agreed between them that Susan would divide it fairly and half would be sent on to Markington. Under the terms of the will Susan inherited a residual legacy of £20,000 which would bring in an income in the region of £1000 a year. The house itself was required to be sold, with John the major beneficiary. According to him, matters were as happy as they could be under the sad circumstances of their mother's death. At the same time he invited Susan and her children to come and stay, rent-free, in a self-contained wing of Markington as soon as Mellington House was sold. She agreed, and he left for Washington thinking he had done the best he could for a sister whose life and lack of fortune had worried him greatly for some years.

He may have been comforted, but was she? Had she not envisaged inheriting her mother's house when the old lady died? Could there have been talk that Mrs Lucas would leave her sadly destitute daughter with something solid at last? John had Markington; should not Susan have Mellington? And did Mrs Lucas promise to change her will in Susan's favour only to be waylaid by her final illness and death before she had the chance to do so? Whatever the truth, one fact was obvious: Susan was left with no home of her own. How unfair life must have seemed to her.

Susan and her children moved to Markington, but the stay was a dismal failure. She hated it and made her emotions clear. They are easy to understand. A proud woman, she would greatly dislike the tinge of charity about the arrangement. Nor were she and John's wife, Laura, who was often at Markington, in any way compatible. Laura Wilberforce, an American, had over the years become known and liked in Markington as a busy, friendly, open person, able to chat with anyone. Susan, by comparison, appeared unfriendly and desperately uncommunicative. Her passion for privacy now verged on the paranoid.

Both sides of the family must have breathed a sigh of relief when she arranged to rent a couple of rooms in a friend's house on the outskirts of Ross-on-Wye in Herefordshire. This friend, Mary Purry, who shares with her a passion for gardening, has, unlike many, stayed a friend through thick and thin. Even now, with the sentencing over and the fraud revealed, she will not discuss 'the strange Susan'. And she took the trouble to visit her in Pucklechurch Remand Centre, a fair distance to drive, every Saturday during Susan's confinement there.

Under the terms of their divorce settlement it had been agreed between Susan and Simon Dale that Heath House would be sold. The judge had ruled that half the proceeds would go immediately to Susan, while the other half would be retained by solicitors pending a marriage maintenance settlement. Simon was allowed to stay until such time as contracts had been exchanged between vendor and purchaser. It was a legal loophole that was to prove their Achilles heel. Each displayed an obduracy only matched by the other, and its existence was to fester in Susan's mind as the years progressed and the battle of getting Simon out grew to titanic proportions.

In 1974 the house was put on the market at the asking price of £75,000. Plenty of people came to look and admire the house, but they failed to make any offers. The estate agents explained that with the country in recession it was a bad time. They might well have added that the plainly unco-operative figure of Simon Dale did not help.

With all the good will in the world, the tiny space at Ross-on-Wye was simply inadequate to house all the Wilberforces. The eldest son, Alexander, was away working his passage through Europe. Sebastian, still at school at Shrewsbury, found the arrangement impossible to work in and moved back to live with his father at Heath House. He had always been closer to his father than his mother, it is said, and was to stay there on and off during his final year at school and during the three years that followed at Hull University.

Although she was to protest to all and sundry that she had no money at this stage in life, it is not entirely true. Not only did she have the £1000 a year income from her mother's trust fund, she was never without hand-outs from friends and family. Together they amounted to considerable sums and would certainly have kept her off the poverty line. Her uncle Robert's wife, Marion, was as generous as ever, giving her £7,000 during the seventies and another £10,000 during the eighties, while Gillian Bence Jones lent her several thousand.

Perhaps for this reason Susan allowed the battle of Heath House to ease off for the next few years while she busied herself finding a new home for herself and the three youngest children, Marcus, Sophia and Simon. She had not long to wait, as a three-year lease with the option of renewal on a semi-detached cottage in the hamlet of Docklow, just outside Leominster, soon came on the market. They moved in during the autumn of 1977. Promptly she renamed the simple farm worker's dwelling Forresters Hall, leaving off the tell-tale word 'cottage'.

At this period in Susan's life, however, there was another reason for her letting slide the sale of Heath House. She had discovered a new passion and, so it is claimed, a new romance. The passion was flying, the place where she learned to fly was the nearby Shobdon Flying Club, and the new man was the club's chief flying instructor, Louis Hillkirk Wood – 'Woody' to one and all. 'Woody' was a character straight out of Ernest Hemingway. He had been a successful commercial pilot, having logged over twenty thousand flying hours in his forty-odd years of the game. He knew all about planes from their earliest days. Although married with a son he was by no means indifferent to other women who, said a contemporary flying companion, found him irresistible. 'Despite his age, he had lots of women mad about him. He used to entertain them in this caravan he lived in on the edge of the field. Susan Wilberforce spent a lot of time with him there. And he used to go and stay with her at Docklow. It was common talk.' That same 'common talk' winked and nudged whenever the conversation came round as to how a penniless woman could afford the expensive luxury of flying. Probably some of the money came from the sale of odd bits of furniture which Susan Wilberforce herself admits to having sold to fund herself throughout life; and possibly 'Woody' allowed her special rates. Again it's an odd match – the much older, heavy-drinking, heavy-smoking man in his late sixties and the delicate, refined lady. The age difference was twenty-three years – tempting stuff to an amateur psychologist, particularly considering the early death of her father.

Three years later 'Woody' died in mysterious circumstances. According to newspaper accounts his body was found by a flying instructor, Stuart Palmer, on a disused part of the runway at noon on 29 December 1979. The coroner recorded a verdict of death by misadventure, accepting the theory that the man had died from exposure after abandoning his car in deep floodwater to reach his caravan on the airfield. Susan Wilberforce gave evidence at the inquest, held at Hereford. It was one of her cars that the dead man had abandoned during the storm. She said he had been a friend since she started flying in 1976. The last time she had seen him was at lunchtime two days after Christmas. 'He was in good health,' she told the court, 'but grumbling about the weather. He was going for his flying medical the next day. He was driving one of my cars because he had an accident in his own last November.'

The inquest also heard that a man from the nearby village of Pembridge, Edward Vaughan, had that evening been standing in his garden watching the floodwaters rise on the road to Milton Cross and been surprised to see an Austin 1300 try to get through conditions which required tractors or Land Rovers. 'I watched it go about a hundred yards and then stall. The driver tried to start it, then I heard him get out of the car. I thought he would come back to the house. The car was still there the next morning.'

Woody's body was found at the western edge of the runway, half a mile from his caravan home and three-quarters of a mile from the spot where he had abandoned Susan's car. The body, Stuart Palmer said, was lying face downwards. 'I didn't recognize Mr Wood at first. He was rather dishevelled. His face had blood on it and his nose was pushed to one side.' Inspector John Martin told the inquest there was blood on the victim's knuckles. 'His trousers were partly down and there was gravel between his buttocks. Moss on the runway was disturbed for four or five feet.' The coroner, summing up, said it appeared that the dead man had taken a short cut to his caravan. 'It was a dreadful night and raining heavily. As he suffered more and more from exposure, he must have fallen a number of times, from the evidence of damage to his body. He got about halfway and then collapsed.'

The verdict did not satisfy Susan. She told another member of the club that in her opinion the evidence had been rushed through, that it implied that 'Woody' had been drinking that night and had collapsed after visiting a pub in Pembridge. She believed he had been deliberately dropped from an aeroplane. His death was most mysterious, she added, and needed a private detective to search out the truth. She would hire one. If she ever did it is not recorded, but it is evidence of her predilection for seeing skulduggery where probably none existed. What is ironic is that seven years later it was suggested by some of those who disliked her around Hopton Heath that she might have done the deed herself. Such is the unfairness of life. But with that gallows sense of humour which is such a strong characteristic of hers, she might even join in the laughter.

And all this time, waiting in the wings except for occasional appearances in the fifties and late sixties, was the central figure of Baron Michael de Stempel.

5

A M·A·R·R·I·A·G·E
M·A·D·E I·N H·E·L·L

SUSAN Wilberforce claimed that Michael de Stempel had always loved her, that she only married Simon Dale to spite him. He claims otherwise, but maintains that he helped her with money all her life. He endorsed a Knightsbridge bank account started by her in 1976, the year she started flying. Moreover, it was his generosity to her that helped bring down his second marriage to Francesca Tesi. So she says. Whatever the truth of these allegations, what is clear is that Susan had begun to turn to him more and more as her own circumstances worsened. The judge in the fraud trial described Michael de Stempel as a 'con man'. What he did not add in such solemn surroundings as a courtroom is that the Baron is pure comic opera, a less padded, less musical Baron Ochs from *Rosenkavalier*, a vainglorious creature, all puff and wind. His voice has been described as that of a 'broken Stradivarius', but in reality it is more like the high bleat of a lost sheep. A fifties' deb remembers him then as a 'ghastly little parakeet bumming off anybody he could, and such a snob it was ridiculous'.

But in fairness, his background and childhood were not the stuff that makes down-to-earth accountants of anyone. His father, Baron Victor de Stempel, was a member of the Russian aristocracy who was compelled to escape his country at the time of the Revolution in 1917, when he was a captain in the Imperial Army. He became a naturalized Briton in 1935, which technically should prevent his son, Michael, from using the title of Baron – not that it ever has.

The dashing Russian officer fled first to Holland, where as *The Times* records 'his main preoccupation was playing bridge with Emma, the Queen Mother'. At one stage, in the best aristocratic refugee traditions, he even taught dancing for a living. But then at Biarritz in 1927 he met – and married a year later – Dawn Beaumont, stepdaughter of Walter Dunkels, a director of the Diamond

73

Corporation. Dunkels was known as 'Mr Diamond', as his company controlled virtually the entire British diamond trade. He was rich, influential, wore a monocle and was besotted by his stepdaughter. Dawn Beaumont was nineteen when she married the Baron, who was thirty-two, as his second wife. Through the influence of Walter, Victor de Stempel was given a job with the Diamond Corporation, under the direction of Otto Dunkels, a cousin. He and his young bride were also given the lease of a house in Chester Place, Hyde Park; again their benefactor was Walter Dunkels. A legal wrangle was to follow that involved the Dunkels and de Stempels plus their son, Michael, who had been born in 1929. It was a court case featuring such famous names as Sir Patrick Hastings (who appeared for Walter Dunkels), Norman Birkett (who appeared for the plaintiff, Baron Victor de Stempel) and Sir Stafford Cripps, who handled the later appeal on behalf of Walter Dunkels. That case in 1937 made even greater newspaper coverage than the recent one.

The marriage between the Russian aristocrat and the young English girl was not a success. Recrimination after recrimination followed their separation in 1932. Baron Victor thought his son was being cared for badly, and blamed his wife for keeping 'bad company'. He wrote to her, 'I only hope that you will soon realise that your disgraceful entourage – so poisonous for a young woman and mother – made me go on living in this house [his separate dwelling] . . . if it comes to my knowledge – even through no fault of your own – he [the boy] is brought up in what I consider to be bad surroundings, I shall not spare anybody or anything to see he is looked after. . . .' He also made it clear that he heartily disliked Walter Dunkels, his wife's stepfather, despite being the recipient of 'hundreds, if not thousands of pounds towards the living expenses of you and your wife' from Dunkels.

According to his wife Dawn, he was extremely anti-Semitic. 'He frequently told me how he had come down in the world through having married me, and having to work and mix with Jews. There were occasions when I was going to my parents' house and he would say, "I wonder who will be there tonight – all the Jerusalem of London, I suppose." The Baron maintained that the Jews were enemies of all the aristocracy. They had killed the Tsar and Tsarina and had been responsible for the revolution in Russia. I used to go out to meet him with welcoming arms but he would say he was tired and push me back, with the remark that I could not understand how he, an aristocrat, felt at having to work for Jews.'

He did not have to endure such feelings for long since the diamond magnate, with the help of his cousin, Otto, had him removed from his job. But in doing so he was guilty of a breach of contract and of slandering the Baron. The jury found for the Baron on the matter of unfair dismissal and he was awarded damages of £6000 – an enormous sum in those days, the equivalent of £130,000 in current value. But though they decided the Baron had also been slandered, the judge ruled that the words complained of were not actionable and entered judgement for Mr Dunkels. Nothing loath, both parties took their appeals to the House of Lords. The Baron won on both counts: the five Law Lords upheld the £6000 awarded him and confirmed the jury's findings of slander.

Through all this wandered the pathetic-looking figure of the Baron's son Michael, known as Mishka. Photographs of the time show him as a soulful boy, solemn-faced and with rather a big head on thin shoulders. Later, he said, 'My father felt that the milieu of an old Harrovian Jewish diamond king was not right for a young Russian aristocrat.' He added, 'I was brought up on the Memoirs of the Duc de Saint Simon. I was encouraged by my father to spend Sunday afternoons writing letters to imaginary Portuguese noble-women – just in case the need arose in later life.'

Michael was also heavily imbued, presumably by the same parental influence, with an obsession for titles and genealogy which could manifest itself in ludicrous ways. 'My grandfather,' he would bleat in later years, his still rather disproportionately large head on one side, his eyes crinkled with emotion, 'was very grand. He was best friends with Tsar Alexander III.' Michael claimed that Franco had decorated him with the Alfonso Cross third class, an award for Christian civilization and Spanish culture. 'I used a very antique Castillian to thank him,' he said.

Such was the over-decoration of Michael's speech and the long, immensely drawn-out nature of his replies while in the witness box during the fraud trial that even the judge became annoyed, and showed it. The Baron, who was noticeably called 'Mr de Stempel' throughout the proceedings, was asked by Timothy Barnes, QC, for the prosecution, if he agreed that Lady Illingworth's house in Grosvenor Square was full of magnificent furniture and pictures. De Stempel raised his head, circled it in the air several times and then bleated: 'Fine . . . well, you should have seen my grandmother's house. Now that –' At which Judge Curtis leaned forward from his chair and said a trifle snappily, 'Mr de Stempel, I have given you enough rope. . . . Would you please answer the question!' The Russian-titled Baron's face collapsed like a blown-out paper bag, and for a few minutes the baroque style of his sentences became more subdued.

The young Catholic nobleman – a description he would agree with – was educated at Beaumont, a Jesuit public school near Windsor. At one time the school was the alma mater of eleven of Franco's cabinet; it has now closed down. From there he did his National Service with the Royal Irish Fusiliers (he was much given to wearing a regimental tie in court) before going up to Oxford to read history. A contemporary, Christopher Moorsom, remembers him as a 'funny little Baltic baron who knew how to present a sword in the manner of the Teutonic knights'. 'He was endearing,' said another Oxford friend, 'but hopeless at the paraphernalia of life. His charm used to paper over the cracks and he had a yawning, seen-it-all-before sophistication. Whenever we had lunch, he would be affectedly disturbed that I had to go back to work.'

But much as he might have wished it, Michael de Stempel was no Sebastian Flyte. What he already was was a confirmed liar, as Judge Curtis was to state categorically. De Stempel says he was at Christ Church – the grandest college in Oxford – but Susan's brother John Wilberforce, who was at Oxford in those years doesn't recall it. In a statement made to the police he said:

> I knew de Stempel was at Oxford, though he himself was not, as I remember, up at a college but doing some other course there. He was not a close friend, so much as a friend of other friends; and I remember him as an eccentric with an obsessive interest in titles and the *Almanach de Gotha*. But it must have been through me that at that period he first met Susan and also Lady Illingworth, who no doubt invited him, along with other people from Oxford, to one or two parties she gave at Grosvenor Square for myself or Susan. After leaving Oxford I may have seen de Stempel once or twice in the early days in London but he dropped out of my life, and I have no recollection or knowledge of him since the 1950s.

Needless to say, de Stempel claims a much closer acquaintance. However, John Wilberforce's memory is at fault because the Baron *was* at Christ Church, albeit only for a year. He was sent down, rumour has it, for flogging a college servant. What he did not get, though he told the police he had, was a degree. Somehow, it struck a note of pathos that a sixty-year-old man should still pretend to have a degree. On the other hand it helped the prosecution to brand him as a liar. 'Poor Michael,' said another ex-deb who visited the court room in Birmingham. 'He was always an upper-class con man!'

Now serving four years in prison, he would at least welcome the fact that she had recognized his background correctly.

From Oxford he went to Spain – hence the antique Castillian – to study the language; he also learned Italian and French. He went on to South America where, according to his own reports, he flourished. Eventually he returned home to England, becoming an economic adviser (without any formal training) to the international division of a trust company, Texas Fiduciary – this, despite the fact that he cheerfully describes himself as 'innumerate and one who never looks at bank statements because they are too depressing'. He became an economic consultant to Costa Rica, he said, which like much of his evidence raised weary smiles in court. For Costa Rica, like him, has a notorious reluctance to make available its bank statements. 'I never know quite what my job is,' he said. 'I suppose I have a dilettante role. Other people follow through the doors I open.'

Although he was supposed to have been deeply hurt by Susan's marriage to Dale in 1957, which he refutes, he himself married the following year. His bride was Cristina Macdonald, described variously as the daughter of a poultry farmer and the daughter of a retired naval officer turned farmer. Whatever the truth, both were pleased to give a number of interviews to the gossip columns of the day. 'We're both very idle,' the half-English, half-Spanish Cristina told the *Daily Express* shortly before the wedding. 'But I wouldn't marry Michael unless I wanted to see a lot of him. Michael has never had a job, and I don't suppose he ever will.' An embarrassed 'economic consultant to Costa Rica' demurred: 'My fiancée is half-Spanish and a bit vague about these things. I have been in the import-export business for about two years. It keeps me quite busy.' Seeing a lot of each other did not prevent the marriage collapsing after six years, though it did produce three children, Tatiana, Sophie and Andrew. They are now an artist, stage designer and doctor respectively.

During the fraud case both daughters came to the court and were seen playing a movingly supportive role to their father. Indeed, on the day before his sentencing de Stempel spent many hours on the arm of his daughter Tatiana, walking up and down the corridors in Birmingham's Law Courts while the jury deliberated on the possible guilt or not of Marcus and Sophia Wilberforce. Here was the once dashing young descendant of an aristocratic émigré (aristocrats, he said, are called émigrés; lesser folk are termed refugees!) now reduced to an aging, exhausted figure dressed in shabby suits, hanging on to the life and energy of one of his children. He was a spent force – once more the little boy lost, the round-faced Mishka of infant years.

Though many people detest his archness, his lies and his colossal snobbery, some retain considerable affection for him. His ex-wife Cristina is one; so, as already mentioned, are his children, who put up the money for his bail by mortgaging their house; and so is his second ex-wife, the ebullient, larger-than-life figure of Francesca Tesi.

He met Francesca in 1967 at the Italian Embassy in London, where she was working as a translator. They married in January 1968, and had one son, Alexander, two years later. It was, the Baron claimed in court, his concern over this son – who was severely dyslexic – that caused him to comply with Susan Wilberforce's demands at a later stage – 'Super Secrecy Sue', as he nicknamed her. The marriage to Francesca began to run into trouble during the late 1970s as his financial generosity to Susan increased. Day after day there would be telephone calls and letters asking for help: she had no money to pay the rates, little money for food, none at all for heating. Francesca, who also calls herself Baroness de Stempel, said of Susan, according to one report, 'She is bad like Lady Macbeth. She is destructive, she is evil. She wanted to destroy everybody. She used to telephone sometimes forty times a day, she was so obsessed with him. I hated her. There were postcards, there were letters. She used to write saying, "I've only got 17p for *The Times*" and he sent her money. She's a useless aristocratic drifter moving from one place to another, a snobbish drop-out.'

Dave Hill, writing in the *Sunday Correspondent Magazine* in May 1990, paints a lively picture of the second Baroness de Stempel: 'I met Miss Tesi at her present home, an elegant garden flat (valued at £175,000) in Swiss Cottage, north London, which she is desperate to sell. She shares it with a Yorkshire terrier and a Siamese cat, and has a painting of Mussolini on the wall.' After the birth of their son Alexander in 1970, things 'went rapidly downhill. "He ruined me financially", said Miss Tesi, "because he was involved with this bitch. She's a criminal, this Wilberforce nonsense. Also, the English aristocracy is really so depraved. All die with drugs or Aids. I don't want to stay in England. Is a shit place. If I was in Italy, I know what to do with that bitch, you know what I mean! Ha!" ' Nevertheless, it was with his second wife he stayed during the nine-week fraud trial. 'She', Michael de Stempel admitted to Mr Hill, had been 'absolutely *marvellous*'.

The Susan de Stempel scandal was not, however, the first time the

Baron had been in the newspapers – apart from social news and gossip columns. On 31 May 1968 he was in the press after being convicted of shoplifting goods worth 18s 6d (92½p) from a supermarket. '£6000-A-YEAR MAN STOLE' blazed one headline – the figure referring to the Baron's unearned income, a considerable one for those days. De Stempel claimed that he was not guilty and had absent-mindedly put the items in his own pocket after his five-year-old son had knocked them off the shelves. The magistrates thought otherwise and fined him £60. What is odd about that story is that the Baron should ever have been in a supermarket. Why wasn't it Fortnum and Mason's? One can just hear the Baron exclaiming 'A supermarket' in the same tones as Lady Bracknell might say 'A handbag'!

Characteristically, he rushed from one woman to another. As his marriage to Francesca Tesi failed, he turned to the figure he had known from the fifties – Susan, secretive Susan. 'If only you had married me instead of Simon a long time ago, when you were asked properly, all these problems wouldn't arise,' he is supposed to have said at this time. On the other hand he frequently denies having had any romantic attachment to her in their youth, apart from a very brief 'fling' which neither heeded seriously. But with the Baron truth, fantasy and downright lies are woven together in a richly coloured patchwork that has covered his entire life.

As 1982 swung into 1983 the intermittent trips to her cottage at Docklow became more regular. He went on paying the bills; Susan was nice to him. Indeed she told me that this period in her life was the happiest she had had. Sophia Wilberforce, who was working in London but paying frequent trips to Forresters Hall, confirmed this. 'We didn't mind putting up with a small cottage because we expected after my mother and Michael married that they would move to a larger house.'

Sophia, of all Susan's children, got on well with Michael. She found him 'funny and generous'. Generous he may have been, but once again his financial ship was sailing into rough waters. Always overdrawn, he replied to one bank manager's request for him to reduce the amounts he owed the bank by answering that the death of his father in Guernsey that year (1983) would ensure him a handsome inheritance. He quoted the sum of £750,000 as the extent of his father's estate. In fact he inherited £175,000 – not a bad amount by some standards, but with his style of spending, woefully inadequate. They would have to stay at Forresters Hall. Although romantically linked with Susan, in her eyes at least, he resolutely refused to share her bed. This lack of sexual passion for her must have been frustrating, but it did not stop her involving him in what was to be the biggest 'problem' of his life – the defrauding of Lady Illingworth. For with hindsight, it can surely be argued that much of the time he spent at Forresters during 1983 would have been taken up with the plotting of this crime. He was, in Judge Curtis's words, 'one of the ready, willing and able conspirators' in the plot.

Two aspects of the case were enough, in the view of West Mercia Fraud Squad, to implicate him seriously: the wording of the bogus will and the venue of the Channel Islands for the 'laundering' of Lady Illingworth's stocks and shares and property. As one concerned with tax havens, the Baron was well acquainted with the islands' relaxed laws applying to financial transactions. Moreover, his father had retired there for similar reasons – the de Stempel family had been badly hit by death duties when his maternal grandmother died.

The peculiarly flamboyant wording of the bogus will was pure Michael de Stempel: it carried his imprint as clearly as if he had signed it himself. For in leaving the sum of £10,000 to her distant cousin, Lord Wilberforce, a past Law Lord, Lady Illingworth was made to say: 'for having added lustre to the family name'. Under cross-examination, John Wilberforce said he found the wording of the will 'quite extraordinary'. With the further discovery that it was the Baron who had procured one of the witnesses for the forged will, a Jesuit priest, Father Dooley, who had taught his son, Andrew, at the Catholic public school Stonyhurst, the Baron's place amongst the accused was certain.

There was a rare moment of amusement at the beginning of the murder trial when Michael de Stempel was due to appear as a prosecution witness against his ex-wife, Susan. The date of a certain telephone call he had received was vital evidence, but all he could say was that he knew it was the night they had had pheasant for dinner. In the face of such vagueness and confusion the police had no alternative but to drop him from the case. Anthony Arlidge, the Baroness's defending counsel, was heard to say, 'Thank God for that – in all my life I have never encountered such tedium as going through the Baron's different statements.'

But if all this paints a portrait of a not unengaging figure – flamboyant, childish, confused, boastful, a *flaneur* in every sense, some could point to aspects that were far from likeable. According to a member of the Fraud Squad the treatment he meted out to Kathy Whelan, the aging housekeeper to Lady Illingworth, and her companion, her cousin Irene Wilberforce, was disgraceful. 'He bullied and shouted at her when she refused to hand over Lady Illingworth's papers and possessions. He screamed at her. He threatened her with the police. She was made to feel terrified. Where were all his fine and flouncy manners then? When she tried to stop him going into her ladyship's bedroom, she was told to stand aside. The whole incident – and they were there for hours and hours – deeply shocked her.' De Stempel maintained that all he wanted was a photograph of Lord Illingworth in Privy Councillor's uniform. On a different occasion he vented his spleen on a bank official in Kensington High Street who refused to hand over the contents of a safe deposit box belonging to her ladyship. Again he shouted and screamed and threatened – this time saying he would take the matter up with the House of Lords. Wisely the bank official took no notice, and it took a letter from Susan Wilberforce to get the necessary release documents sent to her at Docklow.

Yet with all this behind him, de Stempel would stoutly maintain that he had had nothing to do with the defrauding of Lady Illingworth. 'I wouldn't dream of doing any kind of thing against an old woman, particularly an old woman who was my friend. It wouldn't enter my head. It would have been an appalling thing to do.' The police officer to whom he said this added: 'He was all bluff and bluster during interviews. He would say things like, "Come on inspector, we are all honourable men."'

Honour may have been the aspiration of Michael de Stempel's life, but it was the last thing he was to achieve, as his activities over the next two years demonstrate. After six lonely years at Docklow from 1977 to 1983, during which her main source of excitement and male admiration had ceased when her flying instructor was found dead on the tarmac at Shobdon aerodrome, nothing would satisfy Susan Wilberforce except to have Michael by her side.

Ann Devey-Smith has recounted how Susan *had* to have Michael de Stempel. 'It was not love, it was obsession – she wanted him there all the time.' Michael de Stempel, like some mindless moth attracted to the light, flew in and out of its beams. His vacillations infuriated Susan. One moment she thought she had him safely tied to Docklow, the next he would be in London. His excuse was always his son Alexander, whom he loved deeply. Susan did not. She called him 'The Rat' and was unfailingly sarcastic about the boy's dyslexia. And so for months the emotional see-saw continued. She would tell him: 'Bugger off', and then retract desperately.

On one occasion in May 1984 she managed to inveigle him into spending a night with her at an hotel in Paddington – but, as the court heard, nothing happened. The same month she had paid an anonymous £20,000 into his bank account – presumably an early part of her funds from Lady Illingworth – but the money and what the tabloid press was pleased to call 'a night of passion' did not have the effect she wanted. She would have to be more cunning than that. With consummate conviction, she thought again and bided her time.

Meanwhile, no matter what kind of trouble he may have been in, Michael de Stempel could not refrain from seeking female companionship and consolation. All his life he had depended on women; he saw no reason to change now. A long-standing family friend said of him, 'Michael just wants to be mothered. He has always needed that ever since he was a little boy. He needs to live with a woman – not necessarily in any sexual sense. He just needs to be loved.'

In the middle of his involvement with Susan, possibly frightened and aware that he was being drawn into a criminal situation even he could not handle, he happened to meet a former girlfriend, Jane Mackay. A self-professed stickler for dates and places, he says it was: 'June 1st, at a bus-stop outside Peter Jones.' Never one to hold his horses, especially when a rich and available woman was concerned – and Jane Mackay was both – he proposed to her one week later. 'I gave her a ring by Tillander,' he said in court. 'It was the best ring belonging to my family. After this, I think, Susan's behaviour did begin to change.'

It certainly did. Hell hath no fury like Susan Wilberforce denied the man she wanted, denied the title she wanted. What was all the conspiracy about if, apart from money, it was not to bind this man to her irrevocably? She fought back in the way she always fought – with anonymous letters to Jane Mackay's house in Kent, and with endless telephone calls. She even suggested that he was homosexual and despatched gay videos through the post anonymously. When they took no notice, this high priestess of cunning devised a plan that was faultless and brought him running to her side.

Michael de Stempel's Achilles heel was his dyslexic youngest son Alexander, born in 1970. When de Stempel and Francesca divorced, both shared custody of the boy: Alexander spent half his time with Michael at a flat in Hampstead. Now Susan threatened to inform the Social Services Department of the local Camden Council of what a bad father he was. De Stempel told the jury in court: 'She told me that if I did not marry her she would go to the social workers and denounce me as a cruel father to Alexander'.

He panicked and consulted his solicitor, Lord Coleraine, who advised him it was indeed possible that Alexander might be taken away from him. Under such duress de Stempel agreed to marry Susan. Alexander's mother's theory was that Susan had been gradually drawing Michael into a web of deceit by asking for his help over Aunt Puss's affairs. 'She wanted this man so badly. She thought, "I can't have him because he is involved with Jane. So I'll do something drastic. If he won't marry me, I'll drag him down too." ' Others are of the opinion that his involvement in the defrauding of Lady Illingworth was enough to make him obey her orders, albeit reluctantly.

The less than happy groom was told to turn up in Gibraltar: Susan had arranged a marriage ceremony there and bought tickets. She went, he did not – he simply failed to arrive on the given day in August. But Susan was not to be baulked. Another date was fixed and in Jersey, on 11 September 1984, Susan Cecilia Wilberforce married Michael Jossif Victor de Stempel.

If some marriages are made in heaven, theirs was made in hell. He refused to consummate it. Questioned about this by his defence counsel, Richard du Cann, QC, he was asked where he slept when they returned from their wedding.

'I slept in the blue tent,' he said.

'Was there any attempt to consummate the marriage?' Mr du Cann asked.

'By Susan, yes,'

'Where?'

'In her bedroom at Docklow,' replied the Baron, who added, 'I did not wish to live with Susan. I found the idea of living anywhere with Susan impossible.'

Not only was the Baron a reluctant bridegroom, he was a most private one. He wished for no publicity at all. When the new Baroness suggested they put a notice in *The Times* announcing their marriage, he was so angry he threatened that he would sue *The Times* for printing a lie. Nothing daunted, the new Baroness promptly placed it in the *Telegraph* and obtained a hundred copies for distribution to their friends! One of the people she was determined should see it was Jane Mackay. Of the whole episode, a close friend of Michael's said: 'He never wanted to marry her. I think he got into it first as a bit of an intellectual exercise. Then when he found he was in too deep he became frightened and tried to back out. That is when she blackmailed him into marriage.'

*

83

When viewed against the whole background of this story, the sad, ridiculous marriage of the two conspirators seems like a minor, almost comic diversion. Events were destined to get considerably bleaker.

By 1983, the year before their marriage, Michael de Stempel was finding Susan far more secretive than ever before – so secretive, he affirms, that she had her mail left outside in a dustbin so that she would not have to deal with the postman. She saw no one local, he said later on, and few from further afield. Shopkeepers at the local town of Leominster do not recall her. Neither does the pub at Docklow, which is only fifty yards away. The only time the village had dealings with her was on a matter of bees. She was convinced that the bees from her hives had migrated to another colony living in the church tower immediately opposite her house. She caused ructions, as Jim Vickers, retired farmer, curate and dowsing specialist, recalls: 'Her bees came across and she tried to smoke them out of the church. But I said, "Your bees have swarmed on a tomb in the graveyard, not in the church. One lot of bees will not go with another lot. The hive in the tower has been there for a hundred years." But she wasn't having it. She was a bit obstreperous. The children seemed all right and the man who came [the Baron] was all right, but not her.'

Another story concerns Marcus, and is typical of the way of life she had forced on her children from the time they were living in Weobley. One cold day at Docklow he was cutting the hedge in front of the house – a hedge shared by both cottages. The tenants of the other cottage invited him in for some soup, which he was delighted to accept. But the next time he met up with them and was asked in again, he refused. There was no further communication. Susan insisted that her children be as isolated as herself – at home, certainly.

One of the few friends to see her at this stage was Ann Devey-Smith who, after an absence of twenty years, was back in favour again. She lived at Tenbury Wells, not far away, and her friendship was to be cunningly exploited the following year.

By the end of 1983 the financial situation was calamitous, and Michael was showing signs of veering back to former girlfriends. Susan had to have more money, and in desperation she looked round to see from whom she could get it. It takes little imagination to see how readily her eyes fell on her elderly aunt, Lady Illingworth.

From Sophia, who had been living in London at the same address as Lady Illingworth since 1982, she would have known how fragile, mentally as well as physically, the old lady was. From Sophia, too, she might have known that this was the only member of the Wilberforce family who could be relied on for extensive help; others had given and would give no more.

Laura Wilberforce is quoted as saying that they asked Susan to get in touch with Lady Illingworth, to go and see her, but Susan always refused, saying that it would remind her too much of Markington. A few months later the 'special relationship', which Susan argued in court had existed since childhood, would ensure that Lady Illingworth was living with her – though, significantly, John and Laura Wilberforce, now living in Cyprus where he was High Commissioner, were not told of the aunt's arrival at Docklow.

Not only was Lady Illingworth rich in terms of income but her husband had left her a great fortune in the form of silver, jewellery, antique furniture and stocks and shares. When she sold 44 Grosvenor Square in 1967 and moved to Kensington it was recorded that forty-seven vans of valuable furniture, paintings and other household equipment (including three crates of scrubbing soap, five packing cases of old Christmas cards and one crate of Elizabeth Arden Blue Grass scent – the smell of which Susan described as 'quite awful') were shunted off by a storage firm, Giltspurs. The storage bill alone was £100 a week. A great Aladdin's cave of 'goodies' lay there for the asking. Is it any wonder that Susan, who had eked out a precarious existence partly by selling off bits of family furniture, would think of acquiring it? After all, didn't all families behave in the same way? she was to maintain in subsequent conversations.

Irene Wilberforce, who shared York House with Lady Illingworth, was elderly and suffering from arthritis, so offered no objection when it was suggested Aunt Puss go to Docklow for a while. There was nobody of close enough kinship or intimacy with Lady Illingworth to keep a weather eye on her movements and well-being; perhaps Kathy Whelan, but as just a servant she could easily be over-ruled. Accordingly, 'nannied' by Sophia, who was to be paid £100 a week to look after her great-aunt, Margaret Illingworth arrived at Forresters Hall on 29 February 1984.

Susan's 'initial reluctance', and according to Sophia, due only to the already overcrowded conditions at the small cottage, must have disappeared as she thought of the possible advantages to be gained.

Ostensibly Lady Illingworth's trip away from home was to be a short holiday; in reality it turned out to be for the rest of her life. Elizabeth Gregg-Smith, Lady Illingworth's part-time secretary, was shocked: 'There she was one day, next day she was gone – it just seemed so unbelievable to me. . . . She was hijacked! I mean, you don't suddenly come along out of the blue and scoop people up to the other end of the country, together with their belongings and papers, if there wasn't something strange about it – it just, as far as I was concerned, it just wasn't done.' Dorothy Hayman, the loyal 'dogsbody' who had worked at York House for thirty-five years was also amazed to arrive one day and find her ladyship gone. She asked Irene Wilberforce where she was, and was told she had gone on holiday. But as she stated to the police, finding her ladyship's room stripped and denuded of everything a week later was a different matter. This was no holiday. But in their worry and bafflement who could these loyal friends and employees turn to?

Albert Oslar, her chauffeur, recounts that he was telephoned by Kathy Whelan shortly after Lady Illingworth had left York House. The housekeeper was extremely distressed, 'almost in tears', describing how the niece had taken her away and then made two attempts to have all her ladyship's possessions stripped from her bedroom. 'So I asked her', he said, 'if there was any chance of my going to see her, and she gave me the address in Docklow, but said that if I went there they wouldn't let me in – they weren't letting anyone see her. I did think of going,' he added sadly, 'but I thought as I wasn't family – just a driver – there wouldn't be much I could do about it . . . so I left it.'

At Docklow, a small bedroom had been specially prepared for the new guest. Over the next few weeks, up to the fateful will day, Ann Devey-Smith was to see Aunt Puss occasionally. She described her as being 'almost unconscious and like a well-behaved child'. A well-behaved child is an obedient child. When, as the first part of their plan, Aunt Puss was asked to write to her bank in Ripon requesting a cash card, she did so immediately, obediently. All she had to do was sign the letter Susan had typed for her. The great ball of Lady Illingworth's fortune had begun rolling in their direction. It was less than a fortnight since she had arrived at Docklow.

6

L·A·D·Y
I·L·L·I·N·G·W·O·R·T·H

URING all those years of poverty and hardship and near starvation for Susan Wilberforce, what had happened to her Aunt Margaret, Lady Illingworth? Talking at length and most affectionately about her, Albert Oslar is a good guide to his former employer's London life. 'I was driving for Crawford car service in the early days. She had a Rolls in the garage at Grosvenor Square but she didn't like driving it herself. Another customer and good friend of hers was the Duchess of Leinster, who also lived in Grosvenor Square. I used to go and pick her ladyship up from No. 44, which was a beautiful house. I remember – because I liked it so much – that there was a large leather coachman's chair in the hallway. When I first started driving her there was a lot of fuss because they had just discovered a mural by William Kent in one of the upstairs rooms – the drawing room, I think. Lady Illingworth was thrilled and opened her house to the public – that's the sort of person she was.'

The parties, he says, were non-stop during the season. 'She went everywhere – all the embassies, lots of private houses, garden parties at Buckingham Palace, all the big London hotels. As time went on she did less entertaining herself at home, but that did not stop her giving large luncheon parties at Claridges or the Connaught. I was always picking her up from Claridges – I think it was her favourite hotel.'

At weekends she went further afield, to friends in the country. 'She was great friends with a stockbroker called Robert Strauss and often went to stay with him. He had this magnificent estate near Ardingly in Sussex. Another friend was the hotelier Maxwell Joseph. I used to drive her to his house in Onslow Gardens – it was lovely.'

Asked what she looked like, his response was immediate: 'She looked just like the Queen Mother. She had that same sweet smile, and she spoke like the Queen Mother too. She wasn't as small, but otherwise she was just like her. She even wore the same sort of clothes – big flowery hats and flowery silk dresses. And she adored hats. Whenever she went away there were always two or three hat boxes amongst her luggage. She wasn't flash – there was nothing flash about her, except perhaps her hats.'

In 1967 Lady Illingworth succumbed to the persuasive powers of Maxwell Joseph and sold him the house in Grosvenor Square; it was to be demolished and an hotel built on the site. Oslar recalls that time in her life: 'She told me she was very sorry but the house was getting too much for her. She only had two part-time servants by then and I don't think she liked living there alone. It was a big place. I'm sure that's why she went abroad so much.

'One day she told me that she was going to stay with a cousin, Irene, who lived in a big mansion flat at York House, York Place, the southern end of Kensington Church Street. She seemed pleased about the arrangement. I could see why. It was an enormous flat – it went on for ever and you could get lost in it. There was her cousin and there was the housekeeper, Kathy Whelan.'

The housekeeper was represented in court by Sophia Wilberforce as a bossy woman who dominated Lady Illingworth. Did he agree with that description? He exlaimed: 'Absolutely not. Kathy Whelan was not a dragon. She was a lovely Scottish lady who was totally devoted to Lady Illingworth. She was very efficient – she always had Lady Illingworth's things ready for her. If her ladyship was going away she had it all organized. She was good at organizing and she was very efficient, but she was not bossy or domineering. She was a servant and she knew her place. Her whole life had been as a servant. She wouldn't step outside that – she knew how to behave.'

As a well-known rich widow Margaret Illingworth was not without a certain type of hanger-on, especially after the Second World War when London was full of ex-officer types who were unfitted for civilian life. Frequently they found a way of battening on to the edges of society, dependent on luncheon and dinner parties to see them well victualled, returning to minuscule flats at good addresses before issuing forth for the next foray. Her ex-chauffeur recalls the ruse with which her ladyship got rid of one such gentleman. 'She had this chap – he was an ex-squadron leader or said he was an ex-squadron leader – who had invited himself down with her for a few days she was spending on the Isle of Wight. I was to take her on a Sunday morning. I had booked the ferry and was ready to go. Suddenly the telephone rang. It was Kathy Whelan to say the job was off – her ladyship wasn't going. One and a half hours later the telephone goes again and it's Kathy to say the job is on.

'I arrive at York House and there's Kathy with a hamper packed full of sandwiches and strawberries. We get in the car and Lady Illingworth asks me how long will it take to get to Southampton – can we beat the train from Waterloo? And then she explains that she's left this squadron leader waiting in the church, but we've got to beat the train in case he decides to come on his own. "I'm not having these hangers-on," she said firmly, "he's not coming with me for a free fortnight." '

Anxious to amend any impression of a parsimonious old lady, he added hastily that her ladyship was not mean, but generous to a fault. 'I just wanted to show that she was an astute person in some ways. But that didn't stop her being almost overgenerous. Whenever we went to Ascot – and her ladyship loved Ascot – she always gave me £20 "to have a bet with me". She wouldn't take no for an answer.' He rejects the idea of the social butterfly that some people made her out to be. 'She was an intelligent lady. I know in the end her mind started to go, but that was old age. Before, she was as bright as anyone. Took an interest in her investments. I remember going to collect her for a cocktail party and she was reading the *Evening Standard*. She was terribly excited because gold was going up by leaps and bounds. She was delighted because it meant her Kruger-rands were going up in value. And then she suddenly said, "I must show you something", and she disappeared, to return with a solid gold cigarette case. "What do you think of that?" she said. "I bought it at Aspreys." I weighed it in my hand and it must have been all of ten ounces. "I was going to give it as a present," she said, "but I've changed my mind." '

Susan de Stempel maintained to the staff at Langford House, the old people's home where Lady Illingworth died, that her aunt was an alcoholic. Albert Oslar was shocked by this accusation. 'I've picked her up after cocktail parties, I've picked her up at midnight after dinner parties, and there was never any sign that she had been drinking. And believe me,' he said with feeling, 'in this business you know! But Lady Illingworth was never even slightly merry – not with drink.' His defence was well supported by the post-mortem, which found no evidence of excessive alcohol consumption.

Was there no bad side to her ladyship? He thought for a moment and grinned suddenly: 'She could be impatient. Many a time when I've slowed for the lights she would urge me to shoot them, go a bit faster. I had to explain it was more than my job was worth, and she'd accept that.' In some things she was a stickler for form. There was a day, he recalls, when she spoke to him from the back of the car, asking him why his cap was tilted backwards off his forehead. He replied that in getting into the car he had inadvertently tipped it back. She liked to see a cap worn straight, she said. It was straightened.

Two Markington villagers confirm the picture of a delightful woman – indeed a lovable woman. Now in her eighty-third year, but still as bright as a button, Lilian Ross recalls the time she used to stay with her ladyship during the seventies at Markington Hall. 'There was nobody living at the Hall – Mister John was away – but Miss Puss, as we used to call her, liked to come for a few days every now and again. Only she didn't like staying there alone so I was asked to stay with her. My little house is very near the Hall. Her ladyship always went to bed extremely early – by 7.30 in the evening, sometimes. She used to get up very early, too. Anyway, about seven-thirtyish she'd hand me the morning paper and tell me to take it to bed with me – something to read. In the morning there'd be a knock on my door and there would be her ladyship with a little posy of flowers and a cup of tea, telling me that breakfast was ready downstairs.'

It's a charming story that conveys a rather different aspect of Margaret Illingworth from the rich society heiress. Roy Shepherd, Lady Illingworth's gardener, also recollects how generous and thoughtful she could be. 'She was mad about parties – she'd go to Bangkok for a cocktail party. She went there once and when she came back she had this lovely tie – Thai silk – that she'd bought me. She sent me a card, too, while she was out there.'

The details of Lady Illingworth's last few years became a vital part of the whole saga of fraud and theft, as various members of the family as well as employees recounted the end of the seventies and the fateful early years of the eighties. Few, even amongst the hardened, were unaffected. Albert Oslar linked her mental deterioration with the afternoon of a nasty fall in the early 1980s: 'She'd had a nasty accident – a fall – and had hurt her hip badly enough for her to stay at the King Edward's Hospital for Officers and Gentlemen. I went there to see her and took some chocolates with me. She loved chocolates – I'd gone to Charbonnel and Walker to get her favourite truffles – and she was delighted. She treated me like a long-lost son and insisted that I stay and have tea with her. She herself rang the bell and ordered it for me.

'Anyway, from hospital she went to some sort of convalescent home near Guildford. I got a call from Kathy Whelan asking me to go and collect her and take her to Markington. When I got there I found her all dressed and lying on a stretcher. I asked the matron if she should travel, and the matron said no but she's insisting. So I suggested to Lady Illingworth that we get a private ambulance for her – it was more comfortable – and she agreed. We took her to Harrogate and after a bit brought her back to York Place. She was on crutches – well, sticks – for a long time. And that's about the time her memory began to go.

I took her one day to a friend who lived at Datchet on the Thames and stayed outside during the visit. But when she came out she got into another car – not mine. Then, when we went to Harley Street, you'd have to make sure she hadn't forgotten you were there, otherwise she'd hail a black cab. It was sad to see such a lovely lady age.'

At the time of the fraud trial, much was made in court of the gloomy flat at York Place, the huddle of three old women living together, increasingly attacked by age and physical deterioration, endlessly squabbling, imprisoned within their own walls while outside the cheerful bustle of Kensington High Street carried on vigorously. But it was not an accurate picture – merely one painted for her own reasons by Sophia Wilberforce. In fairness, the large, red-brick mansion flat with its long corridors, huge kitchen and seven bedrooms might not have been a young girl's idea of a jolly London flat. Yet much socializing went on: many guests came and went on brief visits to Lady Illingworth and Irene Wilberforce. Albert Oslar did not think it gloomy. There was, he pointed out, a uniformed porter in the block's main reception hall, and 'It was a well-run block of flats.' It had also been the Markington Wilberforces' London base for many years: John Wilberforce stayed there when in London. Even Sophia's godfather, Francis Rose, said he had at one time lodged at York House.

That Sophia's picture was not an accurate one was upheld by Elizabeth Gregg-Smith, Lady Illingworth's part-time secretary from 1981 to the beginning of 1984. Her job, she revealed to the court, was to sort through the mass of mail that had piled up over the months and make some sense of it. There was so much that she had to get down on hands and knees and arrange it into different lots to be filed later. Bills, personal letters, receipts, stocks and shares – all were muddled together higgledy-piggledy. It took her some time to throw away the unwanted papers and arrange the rest into neat accordion files. The Baron, on his famous visit to collect Lady Illingworth's possessions, should have recorded a vote of thanks to Miss Gregg-Smith for making his task that much easier!

At first the secretary found her employer in good spirits. 'She used to take me to lunch at a couple of Italian restaurants in Kensington Church Street where they knew her. Or we'd go shopping together. She was still a sparky old lady who enjoyed the fun and life of Kensington.' She always wore a very beautiful silver watch encircled by stones, recalls the secretary, a neat, fair-haired, quite 'sparky' individual herself. She clearly enjoyed the old lady's outings to Dino's and to Barker's for coffee. She enjoyed, too, the presence of Irene who, though requiring the help of a stick to walk with, was 'a gentle, kind person, quieter than Lady Illingworth, while Kathy was the perfect retainer who was absolutely devoted – yes, *devoted* to them both.' She thought Kathy a deeply religious person much activated by Christian principles. 'Her whole life was their life, if you see what I mean.' She, in common with all who knew Kathy, was angered at the defamation of her character by Sophia and Susan Wilberforce.

A year later she was dealing with an increasingly confused client. Lady Illingworth's sight was failing badly, and her memory losses were more frequent. If a cheque required signing, Gregg-Smith would write it all out and then point to the line where Lady Illingworth would scrawl a very shaky signature. By 1983 she thought her client was incapable of managing her own business affairs: 'She could not see very well and needed to be helped.' They still went out for little trips together, but the old lady had to be assisted across the road. She had taken, also, to asking for her old home: 'She wanted dearly to go back to Markington.' Of course she did. Markington had been where she grew up, where she got married, where she and her husband had delighted in a whole county's affection. What could be more natural than to return there?

Albert Oslar was involved in an occasion made much of in court when her ladyship arrived at Markington out of the blue. It was early February, at a time when John Wilberforce was away in Cyprus and two of his children – William and Anne – were there. On leaving church in Kensington Lady Illingworth, by now subject to intermittent acts of irrationality, had asked her local priest to organize a black cab to take her to Markington. Normally most cabs would have resisted such an order but presumably her wealth was well known at her local church and, urged on by the priest, what cabbie would say no to such a long and well-paid trip? When he arrived in Yorkshire the driver asked for £500, which caused consternation amongst the young people. Kathy Whelan was telephoned down in London, and said she would organize a cheque. Afterwards she rang Oslar and asked him to go and collect her when she was due to come back.

To this day Oslar is incensed that the cabbie had the cheek to ask £500 for a job normally costing £300, but when he arrived to bring her ladyship home he received an even worse shock. She was ready to travel and had been sitting in the kitchen for over an hour. He said, 'Good afternoon, my lady' – his normal manner of greeting – to which she replied with a smile, 'Good afternoon. Have you ever driven me before?'

'Oh, my lady,' he replied, 'I've been driving you for twenty years!'

The trip to London was the last time Oslar saw her. As he says, 'We had a happy drive with her ladyship reminiscing about the past, the great shooting parties they gave in Yorkshire, the Rolls-Royce she used to drive when younger, the fun of Monte Carlo and Switzerland. She enjoyed talking about the past – she could remember that. Anyway, as we pulled up at York Place she looked up and said, "This is it. This is where I'm supposed to be." I got out and handed her over to Kathy Whelan, and that was that.'

A number of people came and went to and from York House at this time – friends of Irene, friends of Lady Illingworth, members of the Wilberforce family. They, like Elizabeth Gregg-Smith, found the once elegant London hostess dishevelled and disorderly. Mrs Gregg-Smith recalls her wearing odd stockings and not always clean clothes. Dorothy Hayman had cleaned the flat for over thirty-five years and was in her own words a 'general dogsbody'; she had enjoyed packing Lady Illingworth's dresses when in the prime of life she went to Monte Carlo, and was distressed by her mistress's condition in later years. 'Sometimes she didn't even recognize me. She was terribly absent-minded. I saw how the secretary had to help her with the cheques, guiding the old lady's hand where she had to sign.'

Susan's brother, John, told the court that he was equally distressed when he saw his aunt in 1983 on a flying visit from Cyprus, and found her very unwell. 'It was no longer possible to hold any intelligent conversation with her. Her mind was rambling and she kept on incessantly asking the same questions. In short, she was very senile.'

'Senile' is not a word much in favour with today's social workers. It is too harsh, too direct, too absolute. They prefer the word 'confused', which is softer and less derogatory. Or so it seemed when another Wilberforce was speaking of her relative. Monica Wilberforce Makra, a cousin of Irene Wilberforce and not a direct descendant of Lady Illingworth, used to visit them frequently. She is a social worker at the Charing Cross Hospital, specializing in the care of the elderly. She admitted that the two old ladies would occasionally 'scrap in a childish way, but they got on very well together'. Latterly she had noticed that Lady Illingworth 'was more and more vague. She did not go out as much and she became mildly *confused*.' She was a warm, obviously sensitive woman who did not like recording what she had noticed at York House, but it was she who was to disclose the most distressing story concerning Lady Illingworth's condition.

She had been at the flat one day, she said, and happened to walk past the open door of a lavatory. Sitting inside 'with her pants around her ankles', oblivious to anyone who passed, was Margaret Illingworth. Could there be a greater change from the rich, popular society hostess whom all London loved to this muttering old woman sitting exposed for all the world to see on a lavatory seat? The harsh indignity of old age impressed itself on all who heard in the court room.

It was a welcome breath of fresh air in court, therefore, when the vivacious and decidedly French tones of Lady Wilberforce, wife of Richard, Lord Wilberforce – one of the Law Lords and a cousin – described her frequent visits to the mansion flat. But she, too – reluctantly, because she was fond of her – had found Lady Illingworth increasingly forgetful and muddled. And when asked the vital question of whether or not she thought Lady Illingworth capable of making a new will at this time, she put her vote alongside those who thought not. When Lady Illingworth suddenly disappeared 'for a short holiday to Docklow' she blamed herself for not finding out how she was. She had written postcards which had not been answered, but she had not telephoned or taken the matter further when Lady Illingworth did not return. 'I should have got in my car and gone,' she said, lowering her head as if in late apology to her old friend whose hospitality she and her husband had much enjoyed at the glittering soirées in Grosvenor Square.

It was the spare, thin, upright figure of Lord Wilberforce who added his impression that the marriage between the elderly wool baron and the young aristocratic butterfly had been 'totally happy'. Furthermore, in his view Lady Illingworth was well looked after and apparently living in contentment during her stay at York House. Not so, argued Sophia Wilberforce, with tears here and there to prove how fond she had been of the old lady.

It was at this stage of Lady Illingworth's mental deterioration that, as related by Elizabeth Gregg-Smith, a curious incident occurred concerning Sophia and Aunt Puss. During one of Miss Gregg-Smith's visits to York Place the matter of the missing handbag came up. Sophia, who had come to live there in 1982 while she worked in London, was also present. Lady Illingworth was due out for lunch and could not find her right handbag. Much fuss and commotion ensued. Finally it was found in Sophia's room, under her bed. The handbag contained £160 in cash and a valuable brooch. Sophia's explanation was that Aunt Puss must have left it there when she came in to talk with her the previous evening.

It was a story that sent flurries of conjecture around the court. How much, some wondered, did it contribute to the jury's verdict concerning Sophia? But it did not stop Sophia's character assassination of the housekeeper. Conditions at York House, she reiterated, were appalling: 'Kathy Whelan was a monster who maltreated the old dear. She wouldn't even let her have a change of clothes or leave the flat on occasions.' It was Kathy Whelan, according to Sophia, who had broken Lady Illingworth's heart by forcibly insisting that the folk at Markington *did not want her*. Sophia also told the police that she had seen Lady Illingworth drunk. 'Drunk?' asked the police. 'Are you sure she was *drunk*?'

'Well, tipsy,' replied the Baroness's daughter, who was likened many times to an English rose by a sentimental British press. But accusations of Lady Illingworth's dependence on alcohol were considerably tempered when Sophia admitted, under cross-examination, that she had been tipsy, too. And Elizabeth Gregg-Smith described how she used to make the old lady a gin and French that was moderate in size as well as strength. She also liked a glass of champagne, but if that were evidence of a depraved addiction to alcohol we should all be alcoholics. The post-mortem on Lady Illingworth, as mentioned earlier, bore out Albert Oslar's defence of his former employer against Susan de Stempel's allegation to the staff at the old people's home in Hereford that her aunt was an alcoholic.

According to Sophia, her muddled but still rational great-aunt expressed a desire to go to stay with her niece at Forresters Hall. Never mind the fact that Susan de Stempel had had, according to John Wilberforce, no contact with her for thirty years – it was to Herefordshire she wanted to go.

John Wilberforce was mistaken, however. There had been the briefest of meetings between Susan and her aunt back in 1971 when Monica Wilberforce, Irene's cousin, married John Makra. Sophia had been a bridesmaid. There had been a family gathering afterwards at York House which Susan did not attend. It was regarded as yet another example of her detachment from the general run of the family, which she had not forgiven for its coldness towards her when she married Simon Dale.

Why did Lady Illingworth go so willingly to Docklow? Would she not have preferred Markington? When questioned on this John Wilberforce, a tall, thin, grey-suited, grey-haired and even grey-faced man, with long, knuckly fingers that he constantly spread in front of him as he talked, admitted with a sort of anguished embarrassment that there had been no room for her at Markington Hall. His own family lived in one part, while the other section had been let off since the previous autumn to his Uncle Robert and Aunt Marion. There simply was not enough room for Aunt Puss. Other offshoots of the family were too distant, and in many cases too old, to take on additional burdens. Without saying it, they were relying on Kathy Whelan to look after her, which Kathy was most ready to do.

One of the saddest aspects of the whole de Stempel scandal, say the police, was the besmirching of Kathy Whelan's character by those subsequently found guilty of the most heartless fraud. Too fragile to figure personally in the trial, she was, they say, an admirable woman who without a doubt loved the two ladies she looked after. As the weeks went by, it became more and more apparent that Lady Illingworth was not coming back, yet Kathy kept her room clean and dusted and 'ready for her ladyship's return'.

The sad litany of the last years of Aunt Puss was in its final stages. Alzheimer's disease had by now commenced its cruel destruction of her mind. Lucidity was intermittent, though not altogether vanquished. An old friend, Everilda Wilberforce, visiting her in the spring of 1984, found her sadly aged but able to converse, though 'Lady Illingworth did not know who Susan de Stempel was.' Quite an irony, considering that both Sophia and her mother were to argue that there was a 'special relationship' between the two.

And why, in this case, should there have been a gap of thirty years, as John Wilberforce claimed, in their communication? It did not add up – or rather it did add up, but to something different and far from creditable.

During 1984 the Baron and Susan made a number of trips to the Channel Islands. One grim aspect of their visits was a certain house on Alderney that Susan had seen and considered as a possible future home. On the ground floor there was a room heavily reinforced with

Markington Hall where Susan
Wilberforce grew up

Lord and Lady Illingworth at
the Derby (Topham)

Simon and Susan Dale with their young family on the lawn at Heath House

Mellington House in Weobley where Susan Dale went after her first marriage ended

Lady Illingworth
looking at a portrait of
her ancestor Samuel
Wilberforce in 44
Grosvenor Square
(Press Association)

Forresters Hall,
Docklow (Shropshire
Star)

Simon Dale shortly before he was murdered (Shropshire Star)

The murder door of Heath House

Baron de Stempel (Newsteam)

(a) *Below left*: Sophia
Wilberforce (Newsteam)

(b) *Below right*: Marcus
Wilberforce (Newsteam)

Simon Wilberforce ('Josh Peters')
base jumping from Notre Dame
Cathedral in Paris (Rex Features)

Some of Lady Illingworth's
antiques which were recovered by
the West Mercia Fraud Squad
(Shropshire Star)

The apartment block in Spain where a flat was purchased in Sophia Wilberforce's name

Langford House — the council-run nursing home where Lady Illingworth spent her last days

Alexander and Sebastian
Wilberforce with Geoffrey
Bowater at the memorial service
for their father (Shropshire Star)

Baroness de Stempel at the end of
the murder trial (Newsteam)

bars. This, Susan suggested, would be suitable for Lady Illingworth
– it would prevent her getting out and getting lost. 'Escaping' is
another word, and it crossed even the Baron's mind. He admits that
he blinked at this sign of Susan's ruthlessness. Perhaps it was his
reluctance on this score, but the purchase of the house, costing
£105,000, was not completed. Twenty-four hours before contracts
were due to be exchanged the deal was called off. No reasons were
given, but it does not take much insight to speculate that even with
bars and locks the deranged Lady Illingworth was more trouble than
Susan de Stempel cared to have. Defrauding her was one thing,
looking after her something totally different – not something that
the other partner in the 'special relationship' knew how to handle
or, more important, was prepared to exercise.

So Lady Illingworth stayed in her small bedroom at Forresters Hall
throughout the spring, summer and autumn. Sophia was paid to look
after her and when she was away visiting her brother in Japan Susan
took over. Occasionally Marcus helped, too, when she 'escaped' and
went scampering up the road outside their cottage. None of the
villagers met her; the family was as reclusive under Susan's
dominance as it had been at Weobley. During this entire time Aunt
Puss did not once see a doctor or a solicitor.

By December the Wilberforces of Docklow were fed up with their
elderly relative. Alzheimer patients are not the easiest of charges,
being subject to aggression, incontinence and wild fluctuations of
mood. Aunt Puss had served her purpose; now she must go. On 6
December the ambulance service at Leominster received a radio
message that there had been a 999 call concerning an old lady who
was causing damage to a window with a hammer. When John
Halliway, the ambulance officer, arrived at noon he was met 'by a
young girl' who 'passed him on to a tall, well-spoken lady'. He could
not remember any men being around. When he asked if a doctor had
been called, the tall lady explained to him that the old lady was not
under a doctor. By this time the police had arrived. To this audience
Susan was pleased to relate the unfortunate incidents that had led
her to call them.

Her aunt had been ill the previous day and had suddenly got
violent. This violence had increased when she saw her niece nailing
up a picture, and she had stolen the hammer – which she had then
used to break the window. More followed along the lines that they
had tried to control her while she had been throwing things around
the house, but altogether it was an impossible task. Accordingly
Halliway himself approached the old lady, whom he found to be

'confused and in need of treatment'. He decided to take her to Hereford General Accident Hospital. The young girl asked where they were taking her, and he told her. Neither Susan nor Sophia offered to go with her. The old lady had no cuts to her head or hands but was, he said, so confused that she thought the ambulance a fine vehicle to travel to Edinburgh in.

At the hospital Lady Illingworth was examined by a house physician. She was cheerful by this time, telling him that she was forty years of age and that her husband was a peer in the House of Lords. Not surprisingly, he found her 'disorientated in time, manner and place', but in 'good physical condition'. It was decided to keep her in, and she was assigned a bed in the Sarah Siddons Ward, an assessment ward.

Three days later she was examined by Dr Aand da Silva, a Hereford psychiatrist who found her reasonable in behaviour but unable to name simple objects like a comb, pen or pencil. She did not know what day it was, what time it was or where she was. He diagnosed senile dementia and gave it as his opinion that she would have been exhibiting signs of it for at least two years.

On 10 December, according to Dr Anthony Orr, Susan de Stempel was telephoned and asked if she would have her aunt back. She declined. In further conversations with the hospital staff she built up an extraordinary picture of Lady Illingworth, saying she was a hopeless alcoholic who had been weaned off drink during her stay at Docklow, that she was a sex maniac from whom no man was safe (at the age of eighty-four!), and that she had a passion for hitch-hiking 'and could walk out any time'. In retrospect it is possible to see in all these allegations the desperation of a woman trying to escape her responsibilities, terrified she might be forced to take her aunt back. Bizarre as they sounded to the hospital staff, however, they got the right message: Susan de Stempel, despite the 'special relationship', was not having her mad aunt back again.

In the hospital the nursing notes tell of a sad old thing asking for her shoes all the time, climbing out of her cot at night to urinate on the floor, puzzled as to why the servants were awake at night. And calling for Kathy, calling for the so-called 'monster who maltreated her'.

From the Sarah Siddons Ward she was transferred to the Canteloupe Ward, which specialized in the elderly and mentally ill, while the hospital staff searched for an appropriate home for her. Pamela Luke, the social worker concerned, saw Lady Illingworth on the 12th and subsequently had several conversations with Susan de

Stempel, who told her that with two children to care for she could not possibly have her aunt back. Of course, as we know, the children were twenty-two and twenty respectively. More importantly, in the light of future events, she said that Lady Illingworth had no means other than her pension; thus the idea of a private nursing home was ruled out. There had been a suggestion that a place might be found for her at a residential home near Droitwich, but it failed to materialize.

When Susan de Stempel failed to keep an appointment with Mrs Luke on 27 December the social worker received a message that a death in the family had necessitated a visit to Scotland. The dates coincide with the death and funeral of Uncle Robert. Susan de Stempel did attend her uncle's funeral, but it was at Markington, not in Scotland, and afterwards she declined to return to the Hall for refreshment. Perhaps she was frightened that she might be asked awkward questions about Lady Illingworth? If so, one can hardly blame her. It was a large family gathering, attended by many who would be most anxious for news of her. How was Aunt Puss? How were they coping in such a small cottage? What was the medical opinion as to her state of health? Could they come and see her? Might not Aunt Marion, Robert's widow, who along with her husband had been such a source of financial help throughout the years, ask embarrassing financial questions? All these and hundreds of others must have gone through her mind on the journey to Markington. She knew there could scarcely be an interrogation during the service; but the reception was fraught with danger. Better by far to depart rapidly.

Shortly after Robert Wilberforce's funeral a place for Lady Illingworth was found at Langford House, a state-funded old people's home in Hereford. Again Susan was contacted by Mrs Luke, requesting some clothes. Two days before her aunt's move to Langford, Susan brought in some clothes. It was evening. She was asked – persuaded is a better word – to see her aunt, but only stayed a short time and reluctantly.

On 28 January 1985 Margaret, Lady Illingworth was moved to her last address. The medical consultant there, Dr Alan Johanssen, found her 'a delightful old lady, not the usual type we get at Langford House. She was very gracious and still quite elegant in her bearing but she was utterly confused. She couldn't answer questions except with a yes or no. She didn't know anyone except matron. She was well into a state of senile dementia.'

The matron of Langford House is a small, energetic Frenchwoman, Andrée Popplestone, who has worked there for twenty-seven years. It is, according to one of her staff, her whole life, and indeed she seems blessed with the unusual gift that some people have for dealing with the elderly. A large red-brick house with many extensions, it is named after Charles Langford, Dean of Hereford Cathedral from 1593 to 1607. It has a mixed history, having been a private house and a school, then requisitioned by the military authorities during the Second World War, until its present designation – a residential care home – in 1947. It accommodates about sixty patients, mostly women. Mrs Popplestone is quite rightly proud of the care and attention given to her old and sick inhabitants, but nothing can change the general feel of the house, situated in an inner suburb of the city, as that of a slight seedy state-run institution.

The old seem to sit in rows silently staring, hardly conversing, yet there are books and television, a bus to take them on outings, and little check-clothed separate tables in the dining room. There are some single rooms; others have two beds; while two rooms, housing four and six beds respectively, contain the advanced cases of dementia and physical deterioration. It is impossible to disguise in these two rooms the smells that attend people in this state. Langford House makes a brave try, but it fails. It fails because to disguise the smell of senility and death requires a lot of money: it means large, airy rooms, huge grounds and a very high staff-to-patients ratio. Langford House has love, but it does not have that much money. Nor does it have that sort of clientele. Small wonder that Dr Johanssen should find Lady Illingworth an unusual figure in such surroundings. Mrs Popplestone added in a statement made to the police and read in court: 'She was extremely polite and gentle with everyone. This part of her was obviously deeply inbred. She was a lady in every way.' But a lady who had no flowers by her bed, no bowls of fruit, no photographs of relatives.

During the twenty-three months she existed at Langford, she received no post of any sort. And only rarely did Susan de Stempel visit the aunt she was so cold-bloodedly milking: possibly every six weeks, possibly less, and certainly not more. Sophia went hardly at all, and the same goes for Marcus; yet Sophia was to shed tears in court over her poor aunt. The sick woman was left to sit in one of those rows silently staring into space for day after day after day. In such brief seconds of lucidity as she might enjoy, what anguish and distress must Lady Illingworth have felt staring round at such alien surroundings. To her the very furniture would tell her she was in a strange place.

Mentally, according to Dr Johanssen, Lady Illingworth did not deteriorate much more; it was her physical state that suddenly went into decline three months before her death. She died of heart failure on 9 November 1986. Had she known how she had been tricked, abused, exploited and then finally tossed away like a useless object, she would have died of a broken heart, not a failed heart.

But even more contempt was to be shown her in death than in the latter years of her life. Margaret Illingworth's proper will, made in 1975, asked that she be buried alongside her husband in the family mausoleum at Bradford. It is sited in an extraordinary place – the veritable necropolis that is Bradford's Undercliffe cemetery. It is now one of the city's Victorian tourist attractions, with nature trails and guides to the textile barons, churchmen and, so wrote Martin Wainwright in the *Guardian*, even a Druid, who lie beneath its eccentric gravestones.

The main Illingworth vault forms a miniature Pharoanic temple carved from millstone grit. Lady Illingworth's husband has his own pillar, topped by a veiled urn, in the next plot but one, with the related family of Baron Holden in between. The grave describes him as 'the beloved husband of Margaret', with the Latin motto *Honesta peto*, I seek things that are honest. Room for his wife's name lies below.

Again it must strike outsiders that, if Lady Illingworth had experienced such a degrading life with her husband, it would be highly unlikely for her to have specifically asked to be buried alongside him.

In any case, she was not given the opportunity: she was cremated at Hereford. Susan de Stempel attended, with two of her children, but there were no flowers or memorial stone. Finally, after vainly seeking Susan's instructions as to how the ashes were to be disposed of, the staff scattered them in the crematorium's garden of remembrance. The £389 bill has still not been paid.

All this did not prevent Susan de Stempel from writing, after a suitable lapse of time (suitable to her criminal intentions, that is) to various members of the Wilberforce family. To the retired Law Lord, her cousin Lord Wilberforce, she wrote: 'Dear Richard, Just to tell you that Aunt Puss died on November 9. She was very happy and beautifully looked after. There were no traumas, she simply wore out.' It was an extraordinary letter, not just for its dishonesty but for the elaboration of it. Susan added: 'That she regained her peace of mind was the greatest triumph of all', and, gilding the lily still further, 'Getting all her possessions out of store gave Aunt Puss great pleasure.' A member of the prosecution team at the trial said privately that in all his legal life he had never encountered such a depraved mendacity as this revealed; there was something unnatural and mentally sick about it. He imagined Susan de Stempel laughing at her entire family for all the slights she had endured from them.

In the forged letter that accompanied Lady Illingworth's forged will, said Timothy Barnes, QC, it was stipulated that no members of the Markington branch of the family should attend the cremation. Susan de Stempel wrote in the same letter to her cousin, 'I was appalled when I saw the state Aunt Puss was in when she came to live here. It was marvellous watching her come back to life.' She then went on to tell of her aunt's wish for cremation and her further desire that her death be kept quiet, with no public announcement. And she concluded: 'There is bound to be a lot of chat and things get distorted in the telling. I am quite sure that a lot of people do not think that Aunt Puss should have been removed from York House. But she was being treated like an animal and had to be moved out.' An animal, it should be pointed out, who was once a rich and generous woman, yet who was found to be on her death overdrawn to the extent of £8000.

Lord Wilberforce revealed that he was 'shocked and distressed' at the funeral arrangements, which were not in keeping, he thought, with Lady Illingworth's previous wishes. She was a devout Catholic who would have been opposed to cremation. 'I would have expected her to be buried in some form or another together with her husband.'

Also distressed and most surprised at the details was Susan de Stempel's brother John. 'It surprised me because before 1984 her intention was to be buried beside her husband.' It further seemed to him to be totally out of character and 'quite extraordinary' that Lady Illingworth would wish to have the news of her death withheld from her friends. Three months after her death, in reparation and at the instigation of Lord Wilberforce and John Wilberforce, the *Daily Telegraph* duly recorded the death of Lady Illingworth in its obituaries column:

Lady Illingworth who has died, aged eighty-six, was an indefatigable hostess at her historic Georgian house in Mayfair, 44 Grosvenor Square, the last privately owned house in the square which was disgracefully demolished in 1967 to make way for the new Britannia Hotel. She was an authority on the history of the house, once the town residence of the Earls of Harrowby, and gave guided tours to the public. It was in the house's morning room in June, 1815, that the Cabinet, the guests at dinner of the first Earl of Harrowby, received the Duke of Wellington's victory despatch from Waterloo. To mark this event, Lady Illingworth would give a ball every June. She herself was a great-great-granddaughter of William Wilberforce, the emancipator of slavery, and always had a keen sense of history. In the early 1960s, she discovered some eighteenth-century wall-paintings behind the panelling in the drawing room at 44 Grosvenor Square which were thought possibly to have been the work of William Kent. The house had been renovated for her in 1931 when she married, as his second wife, the first Lord Illingworth, who had been Postmaster-General from 1916 to 1921. They had no children and when the peerage expired with him in 1942, Lord Illingworth left his property to his wife on the condition that she did not enter a convent. She was a devout Roman Catholic but remained in the lay state and in the 1939–45 War served as Commandant of the Voluntary Aid Detachment (VAD). She was an Associate of the Royal Red Cross. Both Lady Illingworth and her late husband were of sound Yorkshire stock. Margaret Clare Wilberforce was born on November 23, 1900, the only daughter of the Squire of Markington in the West Riding. In 1933 she opened the Wilberforce Centenary Exhibition in Hull and took an active interest in the stopping of slavery in countries where it still existed. Following the destruction of 44 Grosvenor Square, Lady Illingworth migrated down the road to Claridge's where she continued her legendary hospitality.

The Times ran a far shorter notice, four days earlier, when it briefly stated 'Lady Illingworth, second wife of the first Baron Illingworth, died recently. She was thought to be eighty-six.' But it carried a warm tribute from Lord Wilberforce which ran:

Lady Illingworth (Margaret Wilberforce) made a host of friends for herself and for this country through her hospitality at her house at Grosvenor Square and after its demolition at Claridge's. Her generous personality, supported by remarkably good looks (English style), never left her. She was always at home to the Diplomatic Corps, and travelled widely. She was also a supporter of the Red Cross and of anti-slavery causes.

And so Lady Illingworth was laid to rest. But when the sad saga of her defrauding is finally over, might not some member of her family erect somewhere a small stone in token of the abounding generosity of a most warm-hearted woman?

❦ 7 ❦

T·H·E F·O·R·G·E·R·Y
F·A·C·T·O·R·Y

THE year 1984 was one of frantic activity at Docklow – the 'forgery factory' as Timothy Barnes, QC, called it. It took Susan and her accomplices very little time before they started defrauding Aunt Puss.

The first evidence came less than a week after the old lady moved in with them, and concerned Susan's bank account with Lloyds in Hereford. She had opened it in 1974. It was a small account, said a bank official, and frequently overdrawn by about £100. In January 1984 the account was overdrawn by £119. On 5 March the bank's assistant manager, Roger Jones, received a letter from Susan Wilberforce which said she had recently been 'on a bit of a spending spree. This is on behalf of an elderly relation who has recently come to live with me and has lost her cheque card. I shall be fully reimbursed for everything I have bought on her behalf within the next few days.' And so she was, for by 27 March £480 in cash had been paid into the account. Less than a month later another £400 was deposited. Both sums came from a cash dispenser using a card obtained in Lady Illingworth's name.

On 25 April Susan Wilberforce made out a cheque for £444.50 to 'Mount Stevens'. This, according to Timothy Barnes, QC, appeared to be among the first beneficiaries of Lady Illingworth's money. 'Mount Stevens' is actually Mountstephens, a very upmarket dress shop, tucked away in a little pedestrianized street that leads to the cathedral in Hereford. It has been run by Mrs Hall for thirty-five years now and very proud she is of it. She stocks designer clothes, much Italian couture and some Frank Usher. Her clientele is 'very county'. No, she didn't remember Susan Wilberforce personally, she said, but the name was familiar. It would be easy to spend over £400 at Mrs Hall's shop. The clothes are not cheap, but then customers pay for the cut and the label. Presumably that's what Susan – and

104

possibly Sophia – thought when they went on their first 'spending spree'. What is certain is that the clothes were not bought for Lady Illingworth. Both hospital and Langford House staff were struck by the shabbiness of the old lady's garments.

Altogether, more than £6000 was withdrawn from autobanks in less than three months. But that source of income was not enough. For the full exploitation of Lady Illingworth's fortune, forgery was required. Heaven knows how long it took Susan Wilberforce to learn to forge the old lady's signature; suffice to say that, within a few weeks of her aunt's arrival, she was a practised forger. At the request of the Fraud Squad, the Home Office handwriting expert, Dr David Baxendale, examined a number of allegedly forged documents including letters written to jewellers, a stockbroker and solicitors, and a number of cheques. He compared them to a number of documents dating from the seventies and early eighties which bore the authentic signature of Lady Illingworth. There were, he said, 'significant differences. These differences are not such that they can be explained by Lady Illingworth's ill health, infirmity or old age. My conclusion,' he added to a silent court, hanging on every word, 'is that they were not written by Lady Illingworth. They were written by somebody else who deliberately attempted to copy the design of her signature.' They varied in quality, he added with something like professional zest in his voice: 'the least fluent and accomplished are crude, the better ones are remarkably well done.'

If Susan de Stempel had been sitting in court, one feels she would have bowed to the half compliment. What Dr Baxendale's expert opinion shows is the carelessness of a confirmed criminal, taking pains at the beginning but growing slapdash with success at the end. Altogether sixty-seven forgeries were tracked down by the police, but others might still exist.

That forgery was already in her mind, at least from the first days of Aunt Puss's moving in, is proved by the early visit to York House for Lady Illingworth's papers. Both Kathy Whelan and Dorothy Hayman said her ladyship's bedroom had been 'stripped' within a week of her departure. Kathy Whelan, in her statement, said the Baron and his solicitor searched for hours before finding the papers they required. At last they found them, she revealed, under a pile of boxes left on the floor. No wonder the Baron was in a filthy temper during the search – the papers were vital to the plan. Without them how could he know the full extent of Aunt Puss's fortune or, more importantly, who Susan had to dupe in order to get money and goods released? 'The speed with which her money was misappropriated after she arrived at Docklow is an indication of the plan which was put very rapidly into effect. That was the plan for the enrichment at senile Lady Illingworth's expense,' explained Timothy Barnes, QC, at the trial.

During the next few months 'the forgery factory' was kept exceptionally busy. Her signature was forged on documents in order to transfer Lady Illingworth's bank accounts to Hereford. Her assets were moved to accounts made out in the joint names of Susan and herself and to accounts in the name of Susan and Sophia. Eventually, by 1986, there were twenty-three accounts in the sole name of Susan de Stempel.

Letters went to Giltspurs, charging them to release the forty-seven vanloads of Lady Illingworth's possessions that had been in storage ever since 1967, when the Grosvenor Square house was sold. These were siphoned off to three places: Forresters Hall, Heath House and a large barn at Wickton Court, near Docklow. Ann Devey-Smith recollects being shown a great barn full of furniture which had been given them, it was explained, by Lady Illingworth. 'I was told by Susan that her aunt wanted her to have the use of her money and the disposal of her furniture,' she said. One of the first recipients of this sudden avalanche of prosperity was Sophia, Lady Illingworth's minder. The £800 fare for a trip she made to Japan in May to see her brother, Alexander, was paid for weeks before the holiday in cash. Yet one month earlier, when Sophia had needed an operation for the removal of a wisdom tooth, it had been her godfather, Francis Rose, who had paid for it. Why was this necessary, it was later argued, when Lady Illingworth had already indicated that her money was their money? Why, too, pay in cash when Lady Illingworth – who was, according to them, perfectly sane and rational – would have been delighted to sit down and write out a cheque for a great-niece of whom she was so fond? Why, indeed. Because they were still pretending to those few people on the outside world who had contact with them that Lady Illingworth was with them only for a holiday. And though Francis Rose was a friend of the family who had known them for thirty years, he was a solicitor who might conceivably have smelt such a rat that it would have been his duty to warn them off.

That their life was frantic and muddled seems in no doubt. Marcus, when he was not collecting furniture and valuables and ferrying them to auction houses in Bath, Hereford and Leominster, was living back at Heath House. He says that, since it was eleven years since he had been close to his father, he had decided to get to know him again. But the vast empty spaces at Heath House were surely more comfortable than sharing a bedroom with Sophia and young Simon, and listening to the constant rows erupting between Michael de Stempel and his mother.

Crime had not drawn these dependent aristocrats together – rather, it was pulling them apart. Michael, with his usual slippery behaviour, was not always at Forresters Hall. As he put it in court, 'She wanted me to be at Docklow more or less all the time and I didn't want to be there all the time.' Their relationship was 'somewhat strained and most unstable'. She, knowing full well she could not trust him, did not believe his story that he wanted to be with his youngest son, Alexander – a boy for whom she always showed the utmost contempt. She knew his weakness for leaning on whatever richly clad female shoulder might be around.

Also, Lady Illingworth was not as docile as she had been. She had taken, said Susan in a letter written to Sophia in Japan, to 'sitting in the garden in a heat wave with a mohair jacket over her head'. And Michael was 'creating dozens of scenes, sulking in the tent and leaving his luggage in the pub'.

Poor Michael! Ever since Lady Illingworth had arrived at Forresters Hall space had been so limited that he had been forced to sleep in a blue tent in the garden. Sometimes it was so cold, he whimpered, that he had been forced to wear two thick jumpers at night to keep warm. Susan always denied to me in subsequent conversations, however, that Michael slept in a tent. 'It would have killed the grass,' she said with one of her short, sharp and very enigmatic smiles. But Sophia, too, mentions the presence of two tents in the garden, one of which, she said, her mother slept in on occasions. This Feydeau-like scene was one of the few to lighten the whole grisly business and bring a smile – to the barristers' lips at least. The idea of such titled folk carrying their *Almanach de Gotha* and *Burke's Landed Gentry* under one arm, all togged up for a night under canvas, and then next day quarrelling over the disposal of the stolen property of a senile old lady was comic indeed – but black comedy.

Another cause of their disputes, particularly regarding Michael de Stempel, was the tension they were undergoing. With all the sangfroid in the world, a speciality of Susan's, they were aware and had been for weeks that any day Lady Illingworth could go into a decline and die. Her 1975 will made no reference to Susan or to any of Susan's children, bar a small bequest of £1000 to Alexander. It left most of her estate to big brother John. How this wound of deprivation must have hurt, whenever she looked towards the Markington lot and saw them rich, honoured and successful. How unfair it must have seemed to Susan for them to have more money still. Back in 1982, when Sophia was working as a nanny in Oxford, she had always referred bitterly to her family as the 'poor ones' while the Markington lot had all the family money. There was no love lost between the two sets of cousins. The bitterness was a direct inheritance from her mother. The other chief beneficiary of Aunt Puss's will was an Illingworth relation, Lucy Kilfoyle, who lived in South Africa.

Adding to the tension was the risk that if Lady Illingworth died suddenly her executors would want to know what had happened to monies already used by the two conspirators. What about the ever-funding cash dispensers and the creation of joint bank accounts in her and Susan's names? They would want to know why. It became imperative that there should be a new will in which Susan was named as the main beneficiary. Furthermore, it was obvious that they could not simply browbeat Lady Illingworth into taking this action; mentally, she was incapable of it. The new will, therefore, would have to be forged.

Susan – and one can see her enjoying the adventure and the challenge – would take on the physical task of copying the old lady's signature while the Baron would set up the legal side of it. He would get in touch with an old friend of his known to Susan – James Martin Bonar Law, the second Lord Coleraine, a solicitor. He'd known him since Oxford days, and his lordship was godfather to his son Alexander – a simple matter. But a simple matter it did not turn out to be, for they had not envisaged the proper professional etiquette with which Lord Coleraine conducted legal affairs. As this tall, thin, humorous-looking man explained in court: 'I was telephoned on occasions by Michael de Stempel and he said that Lady Illingworth wished me to assist her in making a will, and I told him that I would be prepared to do so. The matter was not taken any further. . . .' The reason the matter was not taken any further was because the good lord made clear that he would like to see Lady Illingworth in the course of drawing up a new will. He had met her once before, years ago, at Lord Wilberforce's house, but had not seen her recently. What consternation his innocent remarks must have caused them.

Lord Coleraine also declined to help when subsequently Michael de Stempel, Marcus Wilberforce and Richard Sexton visited the York House flat for the purpose of collecting papers, clothing and furniture shortly after Lady Illingworth's arrival at Docklow. Faced with Kathy Whelan's defence of her mistress's property and thinking that a title might help, Michael de Stempel rang his old friend asking for assistance. 'I was told,' said Lord Coleraine, 'that there was a housekeeper or some servant in the flat and that person was saying that the possessions could not be handed out. I was asked if I would telephone this lady and say that she must hand them over. I said I would not do so. I did not believe it was correct.'

Another solicitor, Robert Patten, was found to draw up the will, but failed to complete the arrangements due to suffering a heart attack. So this extraordinary document finally landed on the desk of Richard Sexton, a solicitor from Twickenham. Another rare moment of humour later in court was provided by the Baron, who was testy and ill at ease, sibilantly stressing the word 'sir' at the end of every reply. Stung by Timothy Barnes's questions about the finding of a solicitor in far-out Twickenham, he rolled his head and spat: 'You make Twickenham sound like a brothel area, sir.'

On Susan's instructions the will was drawn up on specially thin paper. Thick paper, it was explained, was a phobia of Lady Illingworth's. She also hated the telephone. When examined on this the Baron replied, in part rather truthfully one feels, that he did not think ordering thin paper was suspicious: 'So many people I know have phobias that I would have accepted it at face value. I believe Lady Illingworth also had a phobia about the phone.' What useful phobias they were, Timothy Barnes pointed out – thin paper being a decided help if a signature was to be traced. And the telephone phobia meant that Sexton could not check anything verbally with Lady Illingworth. It had to be done by letter, and these kept coming from April onwards.

There remained but one problem: witnesses. They needed two people of good character and social standing, whose names on such a document would merit no inquiry or raising of eyebrows. But, importantly, these witnesses would have to be innocent enough themselves not to query the strange circumstances attending their signatures. Susan thought of Ann Devey-Smith, her old London friend and nearby Herefordshire neighbour. And then the Baron came up with a splendid idea: why not one of the fathers from his son Andrew's former public school – the Jesuit-run Stonyhurst College, near Blackburn in Lancashire? What a good idea! Never mind that the Baron had virtually no communication with Father Dooley during his son's schooldays. A little matter of slight acquaintanceship with those of whom he was demanding favours had not deterred him in the past; it would not do so now.

Accordingly he sat down and wrote a letter to Father Dooley, reminding him of his son's presence at Stonyhurst and asking a small favour.

Joseph Patrick Dooley, as he gave his name in court, was a burly, well-built man in his seventieth year. He had been ordained in 1952 and always wore his dog collar 'except when I'm climbing mountains', he explained to a respectful audience. He dimly recalled Andrew de Stempel as being a boy who had been at Stonyhurst in the seventies and from whom he had had a couple of holiday postcards in the years since he left. It was, he said, 'a very distant relationship' – he had never stayed with the family or even had a meal with them. Then, out of the blue, 'I had a letter from the Baron – I'd never had one before – saying there was some small service concerning a will he wanted my help on. He would come and see me and discuss the matter.' The priest wrote back that he would do all he could to help.

In court he gave the impression that he had been slightly intrigued by the Baron's letter, and that personal kindness allied with curiosity plus the urge, perhaps, for a break in his usual routine had led him to comply with the request. The weekend of 16–17 June was set aside for the will ceremony. Ann Devey-Smith was invited for the Sunday afternoon. Sophia was back from Japan, minding Lady Illingworth. Marcus was staying the weekend at Heath House with his father.

On Friday the 15th Baron Michael de Stempel travelled to Lancashire. He stayed the night at what Father Dooley was pleased to call a 'local hostelry', where he entertained the Jesuit to dinner. 'The next morning,' recalled the priest 'we proceeded by train via Hereford to Leominster, where we were met by car and taken to Forresters Hall. It was a long house, he described (obviously he was not aware that it was divided up into two cottages), running parallel with the road (which it does), and overfurnished. Very much over-furnished.' This obviously struck him forcibly; he added that there was no order or uniformity to the furniture. 'It was just there,' he said. His own room was small, with a bulky bed and a chest of drawers. He was conscious of paintings hanging everywhere – large paintings that hung oddly in such a small cottage.

He did not meet Lady Illingworth on the Saturday, though he met Sophia briefly. It was a very hot day. The will was not discussed. Meals were taken in a small kitchen at a table set against the wall. It all sounds, to the outsider, hideously embarrassing. What on earth did they talk to the priest about? Old schooldays? The Baron's time at the former Jesuit public school, Beaumont, which Father Dooley would have known? Old Catholic families? Anything but the will and the senile old lady who was carefully kept out of sight by Sophia.

110

The great day was Sunday. Much as she might belong to an old Catholic family, Susan and her children did not practise their religion regularly; they rarely went to mass. In fact, the children were not baptised as Roman Catholics at all; instead they had been christened in the Anglo-Catholic church of St Edward at Hopton Castle, a few miles from Heath House. But this Sunday, what with a Jesuit priest in the house, some religious observance had to be made. Accordingly, after a 'sparse' breakfast shared only with Michael, Father Dooley was driven in Susan's car to a Catholic church near Hereford Cathedral where, in his own words, he 'conducted a service'. Back at Forresters Hall, he went to sit in the drawing room.

Shortly before lunch an old lady was shown into the room. This was Lady Illingworth. He told her who he was, and she smiled vaguely at his name and recounted the names of some of the priests attending her church in London. 'She spoke very, very slowly,' he said, 'searching for every word. There were long pauses. She was recollecting and recalling younger days.'

After no more than ten minutes, in his impression, 'a lady' (Sophia) came to collect her. He did not see her again. Still there was no mention of the will. They had a glass of sherry and then Father Dooley said, 'Shortly before lunch Susan came into the room with a document. Michael de Stempel was in the room.' The priest asked her what he should do, and she signified that he should sign it at the bottom of each page and on the last page. This he did. He was also asked to sign a passport application on behalf of Lady Illingworth, which he did. At no stage, he swore, did he examine the contents of the will or know any of its contents: he suggested in a sharpened tone of voice that to have done so would have been extremely ungentlemanly, in his view. They could not have picked a better person! He had never witnessed a will before.

They had lunch – again a meagre-sounding repast. Good food and wine were not part of Susan Wilberforce's hospitality; she has never been able to appreciate good wine, she claims, since a bad attack of jaundice in her youth. After lunch the worthy priest was driven by Susan, with Michael in attendance, to Leominster Station and put on a train going north. His mention of Michael de Stempel's oleaginous gratitude at the station was greeted with silence by the court.

The second witness had different memories. Ann Devey-Smith recalled arriving at the cottage in the afternoon and finding Lady Illingworth in the drawing room along with Father Dooley, Michael de Stempel and Susan. Tension was running high. It was obvious that they wanted the old lady out of the room. She was asked by Sophia if she would like a walk in the garden, and she said no. Again Sophia repeated her invitation, and again the old lady said no. Finally, and with some desperation, Sophia asked her great-aunt if she would like a glass of sherry. That did the trick, and Lady Illingworth was taken off to the kitchen. The actual words used were damning for Sophia, for what Ann Devey-Smith remembered being said was this:

Sophia: 'Would you like a glass of sherry?'

Lady Illingworth: 'That would be nice.'

Sophia: 'Would you come with me then?' and she led her out of the room.

Onlookers might ask why it was necessary to take her elsewhere for a glass of sherry. Why not bring her one in the drawing room? Because, the prosecution successfully argued, it was vital to get the old lady out of the room while the forged will was signed by the two witnesses. Again, Ann Devey-Smith had never witnessed a will before.

Oddly enough, although wills are common documents in law, few people realize that, in order to be legal, they have to be witnessed *at the same time* as they are signed by the will maker. Despite Father Dooley's evidence, despite Ann Devey-Smith's evidence, the Baron spluttered and swore that he was not a party to the forged will. When asked where he was at the time, he replied: 'I had a feeling that I went to a pub called the King's Head in Docklow.' He spluttered some more, 'I may have had a bath, I may have had a walk in the garden. I was certainly absent throughout any kind of procedure connected with any will.' He further absented himself from the business by saying that it was 'a family matter' and thus had nothing to do with him. But once again the Baron's lies sounded hollow and unconvincing. Even his friends cheerfully acknowledged that he had been a congenital liar all his life.

With the forged will out of the way, the task of relieving Lady Illingworth of her wealth could speed ahead untrammelled. Michael arranged the sale of £28,000 worth of stocks and shares. Letters went to and from banks and solicitors, arranging different accounts in the joint names of Lady Illingworth and Susan Wilberforce. By July all correspondence affecting Lady Illingworth's fortune had been diverted to Forresters Hall. Susan and Michael made trips to the Channel Islands to sound out the possibility of offshore accounts. A Guernsey bank official, Richard Ellis, was told by the Baron, in terms that can well be imagined, that his future wife's account would shortly be £1½ million from an inheritance. That same account in Susan Wilberforce's name had been in existence years previously, but according to Mr Ellis it had never shown a credit figure exceeding £550. Between January 1984 and July 1987 cheques totalling £55,000 were drawn on it. Altogether the West Mercia Fraud Squad discovered a complex network of forty-nine different bank accounts ranging from Herefordshire to Paris and Canada.

The de Stempels' attention then turned to the twenty-eight cases of personal belongings held in the Kensington bank vaults. Susan had told Richard Sexton, the solicitor who had drawn up the will and been appointed to help transfer Lady Illingworth's fortune to Hereford, that the boxes contained nothing but 'old letters, chocolate and fake jewellery'. The good jewellery had been sold, she said in her letter, to pay off her aunt's gambling debts. In reality the boxes, insured for £150,000, contained silver plate, jewellery and a Limoges tea service.

On 3 July the Baron and the solicitor visited the bank to request that the boxes be handed over to them. The bank refused to do so, arguing that they required more notice. At this the Baron lost his temper, considerably embarrassing the solicitor: 'He was beside himself with fury, like a man possessed, because they wouldn't hand the boxes over. He behaved disgracefully towards the staff.'

All was not lost. Within forty-eight hours the boxes were delivered to Docklow and their contents divided up for sale. One month later items from the haul were being auctioned in Leominster, Bath and Jersey. Advertisements brazenly detailing Lady Illingworth's property were placed in *Country Life*. Never mind if the goods did not realize their true market value – what was important was to get the cash into various bank accounts. During the months that followed, the family moved like an express train at full speed through the possessions of the senile old lady, while she was kept shut up in a small bedroom at Docklow.

In August Susan and Michael visited Jersey with the object of selling off Lady Illingworth's valuable jewellery and silver plate. The insurance value of the 'load' was nearly £100,000. The jewellers they chose to act as agents for them were Hettiches, an old-established Jersey firm. Barry Matthews of Hettiches said of the visit: 'At that time we did not wish to purchase the items ourselves but we agreed to sell them on a commercial basis. Susan Wilberforce was made well aware that we would sell these items through the trade.' What, in effect, he was telling her was that if she wanted a quick sale she would have to accept a much lower figure than they were worth. Nevertheless, she indicated that they should go ahead as fast as possible.

The items consisted of diamonds, emeralds, rubies and a distinctive aquamarine brooch. The trade value on a selection of the jewellery was £22,576, though its commercial value would be double that. Some of the jewellery had previously been stored with the London jewellers Hemmels, before Lady Illingworth was taken to Docklow. It was staff from there who identified pieces which subsequently turned up at auctions. They had particular memories of the aquamarine brooch and a gold cigarette case, for they had originally sold them to her in 1934. The cigarette case was the one she had so proudly shown her driver, Albert Oslar, twenty years earlier. The silver was eventually auctioned at Sotheby's for £28,500.

Another visit in August – this time to Guernsey – was with the intention of setting up an offshore bank account into which some of the vast sums they were hoping to acquire could be held tax-free. A joint account was set up in the name of Susan Wilberforce and Lady Illingworth at the Midland Bank, St Peter Port, Guernsey. Richard Ellis, the manager, told in court how he was visited by the Baron de Stempel who informed him (with what *flaneur* one can imagine!) that he proposed to sell £1 million worth of Lady Illingworth's shares and transfer the money into the new joint account. In that way, the Baron believed, the funds in the account would automatically become the co-holder's money on the death of Lady Illingworth. Not so, replied the manager to the Baron's great surprise. Under Guernsey law his wife would not inherit the money in the joint account. 'I suggested that he took advice from either our trustee corporation or a Guernsey advocate,' Richard Ellis said. It is not known whether they did but presumably, as with the will, they did not want too fine a legal eye examining their intentions. There is certainly no record of them having followed Mr Ellis's advice.

One curious point did emerge, however, from the bank manager's evidence. He explained that the Baron had taken out a mortgage at the bank to buy a £105,000 house on Alderney, where he planned to move with his wife and the old lady. 'We agreed to a mortgage of £40,000, which the Baron said would be paid by Lady Illingworth.' So poor Aunt Puss was going to have to purchase her own prison, for this is the house that at the last moment the de Stempels abandoned plans to acquire. Their cynicism was breathtaking. Perhaps, after all, Langford House – with its atmosphere of caring compensating for its shabbiness, its lack of space and privacy – was a better place for an old lady to spend her final months than locked behind bars and looked after – or, more likely, neglected – by her own mercenary relatives.

The list of bank accounts opened and closed down during the active defrauding of Susan's aunt runs to five pages in the prosecution evidence. The later ones are interesting in that they involve the children. Four accounts, one deposit account at the Guernsey Midland, one at the Royal Bank of Canada and two at the Banco de Bilbao, feature Sophia's name as joint holder; three accounts – current, deposit and special reserve – at the St Peter Port branch of the National Westminster Bank feature Simon; while others – current and special reserve – again at the National Westminster, St Peter Port, are in the joint names of Sophia and Marcus.

Such a plethora of accounts can only have been intended to make detection more difficult. The further they spread the proceeds of Lady Illingworth's estate, the smaller chance was there, they thought, of being found out. However, less than two years later all the details of their activities were to lie on Detective Inspector Cowley's desk.

In court the Baron denied he had suggested using the Bank of Canada in order to evade investigation by the Inland Revenue. His explanation for so many different accounts was that he had been trying to protect his wife's aunt's estate. 'I was trying to do my best to preserve and protect Lady Illingworth's affairs which seemed to be financially in a state of chaos,' he claimed. He had to admit, however, that his own financial affairs were at least as chaotic – through inadequacy. His overdraft at the National Westminster Bank had reached nearly £50,000 by October 1984, when he was told the bank would allow him no more credit. 'I am stupidly negligent about money,' he said blithely, seeing no irony in the remark.

The conspirators' attention next turned to the great mass of furniture that had been in store ever since Lady Illingworth sold 44 Grosvenor Square and moved to York Place. That must not be denied them. But the problem was where to hold it while selecting individual pieces for auction. Marcus came to the rescue. Some time previously he had worked as a labourer for Tony Ellerton, who restores half-timbered buildings at Wickton Court, a few miles from Docklow. He had seen that the restorer had empty workshops which could certainly serve as a temporary home. Ellerton agreed to rent them a large barn, and instructions with a forged signature promptly went off to Giltspur Bullens in London, requesting the release of Lady Illingworth's furniture.

Susan had already bought a new Peugeot car from fraud funds but, in the light of heavy pieces to be transported to auction sales, it was decided to acquire a van. For £11,043 she bought a second-hand Mercedes van suitable for transporting small to medium-sized items of furniture. The van now stands locked under the trees at the back of Heath House, awaiting the settlement of the civil action which has still to come to court.

Tony Ellerton remembers the family distinctly: 'Marcus is a nice boy,' he said, 'who had worked for me as a labourer. He did most of the handling of the furniture when it arrived. Occasionally I would see his sister or his mother but in the main they were very quiet, they did not talk to anyone. What they did do was nail material across the windows of the barn so that no one could see in.'

As the pantechnicons arrived with their loads their contents were split up, and a selection loaded on to the Mercedes for sale in Bath, Hereford and Leominster. Altogether eight vanloads, carrying furniture valued at £300,000, were transported from Giltspur Bullens to Wickton Court. Marcus described a lot of it as junk, but the court heard that at Bath one sale alone had netted them £129,000. Some pieces found their way to Forresters Hall and the cottage at Heath House.

At this point it is worth listing what the police contend Susan de Stempel raised from her aunt's estate: furniture worth £150,000 was sold at knockdown prices, while another £135,000 worth was stored at Heath House and Forresters Hall; eighteenth- and nineteenth-century mirrors and paintings were sold for £59,500; £47,000 was withdrawn from Lady Illingworth's accounts using cashpoint cards; silver and jewellery were sold for £45,000; shares and National Savings Certificates brought in £28,000; cheques totalling £15,000 were written. No wonder they had funds for new cars and holidays abroad. No wonder Sophia could luxuriate in a very expensive suit that had been amongst the first items bought with Lady Illingworth's money; the suit was just one of the items of clothes purchased from the upmarket 'county set' dress shop, Mountstephens in Hereford. And, as their main investment, she and her mother could take pleasure from the holiday flat in Spain 'bought on a sudden impulse'. With Lady Illingworth's fortune stowed away they could afford sudden impulses. Yet Susan could barefacedly inform the DHSS that her aunt was totally without funds except for her weekly old age pension. Only a few weeks before this declaration, she had lodged over £44,000 in her and Sophia's Bank of Canada account!

In time-honoured fashion, however, money did not bring happiness. Having forced the Baron to marry her, Susan very soon found him slippery enough to escape even her desperate clutches. Much as she must have expected their jaunts to the Channel Islands to forge an unbreakable link between them, she was forced to acknowledge that in this venture she had failed. The Baron maintained that the marriage lasted no more than two days, and that he had previously never spent more than five days at a time at Docklow. After their marriage in September, he was there even less.

With so much anger and tension between them, it seems extraordinary that *both* should have gone in November to Jersey – where they were married – to see a lawyer. They wanted to get the marriage annulled on the grounds that the Baron had wilfully refused to consummate it. The de Stempels were told that it was impossible, since they did not live on the island. But why annul their marriage so quickly? Was it because they had concealed their new relationship from Simon Dale in case it affected the financial settlement of his and Susan's divorce, which had still not been sorted out? If, it is arguable, Dale had found out that Susan had remarried, he could have instructed his solicitors to press for a larger financial settlement from his ex-wife. She, after all, now had a new husband who could support her. In the fierce war that had existed since the sixties between Dale and Susan – no matter that for eleven years it had lain dormant – any ammunition was welcome. But without the support of the Jersey lawyer the plans of the Baron and his third wife collapsed.

On 3 December 1984, almost three months after their woeful marriage ceremony in St Helier, the Baroness filed for divorce. The Baron hurried back to London and the sympathetic arms of Jane Mackay. But a few ructions still lay in the path of his and Susan's divorce – ructions which again provided a few moments of bleak, black humour in this sorry tale. Never content to leave his women friends entirely – for who knew when he might need them – the Baron remained in touch with Susan.

In July 1985, he arranged to stay the weekend at Docklow and bring back some items he had left in the cottage. The visit was characterized by violent arguments between them over money. He blamed her for adding another £8500 to their American Express account which, as his wife still, she had been able to use. She replied that she had been shopping at Harvey Nichols in London and had lost her chequebook. The arguments grew more violent. As he explained in court, he finally lost his temper when he found his chequebook and cards thrown down a lavatory and his clothing strewn about the bedroom. Not to be outdone, he had broken a few

117

plates and, for reasons unfathomable to the main body of the court, 'put hollyhocks in a bowl of sugar in the lounge as a mild protest'. All good rumbustious stuff.

Susan, he found out, could be just as rumbustious. She locked him in the house after telling him that he was going mad and that she would have him sectioned under the Mental Health Act. Although armed against the world with only a dressing gown, he bravely forced open a window and climbed out. 'And then the police jumped on top of me,' he said. He was taken to a police station and examined by a doctor, who found him to be 'perfectly normal and sane'. He took the opportunity to telephone his dear friend Lord Coleraine, who testified that the Baron had been in some distress.

Ann Devey-Smith had a somewhat different recollection. She said that the Baroness had arrived early one morning at her house, a few miles from Docklow, claiming that Michael (who had been at school with Devey-Smith's brother) had gone berserk. She didn't know that Susan had already called the police; and so acting, she thought, as mediator, she went back to Docklow and saw Michael, who had scratches on his face and was wearing only a dressing gown. 'He was like a child in an emotional state,' she said.

The Baroness arrived independently, now accompanied by the police whom she insisted should arrest Michael. Mrs Devey-Smith said, 'Susan claimed to the police that Michael was going to attack her children. He was very agitated and upset. He didn't look capable of attacking anybody.' She told the court of her surprise at the police presence, but went on to paint a few more significant brushstrokes in this telling little vignette when she described the Baroness's attempts to rouse her recalcitrant husband. 'She was trying to provoke him to attack her, so the police would have some justification in arresting him. At one stage when the police were not in the room she thrust her chin at him and tried to make him angry. It was almost as if she wanted him to strike her.' After the police left, said Mrs Devey-Smith, the Baroness refused to let her husband out. 'Michael was in the drawing room saying he wanted to get out. He went over to the window and pushed it so hard that it gave way and he jumped out.' He was arrested, she added, by the police while scaling the garden wall and still shouting at the Baroness.

Like most of their extraordinary behaviour which almost drew laughter from the court, it also had its grim side. On this occasion the grim note was struck by the Baron's discovery of a large number of blank sheets of paper signed at the bottom in Lady Illingworth's name. He had found them while rummaging in Susan's bureau. It was Susan who had gone berserk, he claimed. She had angrily pushed him away to make sure the bureau was firmly locked, and accused him of searching through her papers.

Neither had confidence in the other's loyalty or fidelity. During this time Richard Sax, who had been the Baroness's solicitor since 1973 except for the significant year of 1984, was acting for both of them. In court he told how hardly a day went by without some new note of instruction; each was obsessed that the other should not learn his or her business.

The war between them rumbled on to its final shots. Michael claimed that he could not serve writs on her. According to him she had changed her mind and now wished to preserve the union. 'It was very difficult to complete the annulment proceedings,' he said in his inimitable fashion. 'Every time my solicitors went around to Docklow, Susan would make everyone lie on the floor and pretend they were out. It was very tedious. Eventually, a team of private detectives on motorcycles followed her taxi when she was in London. They had to drive up on to the platform of Paddington Station and serve the petition through the train window.' Glorious stuff – in other circumstances.

They were finally divorced in 1986. Exit from Susan's life the Baron, the man whom she frequently claimed to me was linked to her by the stars. Astrology has always been a major preoccupation with her. When the marriage in Jersey was arranged, much attention was given to the date and the position of the stars that day. Cynics allowably might smile. Latterly the Baroness has gone in for biorhythms – a similar quasi-science. It is as if the Catholicism in which she was brought up has been replaced by easier laws – laws which, significantly, do not emphasize the individual's choice of behaviour. How can you personally be bad if the stars are wrong?

Her attachment to the Baron lingered on, evinced by a series of rather pathetic letters written in 1985 and made much of in the trial. But after the divorce, the next time they would stand together was as prisoners awaiting sentence in Birmingham Crown Court. All she now has left of their union is her title and that she uses, she maintains, not for snobbish reasons but purely to annoy her successor, Jane Mackay. If so, she still derives amusement from it for, as the years go by, she has shown no sign of relinquishing it – if anything the reverse. Lawyers and others connected with her always address her as the Baroness de Stempel. She has not asked them to do otherwise.

8

T·H·E Y·O·U·N·G
L·I·E·U·T·E·N·A·N·T·S

I was educated at Wigmore School, then moved to Ludgrove Preparatory School, Reading [where Prince William has just started], from seven to thirteen, then on to the Oratory Public School, Reading. I left at the age of eighteen years after completing my A-level course. I subsequently attended Hereford Technical College and retook my A-levels. I subsequently attended Thames Polytechnic, Dartford, for twelve months studying Landscape Architecture but failed after the first year and so it didn't appeal to me to take the course further. As far as my school life is concerned it wasn't over-happy as I didn't do anything athletic and was picked on and bullied. Nevertheless I got through life all right. I have never been flash with money and because of this I have never had a relationship with a female, and I feel that should one get involved you should be able to give them a good time, which requires cash.

Thus Marcus Wilberforce describing his early life in a statement made to the police and read in court.

She was a very quiet girl who came to help nanny a little boy we had adopted. Someone had read the advertisement in the local Oxford paper and passed it on to her. She seemed to have no friends, though there was a brother she saw who was studying Japanese at one of the colleges. And I believe there was a Jesuit priest she saw occasionally. But although a very pretty girl, there was something sad about her. She was lonely. She did talk a bit about her family and we got the impression that there was a deep rift between two divisions of it. One side was rich and the other was poor. She came from the poor side and was quite bitter about it. She referred to a rich aunt but I can't remember if it was Lady Illingworth or not. It must have been about 1981 that she stayed with us for a few months.

That is how Mrs Raynish, the proprietor of a private hotel in Oxford, recollects Sophia Wilberforce, whom she employed as a nanny for her adopted son during 1981.

What sad descriptions they are; particularly sad in that they concern two young people – the two children of Susan Wilberforce found guilty of conspiring to defraud their great-aunt, Lady Illingworth. What they do not show is the fierce loyalty with which they honoured their mother all through what emerged as wretched childhoods. As part of the web she wove around her – a web of deceit and lies and arrogance – it is illuminating to look at the lives (as much as has been revealed) of those so intimately connected with her.

Since she had deliberately chosen to have few friends, children played an important role in Susan's life – she depended on them for the love, affection and support which her own adult world had failed to provide. Marcus and Sophia were the two lieutenants she had appointed to serve her. The two older boys, Alexander and Sebastian, had escaped her domination. The reasons are not altogether clear, but it might well have been that, growing up in the slightly happier days of the first years at Heath House, they were relatively unaffected by the marital conflict. They were able to enjoy an affectionate relationship with their father and thus were less vulnerable to their mother's bitter persuasion when the marriage ended. They also were old enough to have some measure of independence.

All that is known of Alexander is that he went to Shrewsbury, as did Sebastian, and worked for a time for Sotheby's in New York. He studied Japanese at Oxford when Sophia was working in the city as a nanny, and is now employed as a systems analyst in Tokyo. He was not seen in court while the murder trial was on, but arrived for the last few days of the fraud trial. Not so tall as the other boys, and with an odd, almost babyish look and his mother's tiny voice, he yet resembles his father strongly. There are snapshots of Simon Dale that look very much like his first son. Is it snobbery or a wish to be aligned with his young brothers and sister that has made him take his mother's name? After the memorial service for Simon he spoke of his father's love and how much he and Sebastian felt for him. If they really want to honour their dead father, some might argue, why not revert to his – and their – proper name?

In Alexander's absence in Tokyo, the real headship of the family descended on Sebastian's shoulders. It is a position he appeared to enjoy, for it gave him the right to speak with a self-importance that is rare in one so young (he was thirty at the time of the fraud trial). Sebastian is pure Wilberforce, seeming to encompass both the legal and ecclesiastical sides of the family at the same time. In him it is easy to see the nineteenth-century clergyman as well as the nineteenth-century lawyer. Facially he reminds one of the poor curate in Arthur Hughes' painting *The Long Engagement* – there is the same expression of refined agony at the vulgarities of the world. Susan de Stempel was much amused by her son's pomposity. Yet behind it lies a strength that could be supportive in difficult days to come. What has surprised acquaintances is that he became closer to his mother during the fraud trial than he was originally. In fact he appears to have affection for both his father and mother – though he has been heard to express a baffled irritation with Susan. After Shrewsbury he read theology at Hull, but did not enter the Church as he felt his vocation was not strong enough. He spent some time in the wine department at Harrods and working for the Conservative Central Office where, according to the local MP, Peter Temple-Morris, he was much liked. In 1991 he is finishing his articles as a solicitor: the profession should suit him.

It was Sebastian, not Alexander, who put his head in his hands and wept when the verdicts of Guilty on his brother Marcus and sister Sophia were read out in court. He, more than the rest of Simon Dale's children, appears to have the capacity to express his emotions openly.

In the lives of the three youngest children – Marcus, Sophia and Simon – Susan de Stempel reigned supreme. Whatever she ordered them to do, they did; whenever she called, they came. Never was this more so than in the years from 1984 onwards.

But it is possible, too, that the youngest, Simon, born in 1964, was not so profoundly affected by his mother's domination for he seems to have escaped the nest more than the others, though remaining loyal and always protesting her innocence. Unlike Marcus and Sophia, he disliked Heath House and his father so much that he refused to go there more than was absolutely necessary. In this way he became less involved in his mother's battle than the others did. He was also helped by his job as a qualified HGV lorry driver, which took him away from home frequently. Indeed, apart from his physical resemblance to the other male Wilberforces – which ironically comes more from Simon Dale than from Susan Wilberforce, with that tired, sore-eyed look and sparse hair – Simon is most unlike his next eldest brother and his sister. He has more contact with other people and appears to lack the overriding snobbery that has literally ruined their lives. If, as an old friend of Susan maintains, Susan was desperate to prevent her children becoming déclassé and so isolated them from ordinary people, she has failed in Simon who is refreshingly ordinary. Admittedly he has no stong intellectual or professional leanings (in fact, strangely, despite expensive private education, none of the last three children, though intelligent, has displayed any potential for great careers or even vocations) but he appears more at ease with the world than they do.

The one aspect of his life which may, according to some interpretations, give a psychological indication of an underlying desperation is his hobby: low fall parachuting, or base jumping as it is called. Simon uses a pseudonym, as base jumpers do, calling himself 'Josh Peters'. In 1989 the *Guardian* ran an interview with Josh Peters after he had notched up a base jumping first by leaping off Notre Dame Cathedral in Paris. In it he made a number of revealing remarks. He said, 'I'm a perfectly normal person. Base jumping goes on a lot more than people realize. It's very popular. . . . People admire others who do the amazing things they haven't the bottle to do themselves.' Complaining that the British Parachute Association had no right to condemn base jumping as too dangerous, or to compare it with Russian Roulette, which is why the BPA had banned it and any parachutist involved, 'Josh' argued that it was no more dangerous than Formula One racing. 'Base is addictive,' he said cheerfully, and continued:

> It charges your mind, all your senses become very acute, you feel the slightest breeze, notice so much more. Sky diving is all about style, and from 1500 feet, fields and houses look like some dinky town; but from 500 feet, a human being's a human being, and there's not much room for error. You've probably got 80 seconds free fall and then 10 seconds more till you hit the ground. Base is such an intense experience – I can't describe it, I don't have the words, it's like asking someone what making love is like. You just can't explain the incredible buzz you feel. I don't know, I suppose I'm just an earthbound misfit, but I'm definitely much happier above the ground than I am on it.

During the long tension of the trials it was noticeable that, while Sebastian attended as often as he could, this 'earthbound misfit' was absent from court for all but the last two days of the fraud case. Nor, several months after his mother had been taken to serve her sentence at Askham Grange Open Prison, had he seen her or received any communication from her. He has told friends he would like to disappear to America.

Marcus has admitted that since leaving college he has never had a steady job but 'has concentrated on doing gardening in the main and labouring for local friends and their contacts'. A German family who acted *in loco parentis* during the summer of 1983 while he was extending his knowledge of landscape gardening found him very shy.

Margarethe Radau and her husband Wolfgang, friends of the Heath House neighbours Veronica and Geoffrey Bowater, had been asked to arrange some sort of apprenticeship for the boy. According to Veronica Bowater the request came from Simon Dale who was, she avers, far from indifferent to the future of his children. 'He could see the rather hopeless pattern of Marcus's life and asked us to help. We thought of the Radaus who had contacts with landscaping and asked them if they could set up some form of extra training for Marcus – something which he could latch on to and build up into a profession. From general gardening for people he could easily, given more training, have become a proper landscape gardener – not just an odd job man.'

The Radaus duly arranged a three-month apprenticeship with a friend who had a landscaping business in the Black Forest; Marcus was to have a room in another friend's house for which they would pay. 'He was a very quiet boy,' recalls Margarethe Radau. 'He didn't speak very much. It was difficult to get to know him. He went out with our children but there was little contact. He didn't tell us he had finished at college and he could have stayed here longer, but he said he had to get home. He talked about his mother and father and I got the impression he was embarrassed by his father's way of life. He implied that everything had once flourished at Heath House but had since become dilapidated. He said we couldn't come and see him because there wasn't enough room at home, they had so much furniture.' But if Marcus was not very talkative, he was nevertheless quite revealing in what he did say. Frau Radau clearly remembers him asking her family if people lived in castles in their part of Germany. 'Marcus's idea of living was to live in a castle. He hadn't got any standards himself – he wanted to profit from the older generation of his family. He said they – meaning the Docklow lot – expected to inherit a lot.'

Simon Dale wrote before and after to thank the Radaus for their help, but Frau Radau told me that to her knowledge Susan never wrote once to them even though they were paying for the boy. She also revealed an aspect of Marcus not evident in court – meanness. While staying in Germany Marcus had been the recipient of much help from the innkeeper's wife, Frau Klaus. She had done his washing and looked after him, providing him with breakfast and supper. When the time came for him to leave, Frau Radau suggested that he should give the innkeeper's wife a present – a box of chocolates and some flowers. 'He did it most reluctantly,' she said. 'He was not very good about it. He had earned a lot of money out here but he did not spend it. And when he left he didn't even write to say thank you.'

The story does not end there, for subsequently the Radaus came to England to see the Bowaters. During their stay in 1986 it was suggested they should go over to Heath House to see Simon Dale. Early one evening they drove over for drinks with the half-blind architect. As they came down the drive the first thing they noticed were obstacles – logs and such like – impeding their path. They noticed Marcus 'hiding behind a bush' and refusing to acknowledge them, but even more surprising were the events which swiftly followed.

Geoffrey Bowater was driving, with Wolfgang Radau beside him and the two women, Veronica Bowater and Margarethe Radau, on the back seat. Suddenly Susan, with Sophia behind her, came towards them with a blowtorch which she was waving furiously, eyes staring, black in the face with anger. In her sometimes rather quaint English Margarethe Radau said, 'She began scolding us. But Wolfgang, who thought she had gone mad, told her to stop for the blowtorch was dangerously near the tyres. There could have been a fire.' Veronica Bowater says of the same incident that at first she wanted to laugh at the sight of Susan followed by Sophia, both waving their arms in the air 'like one of those many-armed Indian gods', but quickly realized that the hatred being expressed was far from funny. Frau Radau says she had never experienced anything like it – 'her eyes were so full of hatred and so were Sophia's. Marcus was ashamed; he was hiding, not knowing what to do.'

Inside Heath House, over necessarily calming drinks, Simon Dale excused his ex-wife, explaining that she had bad nerves and saying they shouldn't think bad things about her. 'She is very disappointed in me,' he said. Frau Radau said, 'We pleaded with him to get away from the house, we told him it would end badly for him, but he just replied that he had lived there all his life, he was not going.' With hindsight, Frau Radau now says: 'It was a lovely house with lovely furniture but it was a very sad house. We had the feeling that a tragedy would happen in that house.'

The general aimlessness of Marcus's life continued until, dropping all allegiance to his father, he joined the ranks of his mother in the battle of Heath House. From 1986 he was paid £100 a week to help in the general restoration work that Susan initiated. Local friends were surprised when Marcus appeared to 'give up his father'. They surmised that such was the force of Susan's dislike for his father, plus the fact that she now held the purse strings and was paying Marcus for his work, that he had little alternative. He himself has declared that he got 'fed up' trying one-handedly to keep such a large house going.

In private Marcus Wilberforce is a gentle, diffident person and unambitious to a fault. During the long run-up to the fraud trial he spent the nights working at a local baked potato factory supplying pubs and restaurants and the days looking after Heath House. He seemed genuinely not to mind living there on his own and, but for the Lady Illingworth scandal, might have gone on doing so, one feels, for the rest of his life, gradually edging into greater eccentricity as the years went by.

Many local people liked him but found him ultimately unresponsive, unable to make close contacts. He himself admitted to having only two friends – and one of those had been acquired through his elder brother Sebastian. Touchingly he revealed that he had 'two good suits and a dinner jacket' but, apart from the car given to him by his mother from the proceeds of the fraud, little else. He was to maintain steadfastly that he had had nothing to do with the fraud but merely did what his mother told him. He and Sophia never questioned her actions, he said, or thought it strange that Lady Illingworth should make over her fortune to them.

Oddly, in court he presented a different face from his usual quiet demeanour. He was stroppy, even belligerent under cross-examination from Timothy Barnes, QC. He twiddled his gold signet ring in a way familiar to those who have watched the Prince of Wales with his, treating the ring like a circular worry bead. Frequently he would snap back 'So what!' to the prosecution lawyer, which was to do his case no good. Some of those who had visited both trials wondered if he had caught the habit from his mother, who often behaved in the same way under cross-examination; but if so he did it with less panache. Once, just before the fraud trial and conscious of the strain the family was under, I asked him if he would like to have a mass said for them. As all Catholics know, mass is said for a variety of reasons and often just as a way of asking for good luck. To my surprise he said very coolly: 'I don't see the need for anything like that.' Does he now? For he, too, is caught up in the same 'revengeful' civil action as his brother Simon. And, like Simon, he has expressed a view that when it is all over 'I'd like to go to London and fade into the crowd.'

The first lieutenant of Docklow was Sophia. As enigmatic as her mother, she is also, seemingly, as aimless as her brother. Susan's only daughter is an extraordinary creature to describe. Sitting demurely in court, a high white frilly collar encircling her neck like a pie frill,

Sophia Wilberforce seemed, every inch, as one normally coarse journalist put it, 'the lass with the delicate air'. Indeed, many were captivated by the dark curly hair and blue eyes – 'like Elizabeth Taylor in *National Velvet*' was another journalist's description. Yet if the evidence is to be believed – and the jury had less hesitation about her role in the fraud than they did over Marcus (the verdict was 11 to 1 in a majority vote, 10 to 2 against Marcus) – she played a vital role not only in persuading Lady Illingworth to come to Docklow but, on the fateful forged will day, in energetically tempting the old lady out of the room with the offer of a glass of sherry.

It was Ann Devey-Smith who swore in the witness box that Sophia had been instrumental in getting the old lady out of the way. Sophia told the police in an interview that it was a total lie. When the two women were in court together the temperature dipped appreciably, even though yards separated them. The 'English rose' busily filled a page of notes as the erstwhile family friend gave evidence which was clearly damaging.

Like her brothers, Sophia went to a village school – not Wigmore but one in Craven Arms. From there she went to the Ursuline Convent in Brecon, but left without taking A-levels – due to her mother's inability to pay the school fees. If Marcus had disliked being bullied, so surely must Sophia have resented her insecurity as a pupil. Like Marcus she went on to Hereford Technical College, where she did take two A-levels.

It was just over a year since their mother had settled at Docklow, and presumably there was for a short space peace in that troubled house, with both brother and sister busy at their studies. Prompted by Sebastian she took an entrance exam for one of the Oxford colleges, but failed. Did this reinforce the isolation in which she had grown up? She appears to have made as few friends in life as her brother. Rather she seems to have spent a considerable amount of energy trailing round elderly relatives. It is hard to suppose that it was much fun for her living at York House during her two-year work period in London from 1982 to 1984. Why did she not choose to share a flat with other people of her own age? Sebastian was already in London and could surely have helped.

Suffice it to say that Sophia seems most ready to have been at her mother's beck and call from the age of twenty-two onwards. There is no sign of her having made any of the usual youthful dashes for freedom and independence. The small, dark carbon copy of her mother remained anxious to please, undetached from the umbilical cord. Even her conversation is like her mother's. During the fraud case she complained that she was aging rapidly, that her body was 'going'. And with a humour most reminiscent of her mother she hoped, she said, that the jury 'had not had too much red meat for lunch, making them more savage in their verdicts'. She told another journalist that she rather liked working, as though it were some strange aberration that she had suddenly found attractive.

Just as her brother had sworn that he followed his mother without questioning, so she swore the same. She would not query her mother's good luck in inheriting Lady Illingworth's fortune; indeed, she never discussed money with her mother. All she knew was that when times were hard her mother, who loved furniture, was forced to sell off family heirlooms.

Sophia is more nervous than she appears. When first arrested on a combined charge of murder and fraud in December 1987, she had a nervous collapse while in custody. Significantly, her defence counsel handed the judge a letter – presumably from a doctor or psychiatrist, as is usual in these cases – before he sentenced her. Also, such was the discord between mother and daughter when they were sharing a cell in Pucklechurch Remand Centre that they asked to be separated from each other. Recrimination had severed the umbilical cord at last. Even so, Sophia still maintained a deep even passionate affection for her mother.

They might not *like* their mother – Sebastian has been heard quietly to express reserve about her – but all five admire her fiercely. They see her as the guardian who protected them against the roughness of the world. 'She is a wonderful mother,' said Sophia. 'She is the most intelligent, witty, humorous woman I have ever met.' The obvious answer to that is that Sophia was not allowed to meet many women of her mother's age – witty or otherwise. Moreover, it was a remark made before Sophia was found guilty of conspiracy to defraud. Would she say it again now?

It was her mother's idea rather than her own, swore Sophia in the last telling piece of evidence against her. She was alleged to have asked a friend, Barbara Ann Smith, to look after some documents in April 1987. During a visit to Pucklechurch the friend was begged to keep the documents safe – and secret. Not unnaturally Mrs Smith asked the advice of her husband who, fearful of involvement in a serious criminal case, persuaded her to take them to the police. They were discovered to be documents relating to various bank accounts that Sophia shared with her mother in the Channel Islands and to the purchase of the Spanish flat in Alicante. It was an interesting point, which raised the notion that the mastermind and the two lieutenants were aware before the murder of Simon Dale that the net might be closing in on them.

Time and again, whenever both Marcus's and Sophia's defence counsel argued that their clients had no knowledge of the fraud and forgery, the question popped out – like an irreverent jack-in-the-box – what then *did* they talk about? Imagine the scene: the small, vastly overcrowded cottage at Docklow, the three grown-up children sharing the same bedroom while Lady Illingworth was there, the sudden arrival of new cars and foreign holidays and cash – yes, actual cash in hand. Surely, argued those following the case, the children must have discussed this avalanche of goodies, this extraordinary volte-face of luck amongst themselves? Did nothing arise from those conversations that made them doubt the legality of what was happening all around them? Did nothing in the forlorn appearance and behaviour of Lady Illingworth make them question their mother's activities? 'Aunt Puss went out of her mind,' said Marcus in his evidence, as if it happened one day with no before or after – just like that. And surely they must have conversed amongst themselves about the 'dumping' of Lady Illingworth in a state-run old people's home? Why was there no family funeral? They had been brought up to know how extensive the Wilberforce family was. Did they merely discuss the performance of the new cars and the expensive clothes their mother was buying them – or bribing them with?

This was the fact – what *did* they talk about – that stuck in the throats of ordinary onlookers in court, that stuck in the throat of those who followed the case via newspaper reports, that surely stuck in the throat of the seven men and five women who constituted the jury. Added to this was the realization, never once referred to by their defending counsel, that these were not children at all. They were adults. Marcus was twenty-three and Sophia twenty-two when they neglected to accompany Lady Illingworth on her last journey in December to Hereford General Hospital. The Jesuits at Marcus's school and the Ursulines at Sophia's convent would have acquainted them with the Catholic belief that a child is capable of sin after the age of seven. Treble that number and you have two adults each protesting a child's innocence. On 21 April 1990 they learned they were children no longer – not in the eyes of the world outside Forresters Hall, Docklow.

During the weekend of the murder trial – July 22–24 – I went several times to see Marcus and Sophia at Heath House. They had kept away from Worcester for the main part of the trial fearing press harassment. On the first occasion we sat in the kitchen drinking coffee and chatting about the hard time the prosecution was having. They seemed to feel no embarrassment about being 'in the murder room' or at least they gave no impression of such an emotion, or of the fact that anything other than the normal domestic routine had ever happened in it.

On the second occasion Sebastian was present and the atmosphere much charged with tension as he made clear his feelings about journalists and the press in general. We drank wine in the beautiful panelled drawing room. But despite their superficial assurance they seemed pathetically young and isolated. They agreed to come for lunch on the Sunday. If I drove over I could leave my car at Heath House and together we'd go in the Peugeot Estate to some pub they knew which was supposed to have good food. As it turned out the food was not especially good but, dutifully, like children on their best behaviour, they ate it all up. So much so I wondered if they had had any proper food for days! That and the inordinately fast, almost reckless, way Marcus drove the car were the only extraordinary features of the day. Certainly there was nothing to suggest that their mother was in custody charged with killing their father or that Heath House was the scene of the crime. The whole experience was surreal, like a sequence in a film.

❦ 9 ❦
A G·E·N·T·L·E G·I·A·N·T

CERTAIN years have certain characteristics – as true of Susan de Stempel's life as of anyone's. If 1984 appears in retrospect the year of deceit, the following years, 1985 and 1986, were totally different. Both, as her profusion of letters indicate, were years of desperation. Apart from the letters needed to carry on the deception regarding Lady Illingworth's funds, all the rest convey the atmosphere of a woman in mental and physical trouble. Turbulence is a better word to describe her mental state. Above all, they indicate a lost woman with no friend to talk to. Some of the extraordinary claims can possibly be explained by the fact that she was going through a mid-life crisis at the time they were written – she was fifty-one in 1985, and the contents of the letters are typical of various menopausal symptoms. Some are part of the web of deceit she was committed to, yet so weird that they suggest a woman isolated and racked with guilt and exhaustion. A moralist might argue that the defrauding of Lady Illingworth carried with it the seeds of its own destruction. Be that as it may, Susan de Stempel was a deeply unhappy woman – though never without that amazing gallows humour which is, possibly, her greatest defence against the world.

Following the weekend during which he witnessed the forged will, Father Dooley wrote a polite note to his hostess thanking her for her hospitality and saying he would remember her in his prayers. It was the only time they had met, and he did not expect to see or hear from Susan again. Much to his surprise, he received an agitated letter from her the following year saying that she was on the verge of despair over the breakdown of her marriage to Michael de Stempel: 'My life is in shreds. . . . Michael and I were married in September in Jersey. Almost immediately afterwards he became mesmerized by the wretched rich widow, and has been living with her ever since. Every word he says about anything is a lie. He has always been a pathological liar but now things have got completely out of hand.'

In another letter she told Father Dooley she thought Michael's

131

finances were in a chaotic state and that he might be mentally ill. And in yet another missive she advanced the most incredible notion that she had become pregnant by Michael and lost the baby. 'We spent the night in an hotel in Paddington', she wrote, 'and I became pregnant. He promised to come up the next day but didn't.' This was at the age of fifty-one which is, though not unknown, an unlikely time to get pregnant. It is well noted, however, that menopausal women frequently desire a last baby before becoming infertile. The priest told the court, 'I found the letter extremely embarrassing. I wrote a very noncommittal reply, not really giving any advice other than to say that I would say a few prayers.'

Another man she wrote to informing him that she had become pregnant but 'lost it' was Richard Sax, her old solicitor whom she had resumed consulting in January 1985. Poor Sax. This was the time when he was constantly bombarded with letters from either her or Michael. If she was not complaining about Michael's behaviour, she was abjuring Sax to reveal nothing of her activities to the Baron. She was frightened, she wrote, that de Stempel might be able to get his hands on some of the proceeds of the sale of Heath House. It must be taken into account that she had not yet obtained a divorce from him.

But what is obvious from the letters to Sax is that she had resumed the legal business of evicting her ex-husband, Simon. It had been allowed to slide, but now, with both Michael and Lady Illingworth gone, what could she turn her attention to but the disposal of Heath House? And, despite the new cars and considerable funds that she now possessed, it was important to keep up the act that she was near destitute. Presumably she reasoned that an eviction court would take less notice of the claims of a rich ex-wife than those of a poor ex-wife. She may also have been concerned to keep her funds secret lest members of the Illingworth family heard of her *unexpected* good fortune and started checking. In April she wrote a letter to Sax which ended, 'Yours frozen, broken bones, starved, almost destitute, disillusioned, in need of a quick removal of a husband, painlessly, cheaply and above all speedily.' The broken bones referred to an accident when she had shut her hand in the door of the new Mercedes van; the rest is typical of the letters she wrote to him.

Sax was asked in court if he thought his client was 'intolerant of others with different views and capable of lying'. 'Yes,' he replied, with a slight indication of distaste at being asked to rat on a client. But he made clear that, liar or not, Susan de Stempel was a fascinating woman. 'Never in twenty-five years of legal work,' he said, 'have I met a client like her.' Her speech was like her letters, he added. She was not frightened of calling a spade a spade: Michael de Stempel was an odious bumprick and there was no way that Simon Dale was going to bugger up Heath House by turning it into an institution for history scholars. 'Her letters are always very interesting,' he said in his neat pin-striped voice, looking over the top of his half-moon spectacles at Richard du Cann, QC – defence counsel for Michael de Stempel – who returned the gaze over similar half-moon specs.

Fantasy followed fantasy. Throughout the year she had suffered from varicose veins in her legs. But varicose veins, as everyone knows – everyone in her milieu, anyway – are a lower-class ailment. Only servants have troubles of that kind from having to spend long periods standing in shops and kitchens. It was to her, therefore, a deeply degrading affliction, and one that the Baroness was not prepared to accept. Accordingly she wrote to Sax in October saying that she had to have an operation for cancer and needed to 'get matters straightened out'. But even with this grim news her obsession for secrecy manifests itself: 'I do not want to say anything to anyone. I've not told Michael as his network of lies is greater than I thought.' A surprising sentence follows: 'Simon would be sorry but would use the information to stall about the house.' Further letters informed Sax that 'it's only my willpower that keeps me alive' and 'it was hope that kept me being spared the shipwreck of old age'.

As the time neared for the operation at the Radcliffe Infirmary in Oxford in early November, she wrote to him again saying, 'If I snuff it please thank Martin [Lord Coleraine] for me'. She told him that she had medical insurance, so 'I do not owe one penny except to you lot' and ended the letter on another typically eccentric note: 'Do you know any good books on the art of haunting?' In the same note she added, 'The medical profession think that the end is nigh, weeks rather than months.'

But she survived – most people do survive operations on varicose veins! – to write yet another letter: 'I am out of hospital but can hardly stand.' The operation, she disclosed, had lasted three hours and she would have to go back for another one in mid-December. When the hospital asked for her next-of-kin she had replied, 'I have a husband but don't know his address.'

No wonder poor Sax, who obviously had a kind heart, was troubled for this poor damsel so deeply in distress. Characteristically, she did not tell him that she had contacted Michael and asked him to come and look after her but he, having slipped the net, was not going back into it. He did not respond even when she wrote the most heartbreaking letter to him: 'I refuse to be cast aside by you in this way . . . I do belong to you, rejected and abandoned as I am. And you belong to me, as you will find out one day, my beloved.' Not even the astrological links which she thought bound them together for life were strong enough to bring him back to a woman he had learned to be frightened of.

At the beginning of January 1986 she wrote a three-page letter to Sax saying that she had had the offer of a house in Spain and so had gone abroad to convalesce. 'I would be very grateful if you would not tell Michael I am in Spain.' And then – obviously because she could not stop herself referring to him again – she added, 'I do wish you and Martin would persuade him to see a psychiatrist. I did hope to have a happy marriage before the geriatric floozy in Kent [Jane Mackay] got her claws into him. The whole of London has been told that the baby I conceived was not Michael's . . . could you please stop him molesting me in parks?' She ended her letter, 'I also believe in fidelity in marriage.' What she did not believe in, as poor Sax was to discover, was fidelity in letters. The house in Spain that she referred to was the flat that she and Sophia had bought in Alicante. Both Marcus and Sophia had had to deal with a very depressed mother, particularly in the latter part of the year, so they were relieved when, on a visit to Spain in December 1986, she had suddenly decided to buy a flat. They thought it would be good for her depression. It did not occur to them to question where the money came from. According to Marcus, his mother had had a sudden windfall.

In the middle of July 1986 the last proceedings of her divorce from Simon Dale required her to make a sworn affidavit regarding her finances. Again she could only tell a lie. In it she referred to her two accounts at Barclays Bank but omitted any reference to the numerous accounts she had by now accumulated in the Channel Islands. She continued to press Sax for a legal settlement regarding Heath House. 'Gird up your loins,' she told him, for the battle – a battle that had lasted fourteen years but must, she urged, now have a stop. Despairingly she ended another letter, 'Do anything you like but get it done – the last of my youth has gone.' In the spring of 1987 Sax wrote to her that the end was in sight. 'The matter is not yet in court but it will be soon.'

The end was in sight, but in a manner no one could have envisaged – certainly not poor Simon Dale.

*

What had happened to the ardent amateur archaeologist since that angry summer of 1973 when Susan had finally quit the house 'taking only her handbag' for life at Weobley? Over the years this 'gentle giant', as he was affectionately called, had achieved a remarkable *modus vivendi* in view of all his handicaps – lack of sight, poverty, isolation, immobility. His passion for the house had not abated – rather it had grown and become the dominant feature of his life, taking the place, it would seem, of the family he had lost. He dug ever deeper into the history of the house and surroundings, quarrelling frequently with professional archaeologists whom he asked to verify his findings.

Adrian Tindall, archaeology officer for Hereford and Worcester County Council, said: 'Mr Dale believed that Heath House was the site of a very important native British settlement. He had suggested there were connections with a variety of legendary figures and local traditions.' Dale, he continued, had constructed his elaborate theory concerning King Arthur and even, astonishingly, an Armenian settlement dating back to AD 400 from documents, folklore and legends. It was twice put to the test by archaeology experts. A trial excavation was made of the site, with inconclusive results, and then, in February 1987, Tindall himself visited Heath House. He found little, he said, to support Mr Dale's theory. 'Our conclusion was there was no evidence to substantiate it. But Mr Dale did not see it in those terms. I'm quite certain that he did view the archaeological world as forming a conspiracy against the publication of his work.'

What Tindall did find on his visit was an irate Baroness who, as he walked up the drive to the road after leaving Dale, stepped out from behind some bushes and confronted him. She asked him what he was doing there and he told her that he had been invited by Dale but on visiting Heath House had found that there was no archaeological interest in the site. 'As the conversation continued, I began to get the impression that she was rather odd. She said that Mr Dale was very violent, had threatened to kill her, had dug a grave for her and kept large quantities of cyanide in the house.' The serious, slightly pedantic expert continued: 'I *think* she said that Mr Dale had tried to murder her, rather than threatening to do so. She admitted that she had intercepted his mail.' She explained the presence of a jemmy hanging over one arm by saying that she always carried it for protection from Dale. It was a jemmy that the police later suggested could have dealt the blows that killed Simon Dale in September.

As well as the local archaeological officer, Dale also bombarded any public figures he thought might help him in the true investigation of Heath House. Peter Temple-Morris, MP for Leominster, was one. He regularly received letters from Dale attempting, as he said, 'to overturn British academic opinion built up over the centuries as to the site of the seat of King Arthur and the Round Table and the kings of the period. He maintained that one of the courts of Arthur was actually held on his site. The problem was the academic world did not react warmly to this.'

Personally Temple-Morris found Dale an engaging figure – pleasant, affable, though locked away in such abstruse thought that not many could follow him. 'He was the sort of chap better for lunch rather than dinner – he could become rather heavy going once launched into his pet subjects.' Temple-Morris had also met Susan once in 1982, when she had come to one of his 'surgeries' and complained about Simon Dale's brutality and obduracy. He found her 'a very quiet woman, demure, not very assertive'.

Robert Clifford, who had been best man at the Dales' wedding, paid a visit to Dale in the eighties and found the ex-architect a changed man, no longer the 'amusing and amused' person he had known. 'He was bitter about the way she had taken his children from him. "She's turned them all against me," he said. She was even using them against him, helping her harass him the whole time.' But apart from the bitterness – which Dale revealed but occasionally – he still preserved his sense of humour. 'He never held it against you that you did not agree with him. He had this complete Roman camp mapped out in the house but you did not have to go along with his findings.' Robert Clifford's second son, Daniel, is a stonemason who, his father recalls, had many happy arguments with Dale over the existence of a tunnel that went between Heath House and Hopton Castle. Neither could agree on the precise direction this tunnel would take and it was too gaseous to explore. The great tragedy in Dale's life, thinks Clifford, is that there was 'no rein over his imagination that sight would have given him. There was nothing to haul him back to common sense.'

As a young student Rupert Bowater, son of Geoffrey and Veronica Bowater, also found Dale entertaining and erudite company. 'He was a nice man fond of explaining his theories. I found him very easy to get on with.' Perhaps in Daniel Clifford and Rupert Bowater Dale found, temporarily, the companionship of young men that he would, in fairer circumstances, have enjoyed with his own sons.

An extraordinary paradox emerges from studying the lives of Dale and his ex-wife. Although Dale was a man poverty-stricken (he was on state benefit, with a special disability allowance for the blind), sightless except for the weakest of tunnel vision, isolated, without a car and living in a remote area, he had more friends than the woman who hated him, who lived with children and cars twenty-seven miles away.

Veronica Bowater, who was the unofficial leader of Simon's friends – foremost in the 'Look after Simon' group – was horrified at the picture presented of him during the murder trial. So were a large number of people who had come to like and admire the large stooping figure regularly seen striding fearlessly across the fields or walking unconcernedly in the middle of the road. 'I never once saw him lose his temper or complain,' said Mrs Bowater. 'If he ever mentioned Susan it was always with sympathy. It wasn't really her fault, he implied – she was mad, had been dropped on the head as a child. He was not a bitter man, he was friendly, gregarious and welcoming.' And, she added, within the limitations of his finances, generous to a fault. Many were the times that he would ring up and say in his very deep voice, 'Would you like a crumpet tea?' It meant that he had walked all the way to Leintwardine, three miles away and back, to get the crumpets from the local baker.

He was also famous for producing the best baked potatoes in the county, attributing their excellence to the Aga cooker in the kitchen. 'It became a habit for one of us to ring others in the group,' she disclosed, 'and fix a day to go over and see Simon. One would take a quiche, one a salad, somebody else the cheese or pudding and we would arrive together at Simon's house, where he would greet us with a bottle of wine.' He treated all his handicaps, she added, with style. Indeed, style was important to him. He might have the most darned sweater in the world – she was always replacing new patches over old darns, darns over darns – but she remembers his clothes as once having been good. 'He always had good shoes and nice tweed suits and fawn Daks trousers – old, certainly, but still stylish. Looking at Simon you could tell he was a gentleman.'

She laughs at two recollections which, more than most, characterize her late friend. 'We used to sit with Simon in the big hall, as it was called, on the south side of the house. At first it had been desperately unfurnished, but we rummaged around upstairs and brought down some chairs to make it cosier. We also hung up some curtains because it could be decidedly draughty. There was this huge fireplace which burnt trees rather than logs and sometimes it would smoke abominably. Then we would say to Simon, "The brick, Simon, the brick". Whereupon Simon would take this brick tied to a length of rope, climb up on the roof and let it down the chimney, banging it from side to side to clear an air passage for the smoke. It was incredible, this virtually blind man up on the roof, but he never minded. It did the trick marvellously.'

The other story concerned his culinary practices. Despite his blindness, she said, Simon always cooked himself an evening meal. Others, too, have emphasized how important a role food played in his life. Understandably. He always made his own marmalade each year. One year, trying a new recipe, he rang her in a little agitation to ask her to come quickly as his marmalade had gone wrong. On arrival she found that the newspaper he had used to cover the oranges overnight had also gone into the pan. 'We both laughed about it, Simon as much as me.' He could be chided about his obsessions. 'We could say to him, "Oh please, Simon, not your Armenian loos and Arthurian tables" and he would laugh and desist.'

Ken and Jane Davison, members of the same group of friends, were also horrified by the picture of Simon given in court, in particular, tales of his transvestism. In all the times they had visited him and been asked to close the windows in his bedroom when the weather demanded it, they had never seen any sign of women's clothes. But they had an interesting anecdote to recount which never came up in court, though it does tie in with a story told at the committal proceedings.

According to Ken Davison, a local farmer who had known both Susan and Simon for some years, Dale told them not to be surprised if they found him dead. 'If you ever find me dead, you'll know who's done it.' On another occasion he said, 'I think I'm probably going to get knocked off.'

Davison remonstrated, 'Oh, come on, Simon – don't be damn stupid. That sort of thing doesn't happen now.' He added, 'Who's going to do it? You don't think your wife is going to do it, do you?'

Dale answered, 'I don't know, but I understand that a contract costs two thousand quid and she's taken a contract out on me.'

Could Dale have acquired this information in a roundabout way, following a Sunday lunch party given by Ann and Terence Devey-Smith at which Susan was present? According to Roberta Mitchell, one of the guests, Susan inquired at this lunch if anyone knew of a hit man who could get rid of her husband. Nothing was made of the story, and it is easy to see why: it had been a good lunch with plenty of wine, and a whole table bemoaning in a light-hearted manner how difficult ex-partners of both sexes could be. Yet, retold, it could well acquire sinister overtones – particularly in the light of what happened.

As the year progressed, Susan's anger deepened. There she was every day, helped by her two lieutenants, working themselves to exhaustion painting up the house while 'his highness sits in a deckchair in the garden'. Her anger was such that it showed itself everywhere. She wanted him to be as isolated as herself. She hated seeing him have guests. They in their turn had come to expect harassment as part of the scenario whenever they went to see their friend.

Ken Davison, who remembers Susan years back as a laughing, vivacious woman, was keenly aware of the difference. He cites a lunch party Dale gave, which he attended. 'The Baroness was furious and showed it by driving round the house at terrific speed in her estate car.'

Veronica Bowater recalled a day when she visited Heath House, only to be accosted by Susan 'shrieking incoherently'. She noted what a temper the woman had. 'I called her Mrs de Stempel, whereupon she drew herself up and said "I am the Baroness de Stempel." She made it perfectly clear that I was trespassing in her house. I saw her kick our car. I thought she was unbalanced. Later she began to telephone me at home, saying she intended to have Simon out by Christmas.'

The same was said to Michael Sargent, a local bricklayer, whose wife answered an advertisement Dale had placed in a local newspaper for a reader and part-time assistant. Waiting in the grounds while his wife was being interviewed, he was approached by the Baroness who in no uncertain manner informed him that she was the owner of the house and that it was foolish of them to waste any time on Dale since he would not be there much longer. 'She told me,' said Sargent, 'that Mr Dale was squatting in the house and would not be there within fifteen days.'

Day after day the harassment went on. Milk and post had to be left at the end of the drive, since neither tradesman would attempt to get his van or cart down the drive and encounter what obstacles had been placed in it. With Illingworth funds, Susan now had all the money she needed to spend on paints and materials for renovating the exterior of the house. Scaffolding went up on the south side so that the top windows could be painted. She herself tackled the garden.

While she still pretended to the rest of her family that she was as poor as ever – even to accepting a gift of £500 from Aunt Marion, her late uncle's wife – in reality she had ample resources. But as the summer continued, the storm clouds gathered. The tragedy that the Radaus had predicted struck on Friday, 11 September. It was the third anniversary of Susan's ill-fated marriage to Baron Michael de Stempel. That night someone came knocking 'on a wee small door'. In almost the last action of his life, Simon Dale, the gentle giant, opened it and fell back under the first blow from his killer. . . .

⚜10⚜

T·H·E I·C·E
Q·U·E·E·N

A Baroness and two of her children were accused yesterday of murdering her former husband who was found battered to death in his country mansion. Baroness Susan Cecilia de Stempel, fifty-three, her son Xenophon Marcus Wilberforce, twenty-six and daughter Georgina Sophia Wilberforce, twenty-five, who live at Forresters Hall, Docklow, Herefordshire, were all remanded in custody for a week by Hereford magistrates. . . . The four times married [*sic*] Baroness appeared in court in a checked shirt and anorak, and was described as a housewife. Her son was described as self-employed and her daughter as unemployed. All three are also accused, along with Baron Michael de Stempel of Upper Park Road, London, NW of plotting to defraud the Baroness's late aunt, Lady Margaret Illingworth [*sic*]. . . .

So ran the news item on 7 January 1988 in the *Daily Mail*.

The Hereford magistrates, after a two-minute consultation, had had no hesitation in remanding them all in custody for a further seven days. Due to the seriousness of the charge the Baroness was accompanied by a policewoman, who sat at her side throughout the proceedings.

Not unnaturally, by now the national press had pricked up its ears and realized this was an unbeatable story: titles, murder, isolated mansion in deepest rural England, missing millions – all the best ingredients for several front pages. But what the press was to find through the labours of its reporters was a story so convoluted, so intricate, with such a difficult chronology and containing such bizarre details, that few in the end would understand it fully. Few, even within the family, if the truth be told, understand it now. When all the rumblings were quiescent for a time, a distant cousin grumbled to a friend that not even he, with some inside knowledge, knew all the ramifications of Susan de Stempel's life or her motivation. She had been as secretive with her own family as she had been with the rest of the world.

Over the next few months the police were busy and so was Hereford Magistrates Court. On 27 January 1988, charges of murder against Marcus and Sophia Wilberforce were withdrawn after a submission by the prosecution. The Baroness alone remained accused. All three, however, were further remanded in custody for a week on the fraud charge. So was the Baron, who was remanded in his absence; he was being held at Gloucester Prison. Less than a month later the pattern had changed a little, for it was announced on 25 February that Baron Michael de Stempel had been granted bail of £240,000 by a High Court judge in London. As is normal, in such cases, there was a condition of residence and a requirement that the Baron should not contact prosecution witnesses. At the same time – and how sour it must have tasted to them – an application for bail on behalf of Marcus and Sophia was turned down by Hereford magistrates, who stipulated that the Baroness and her children should remain in custody. It was not until 15 April that Marcus and Sophia won their battle for bail, which was granted them by a High Court judge in the sum of £190,000 each.

By the middle of the month the Baroness was the one remaining figure held in custody. She was to remain in custody for a long time – 868 days precisely – until sentence was passed on her on 21 April 1990.

While both investigations continued their separate paths, the murder case was a simpler matter to process than the fraud case, where hundreds of documents as well as overseas trips were involved. Thus it was that committal proceedings, expected to last three days, were booked for Bromyard Magistrates Court for the beginning of the new year on 4, 5 and 6 January.

Bromyard is a small, dusty market town to the east of Leominster. When surprise was expressed that it had been chosen as the venue of an important murder case, the argument was – amongst the locals anyway – that it was a good enough distance from Hereford and Leominster for the magistrates to be unaffected by the wild stories that had been circulating in the area about the case.

The weather was bitterly cold, so much so that some of the shabby old building's lavatories were frozen up. Not that the icy conditions deterred the picture-hungry photographers, who were in position from eight o'clock onwards every morning to get a picture of the Baroness as she arrived in a police car with a policewoman by her side. 'I see she's got her chauffeur-driven car,' was one cynic's remark as the Baroness, all smiles for the press, swept into the courtyard one frosty morning.

They duty of a committal hearing is to establish whether there is a *prima facie* case – that the prosecution has a 'case to answer'. If the magistrates so decide they can throw out the evidence and dismiss the case altogether; so much depends on it. David Crigman, QC, a small man but with a well-produced voice sounding bigger than himself, spoke for the prosecution; Anthony Hughes, tall, fair, as totally unlike Crigman as a stage director could wish, appeared for the defence. Reporting restrictions were not lifted, which meant that the press could record the findings of the magistrates although not the details of the case.

At 10.30 on Wednesday morning, 4 January (almost a year to the day since the Baroness had first been charged with murder), the prosecution opened its case against her. Some of the people in the public seats, had travelled from the area around Heath House, so as to report back to their friends and neighbours in the 'Look after Simon' group. Later they were keenly to attend the murder trial.

Rapidly, reading when necessary from witnesses' statements, David Crigman outlined the Crown's case: 'Dale,' he said, was a man whom the defendant 'had grown to hate beyond all sense and reason. The method of killing was a series of blows, not less than four, to the head and neck. One or more blunt instruments were used to effect the injuries caused. The fatal blow was a blow to the neck which fractured the larynx. Heavy blows were inflicted on the scalp. The place of the killing was the kitchen at Heath House. That is the house . . .' he paused for a moment, tellingly, 'over which the defendant and her ex-husband had fought for over fourteen years, in which the victim lived, and the defendant was despairing of ever getting her hands on the property again. The prosecution says that the evidence discloses an obvious case for this defendant to answer. One, she had a deep-seated hatred of the deceased. Two, she had expressed a wish to see him killed. Three, there is evidence of irrational behaviour over a long period of time. Four, there is a link between her and one of the likely murder weapons. Five, on the night when Mr Dale was last seen alive, this defendant was seen surreptitiously hiding in the grounds of Heath House, waiting for visitors of the deceased to leave. Six, she had a very well-used means of access to the house and this is a case of violence where there is no forcible entry to the house in question and nor was anything stolen. The deceased lay on the floor with £25 untouched in his pocket.'

Equally rapidly, to a now silent, attentive court, he touched on Susan's marriage and divorce from Simon Dale. 'The marriage was not a success and ended in divorce. The children took her side rather than Dale's. There was a deep family rift, and there was a state of bitter acrimony.' He said that there was a profit motive to see him gone. So intense were her feelings that from 1985 to 1987 she was unable to stop herself from letting other people see how much she despised Dale. 'A titanic battle' for occupation had taken place over fourteen years, with Dale displaying an obstinacy on a par with that of his ex-wife. A judge had directed that Dale should move out of the property within two weeks of its sale, but no buyer had been found.

With the same despatch Crigman dealt with the murder night. He told the court of the visit of Susan Evans and Ben Scott. The defendant, he emphasized, was behaving quite irrationally. It was a dank, wet night and she waited in the grounds while Scott and Mrs Evans were seeing Dale. When they left, they saw that she had hidden herself in the area of the archway. She was watching every move in the house and knew exactly where they were at all times. Crigman paused to dwell on the alibi she offered. Although Mrs Evans and Scott reckoned they were there for two and a half hours, having arrived at six o'clock, she was still there when they left. Despite this and the distance of twenty-seven miles to Docklow she claimed, he said, to have been back in Docklow before nine o'clock. She also admitted, for reasons she could not explain (a point which was never taken up), that she drove from Heath House with her car lights off until she got to the road.

More followed concerning the actual murder. 'The defendant waited until his visitors had gone and then went in. It is in the lobby that she struck him. He would have no warning about the impending violence. Afterwards she drove up the drive without the lights on the car. Whether Mr Dale ever knew who attacked him, we do not know. From then on, the defendant was as cool as a cucumber.'

Normally Susan de Stempel would put her car in the garage attached to the cottage so that Dale would not see her, but on Saturday she put her car in front of the house where 'there is no doubt she felt it belonged. She had the confidence to stay alone in the grounds and Dale could do nothing about it any more. On that Saturday morning,' Crigman urged in the rhetorical manner so familiar in law courts, 'we ask what was she doing there? Was she covering her tracks? Only she knew the answer to those questions and she is not telling. Like many a killer before her, she could not stay away.' She had driven there from twenty-seven miles away, staying there alone, and then left.

On the second visit Simon went with her. They took some ladders. It was yet another unexpected visit for no genuine reason. On the Sunday morning she decided that the chimney at her home in Docklow had to be cleaned. She had spent part of the morning cleaning the poker. The poker is from Heath House and is part of a set. After the killing, it was found in the defendant's car. She didn't tell the truth as to why she was cleaning it.' Crigman dwelt on her reaction to the police visit informing her of her ex-husband's death. He told the bench of two women and one man that Giselle Wall, the woman who first found Simon Dale's body, had found the kitchen enormously hot due to the cooker and boiling ring of the stove being left on. Was it not significant that Susan de Stempel's first reaction to the police tale of her husband's death was: 'Has he burnt the place down?'

The evidence piled up against the Baroness. There were nine hours of interviews on tape. She had denied from first to last that she was in any way responsible for her ex-husband's death. Only one witness was called by the prosecution to give live evidence to the court. It was the Baron de Stempel. At this time little was known of the fraud case, so little was read into the careful non-communication between ex-husband and ex-wife. The Baron was anxious not to engage in any eye contact with his third wife, while she maintained the frigid coolness that was fast becoming recognized as her main characteristic in public. But what he had been called to say was vitally important to the Crown's case.

In the usual preamble that occurs at the beginning of any witness taking the stand, he stated that he had married the defendant on 11 September 1984 in St Helier, Jersey, but that the marriage was dissolved on his petition on 3 December 1986. He said that he had received a telephone call from either Susan or her daughter Sophia – he couldn't be sure because they had identical voices, in his opinion. The call came at eight o'clock in the morning and the gist of it was that Simon Dale was dead. 'It was implied,' he said, that Simon Dale had been attacked and was defending himself against a possible intruder. The owner of the voice was 'quite cool, stressfully cool'. There was mention of a trust fund of Sophia's during the call. 'I didn't understand it and I was very shocked. I was very upset. I thought there was an attempt to involve me in something I was not involved in. I was extremely worried.' There was talk about a solicitor, Richard Sax, whom they both knew and then the Baron reiterated the fact that 'it was rather a taut conversation and I really wished very much not to hear it. I greatly feared that I may be involved in something of which I had not the slightest knowledge.' He added that Susan had considered 'for the last twenty years that it was inevitable that Simon Dale would die. I do not mean by her hand,' he blustered quickly. 'It was an idea running through her mind. I do not think she would do anything against him. It was a thought.'

The Baron further disclosed that he had been asked if he would go up to Herefordshire and give them 'moral support'. This he jibbed at, explaining, 'I was asked if I would go up to Herefordshire in an extremely stressful situation. I did not agree to go. My relations with Susan Wilberforce were non-existent. The defendant had me falsely arrested and tried to have me certified on 17 July 1985.'

What was so crucial about the telephone call to the Baron was the date on which it was made. Was it Saturday, 12 September or was it Saturday, 19 September? If the former, it would reveal that Susan (or the speaker) had knowledge of Simon Dale's death *before* the police visit to Docklow in the early hours of Monday morning. On this matter of primary importance the Baron displayed that bleating incoherence which was to bring forced smiles of irritation to lawyers' faces in the subsequent trials. He could not remember for sure. Ah yes, on reflection he thought it might be the 19th, because he recalled that that day he had gone out and bought a pheasant for dinner as his son was coming. Yes, he thought it was the 19th – but he could not be sure. What he *was* sure about was that on the weekend of the murder he had gone to see Jane Mackay in Kent, and he produced his train ticket for the police to retain as proof. So what might have been the conclusive piece of evidence in the entire allegation ended up with the rest of the circumstantial evidence that the police had gathered.

Crigman, who must have been deterred by the Baron's woolliness, moved on instead to other witnesses' statements, like Giselle Wall's which disclosed such details as: 'Mr Dale was a man of regular habits. For his breakfast he would have toast, butter, marmalade and coffee with milk. He was a very careful man with a limited income. He would always wear leather slippers in the house.'

Briefly Crigman outlined the early-morning visit by the police, when the Baroness had appeared so calm and collected. He pointed out that, when arrested on suspicion of murder, she had replied, 'I

146

have nothing to say whatsoever.'

He read from the statement of Linda Williams, a home help who visited Dale once a week, that in her opinion, though he was blind, he was capable of preparing his own food. She also referred to the malevolence of the Baroness. 'During my visits,' she went on to say, 'I have seen numerous obstructions and have moved large objects including bricks, polythene sheets, rubber, branches or grass placed in the drive. He would never let in anyone he did not know. He was always very conscientious about security.' Talking about his everyday life, she said, 'He was a careful man, who always ate everything. He had a keen sense of smell. Meals were the high point of his day. He ate his evening meal at about eight o'clock.'

From statements made by the Baroness to the police, Crigman informed the court that by 1962 the love had gone from the marriage. 'He became violent,' she said, 'and on one occasion he dug a grave in the garden . . . I very much feared for my children.' She was, she swore, the victim of frequent assaults by Dale. He knocked her off a chair, punched her in the back, kicked her on the floor. 'I was absolutely terrified of him. He was very big. He seemed to get bigger when angry.' He was obstructive in her attempts to sell Heath House, so much so that by March 1985 'I personally felt that Heath House would not be sold. Whilst being at work [on the house] we have all experienced constant harassment from Simon. His attitude whilst work was going on was belligerent.' She also admitted, Crigman read to what by now was the quietest, most attentive room in the whole of Bromyard, that on two occasions she had struck Simon. 'On one occasion [and behind Crigman's plummy tones one could hear the cool, level timbre of that small voice talking to the police] he was being thoroughly obnoxious going on about something unimportant, laying down the law. I couldn't stand it any longer. I picked a piece of coke up and threw it at him.' What her statement did not reveal was that Dale had been forced to see his doctor over the abrasion on his face caused by the sharp-edged coke. 'On the second occasion Simon had kept on at my son Marcus while I was carrying out some repairs at the house. Simon was shouting and chasing Marcus. I intervened and we collided. I attempted to kick him in the testicles. I missed and kicked him in the groin. I went to protect Marcus.' She wound up this interview tape by saying, 'I am absolutely not responsible for the death of Simon Dale and I have no knowledge of his death whatsoever. I have now received the keys of the property, which I anticipate I will continue to redecorate with my children.'

147

The trust fund of £4000 set up by Francis Rose, Sophia's godfather, was referred to when it was revealed that Susan de Stempel had used this as collateral to obtain a loan with which to pay for vital roof repairs to Heath House. When the time came to release the money to her Dale was again obstructive as a co-trustee, refusing to sign the necessary papers as he deemed the money would be wasted on his daughter.

Briefly, but as tellingly as possible, Crigman referred to the Sunday lunch party given by the Devey-Smiths and attended by Roberta Mitchell, a self-employed interior decorator from Knutsford in Cheshire, at which she claimed that Susan had said, 'If I could find out how to hire a contract killer I would get rid of him.' Everyone joked about the matter and some said they would share the cost. According to the witness Susan was cool, quiet and 'had a dry sense of humour'.

Statements from Susan's Herefordshire neighbour Veronica Bowater, from the archaeologist Adrian Tindall, from Dale's past assistant, Susan Evans, and present assistant, Mary Jo Corfield were all built up by the prosecution to make a damning indictment of the defendant, who sat as coolly as ever throughout the readings. In the shabby, dusty room the darkness of her hair occasionally took on an almost fluorescent glow when contrasted with the paleness of her face. She listened, even sometimes looked, but appeared not to give a damn for the world against her. Intrigued, the press watched and noted. The myth of the 'Ice Queen' was in the making.

The second day began dramatically enough with a statement from Susan's youngest son, Simon, used by the prosecution to establish the hatred that existed between father and mother. In it he swore that he recalled an incident when his father beat his mother so hard that blood flowed. The attacks were stepped up as the divorce neared. 'I learned to avoid him,' he said cryptically. He gave a detailed account of the Saturday, 12 September, when he accompanied his mother to Heath House and revealed that part of his day had been spent at Shobdon airfield, where he and Susan had learned to fly. The three magistrates heard in detail about the discovery of the body by Giselle Wall and all the attendant activity that followed as Crigman read the medical evidence, provided by Dr Peter Acland, pointing out that the injuries to Dale could have been caused by the jemmy that the Baroness always carried with her.

Now it was the turn of the defence to assert itself as the tall, confident figure of Anthony Hughes rose to address the court. In a voice less resonant than that of his protagonist, yet equally authoritative, he denounced the whole business as 'a colourful, picturesque tale that would fit happily into a novel or soap opera. The sheer volume of papers might suggest a case,' he continued, 'and there is an enormous amount of detail that has been carefully summarized which' – he paused effectively – 'adds up to very little. Is it evidence that a jury can be *sure* of. . . . There is no direct evidence at all to link this lady with the case.' Moreover, was the indirect evidence that compelling? he asked with a shrug of the shoulders. In his contention it was not. 'There is evidence of a dispute which is said to provide a motive not just for dislike but violent murder. The murder most likely took place on the Friday night and you have evidence that the defendant was physically present at or about the right time – *but that is all you have got.'*

Warming to his task – almost enjoying it – he then proceeded to deal with the prosecution's case: there was a long-running dispute about the house, but the Baroness had pursued the sale of it in a desultory manner rather than in a more forceful way. At the time of the divorce a judge had ruled that the house should be sold and ordered the deceased to leave. Dale had no right to be there. 'The courts at the time of his death were considering an application to eject him from the house lawfully and sell it. He was going to have to move, there was no need for violence.' The Baroness was not pursuing the claim with any urgency – it had gone on for years and she was quite prepared to accept the true value of the house. The reason she was keeping a watch on the house was because she was worried about Dale's schemes for digging deep beneath the structure of the house or turning it into a conference centre for medieval historians. She did not want people to get the impression that the house was his. There was evidence of all this, Hughes said, but did it get within a hundred miles of murderous intent?

Furthermore, why should people be shown around her house? We would all be cross if the same thing happened to us. But being cross was a long way from murderous intent. It was easy to attach sinister connotations to everything – to the surveillance, for instance, but only if you were looking for the sinister. She had been known to call the locals 'old cows', but after fourteen years did she not have some reason to be cross with the situation and those who took Dale's side?

The court had heard of acts of violence but what did they amount to: (1) she took some egg-shaped coal and threw it at him; and (2) she aimed a kick at his crutch. Both events, exclaimed Hughes, had happened months before the death. The lunch party at which she was heard to ask about a contract killer took place *two years* before the murder. It was also part of a general conversation at which people were talking about the problems caused by their ex-partners. Disclosing an aspect of the humour that has always characterized her, he told the magistrates that Susan had invented a story that she was seeking a bugging device for Heath House. She had even had a receipt printed in Hereford for a bogus firm she named 'Catch Him At It Surveillance'. It was sent to Dale at Heath House, who was reported to have roared with laughter about it. Significantly, added Hughes, there had been no real violence between the two of them since the marriage ended fourteen years earlier.

Coming to the link between Susan de Stempel and the jemmy, he admitted that there was clear evidence linking her with the tool – but was there evidence, he queried, that it was used as the murder weapon? Dr Acland had given his opinion, when shown a variety of pokers and the like, that the jemmy fitted the wounds better than the others, but he couldn't link the jemmy *specifically* with the wounds. It was found in its place in the cottage on 16 September, three days after the body was discovered, bearing no trace of blood, tissue or body fluid, nor was there any evidence that it had been cleaned. It would have had to be cleaned on the Saturday, since by Sunday the police were in control of the house. And in driving to Docklow, twenty-seven miles away, would there not have been ample opportunity to dispose of it if it had been the murder weapon?

The Baroness was there on the night of the murder; she had been seen by Dale's visitors and had not hidden from them. With her was her son Marcus. To have been so open was not the act of a murderess. Nor was there any sign of blood, fibre or tissue on her clothes, the tools or her car.

Penultimately, Hughes produced an argument that suddenly had the whole court buzzing. 'There was evidence,' he said, 'that someone else went there after Susan de Stempel, Evans and Scott had left. Five sherry glasses were found in the kitchen. Dale and his two visitors had used three of them. If Dale had already drunk from a fourth – as was his habit at six o'clock – before they arrived, it left one extra. Had the killer drunk from it? Altogether, none of the prosecution's statements added up. The accusations could be directed at any other member of the family, said Hughes. Marcus and Sophia could have done it. In his submission there was no case to answer.

While the court was still agog with Hughes's astonishing disclosure of the unknown guest, Crigman made his final appeal to the magistrates: 'The suggestion that there is another visitor to the house at the end of the evening ignores the whole body of evidence that I have read out. This is no ordinary stale, sad marriage. This is a living, continuing, bitter dispute over a house which has great emotional and financial meaning to the defendant. This is not dislike, this is not mild hatred, it is deep-seated – of a very real intensity.' Pausing after this emotionally charged attack, he continued, 'The evidence shows unequivocally no forced entry. This person knew how to get in. There was nothing stolen. It is of importance that lying in the wallet in the pocket is £25. This was a deliberate and sustained attack. The person who attacked him did so for a reason that has nothing to do with theft.' Again he paused dramatically. 'There is an undercurrent going all through this case – Mrs Corfield, Mrs Wall, Mr Scott, Mr Sargent and Mrs Evans – of a deep and intense hatred by this woman towards her ex-husband. There are further examples of a whole series of irrational acts by this defendant towards her ex-husband's visitors. Simon Dale feared for his own safety.'

Crigman asked why it was that the Baroness was still in the grounds of Heath House at 8.30 p.m. 'We know that she was hiding. She kept herself and Marcus out of the way. She was in that archway, listening and watching. She could give no satisfactory answers to these questions.' His voice shifted a note, hardening as he said, 'For two to two and a half hours in the rain she was waiting, watching and listening. We have evidence which shows how this lady was behaving in these critical moments prior to the affliction of those wounds. We have a plain circumstantial link. This was a murder without witness.' The wounds to Simon Dale's head and throat were consistent, he said, with wounds inflicted by a jemmy. Tindall's evidence was vital in this context. 'That weapon is a weapon seen by a witness in this case. She had even said to Mr Tindall that "I carry this to use on my husband if I have any trouble with him." '

The last telling point he made was that the Baroness returned to the scene of the crime. 'Not only could she not keep away, she was there again on the Saturday. On the Saturday morning, she was quite content to stay there for twenty minutes alone.'

While the magistrates retired to discuss their findings, journalists and public alike were still taken up with the question of the fifth sherry glass. Surely this were proof that somebody had come after the visit by Scott and Mrs Evans? Did Simon Dale have any enemies? Could he – extraordinarily – have had a lover? Nobody had mentioned any emotional attachments, but after all he had been a man living alone for the last fourteen years. Wouldn't it be natural for him to have someone somewhere? She had said he was a highly sexed man – surely, then, there was an unknown woman lurking in the background? Or perhaps it was a homosexual relationship? Again, she had said he wore lipstick and high heels and women's clothes. That could point to a homosexual relationship, with a sudden row blowing up. Heath House was in an isolated place. Who could possibly know what went on there at night?

There were those who deemed the defence had succeeded in its object – there was no case to answer. 'Forensic' was the word on many lips: there was nothing to link her with the crime; no blood, tissue or hair was found on her, her clothes, her car or even the cottage at Docklow. There was nothing, absolutely nothing on which the police could base their case except a history of hatred. 'And that could make murderers of us all,' said one onlooker, shaking his head as if at some sad personal memory.

After a retirement of seventy-five minutes the magistrates had come to a decision. The court settled, Susan de Stempel stood to attention, her back as straight as a bookend, as Gordon Powell, the chairman, was asked the magistrates' findings. Looking neither to left nor right, and certainly not at the Baroness, he said clearly in a voice that could be heard in every part of that old, dusty room: 'The magistrates find there is a case to answer.'

Journalists hurried to report this one allowable fact while the photographers took up their positions at the back of the court. The Baroness, impassive as ever, turned away escorted by police.

Suddenly the whole case had become more serious. The wheels of justice might grind slowly, but they were now set in a direction that would eventually take all concerned to Worcester Crown Court on Tuesday, 18 July 1989.

Following my first visit to Susan de Stempel in custody, when I was accompanied by her youngest son, Simon, I went the second time to Pucklechurch Remand Centre on my own. It was a pleasant July day, a few months before the committal proceedings. The remand centre, like so many of its kind, is a large, ugly building sited next to a small industrial estate outside the village of Pucklechurch, near Bristol. The women's block was separated from the main block by beds of flowers kindly in purpose, unsuccessful in reality. For, once past the huge outer gate, nothing prevents a prison or a remand centre from looking and smelling of its job. The paraphernalia of locking and unlocking doors, the solidity of the walls, the uniformed staff, all contrive to make it a secret, withdrawn world in which the visitor feels acutely uneasy. Old claustrophobic nightmares raise their dead heads and threaten to come to life again. If the relationship between a hospital patient and visitor is often a strain, so, even more in prison surroundings is the artificial propinquity of the inmate and his or her visitor. Nervousness is palpable.

Yet, in keeping with her character, Susan de Stempel displayed none of this. Escorted by a female prison officer she came into the room with its cheap tables and chairs arranged in a single line. A 'screw' sat so close that any attempt, if that had been the intention, at subversive dealings would have been absurd. The effect was to make conversation a whispered exchange of half sentences and sudden jokes from which laughter would crackle in the room like fireworks.

The line was not full – there were spaces here and there – but in the main the heads bent so close together across the card-sized tables were young, very young. It never came up in conversation, but a hard fact about prison life for an older woman is how much she is surrounded by young girls. Middle-aged women prisoners find few inmates of their own age and, in the case of an aristocrat, even fewer of their own class. If she had not been a recluse before, there is much in prison life that would have turned Susan de Stempel in that direction.

She looked pale, as she had all through the long obstacle race of remand hearings. Around her neck she wore a white scarf, which she constantly rearranged. It became a sort of symbol to me, as each time I visited her she seemed to be wearing it. At the back of my mind I fantasized as to whether for her it was a form of noose which she was subconsciously arranging. The less fantastical side of my brain, however, argued that that was absurd – here was a once good-looking, if not beautiful, woman who was merely concerned to hide from sight the ravages that age had wrought on her neck.

How was she? As well as could be, she answered in that tiny voice which was always so difficult to hear. She had a habit of flicking her eyes to left and right, not dramatically but just checking, checking. She openly dismissed the 'screws', as she called them, in a way that she might well have used to dismiss the nuns at school. I thought of Sidney Carton in Dickens's *A Tale of Two Cities*, and imagined her cool disdain in front of the guillotine. My reaction, I had found when talking to lawyers and solicitors and friends, was not uncommon.

She can and does inspire – arouse – gallantry in those dealing with her, and even in those opposed to her.

Pucklechurch was pretty ghastly, she said. But not as bad as Risley. Leaning forward, the hooded eyes less blue in close confrontation, she embarked on the story of her first night in Risley. For some obscure purpose, she said, but probably just sheer nastiness on the staff's side, she had been placed in the hospital wing of the centre. The filth was unbelievable – unswept floors, dirty windows, unwashed paint. She awoke in the middle of the night to see the most amazing sight of her life: arranged in two armies were lines of cockroaches and mice. The mice moved towards the cockroaches and then stopped. They moved again a shorter distance and then, without preamble, they turned and fled. The cockroaches had won! I gasped and she laughed. Nothing could beat a cockroach, in her opinion. It was a story which, if nothing else, served to illustrate the truly dreadful conditions there. Fingers always at her neck arranging the white woollen scarf, she was determined that the authorities should do something about improving conditions.

Life at Pucklechurch, she explained, was bearable if you ignored the lesbianism and drug-taking. She was in a dormitory of twenty-four, of which half were lesbians, 'humping' each other, while the rest were 'chasing the dragon'. The up-to-date slang sounded odd on her lips.

She had, I noticed, a very thin, straight line of a mouth that turned down at the ends. In repose it is a bitter face rather than a sad face. Yet when she laughed she did so with enthusiasm and an almost childlike glee. Now in her mid-fifties, she carries more of the child tucked behind the aging skin and thin bones of her face than do most people of her age. The same quality even extends to the way she sits and moves, to the hands held carefully by her side when she stands. Again and again one could envisage the quiet, dutiful girl standing before her nanny or, later on, the nuns at her convent. But of course, as her history showed, she was neither dutiful nor obedient, only quiet. What was it one of the nuns at St Mary's Ascot had said of her? 'A difficult, obstinate, quick-tempered girl.'

We talked about a few friends we had in common, and I noticed that she rarely had a good word for anyone. It was a mark of her bitterness about the world that she seemed untouched by any charitable feelings towards others. But she swung back into good humour when we discussed my next visit. If I came dressed as a nun, she suggested, I could stay for a much longer time than the normal half hour. That would constitute a different type of visit altogether.

154

I could come as her spiritual adviser and be allowed to stay for hours. I was a Catholic, she prompted – surely I wouldn't find the deception difficult? What a hoot, what a laugh. What a marvellous joke against the screws. What a marvellous joke against authority. How well it all fitted in with the details of her expulsion. I feel sure that if I had carried out her suggestion she would have met me in the visitors' hall without blinking an eyelid. But the next time I saw her 'inside' was after the murder trial, when she had been transferred back to the hated Risley.

The weather for the murder trial, which began on 18 July at Worcester Crown Court, was as hot as it had been cold for the committal proceedings. Nothing would be done by halves, it augured – not even the temperature.

Set bang in the middle of this old cathedral city, the Crown Court is a classical building with Ionic columns supporting a hefty portico placed in front of a modern aluminium window with swing doors. A somewhat indifferent statue of Queen Victoria holding a sceptre looks in a southerly direction over a city that still retains vestiges of charm, particularly round the cathedral and river. Today Worcester is a place as well known for its racecourse and cricket ground as it is for its fine china.

The court building is dominated by a vast entrance hall used as a main meeting place, where barristers flap to and fro like rooks in their black-gowned way, some smoking a last cigarette before disappearing into the smokeless region of the actual court. Every morning during the trial a couple of volunteer women supplied coffee, tea and biscuits to those who needed them and within a day their table had become the favourite meeting place.

Inside the courtroom itself, a white-painted gallery runs round three sides of the room, its gold balustrading standing out against the terracotta walls. Below, the wood panelling is painted white. The ceiling is pale grey, and at the time of the trial the large plaster crown placed over the high judge's seat was badly in need of dusting. It was always infernally noisy, with a tumult of traffic and pigeons outside – so much so that on one exceptionally hot day they were forced to shut the windows in order to hear the quiet tones of the Baroness.

The press and public sat upstairs where the door to the gallery squeaked abominably and took hours to open and shut discreetly while the case was going on. The jury was placed directly beneath the gallery so that, peering over the top of the balustrading, we spectators could see their plans and photographs. During one very hot afternoon I could have sworn the plans looked upside-down at one of the juror's places, but I could have been mistaken. The dock stood firmly in the middle, with steps descending to the cells below. It was a court in which one could justifiably expect to hear the famous old phrase 'Take him down', and like all courts it had enough exits and entrances to delight a budding Feydeau.

None of this, however, prepared one for the sheer solemnity of the occasion as the bewigged judge in his red gown crossed with a broad black sash and white Quaker's kerchief at the throat was ushered in, followed by the High Sheriff. With his high, stiff military collar, the Sheriff must have suffered agony as the days sweltered on.

The Baroness sat in the middle of the dock, flanked on either side by wardresses. That first day she wore a pale blue and white striped seersucker jacket and skirt, with a striped blouse and dark brown shoes. Sometimes she varied the outfit by wearing a darker, floral-patterned skirt; at other times she wore a plain jacket. Sophia had bought her three matching outfits before the trial commenced. Always there was a high neckline to the blouse she wore. Whoever instilled in her the notion that a woman's looks are gone when her neck is gone had performed her outdated task most successfully.

Day after day during the eleven-day trial the thin, slight figure sitting in the dock as the gruesome details of her ex-husband's murder were debated rarely moved or showed emotion. Perhaps she showed a little curiosity at times. What lesser mortals were these parading themselves in such a banal fashion? Every so often she would put on a pair of dark-rimmed spectacles and stare momentarily at the witness giving evidence. The hardest stare of all was for the jury when they filed in for the first time. She looked long and carefully, assessing each one in the cool, dark recesses of her mind. Then off came the glasses and they were carefully tucked away in their case: it was a neat, inhibited action that suggested much about her.

From time to time during the long, hot days she would kick off her flat-heeled shoes and sit unconcernedly in stockinged feet. Every now and again she would make notes on a reporter's pad, writing first at the bottom of the page and travelling up. These notes she would pass to her solicitor or barrister. As the poet of her part of England, A. E. Housman, has termed its landscape 'the quietest under the sun', so too could she, in the heat of a blazing English summer, be considered 'the quietest woman under the sun'.

But even the Baroness on that first day showed a little nervousness when at 11.25 she was asked formally at the commencement of the trial if she was Susan Cecilia de Stempel. Those, however, who had come expecting a fine day of legal theatre were disappointed, because, while the jury were out, there was a plea from the defence requesting that the matter of the fraud be *sub judice*. She had relied on legal aid for her defence, which by the luck of the draw was led by the suave, highly competent figure of Anthony Arlidge, QC. Famous for his successful prosecution of Jeremy Bamber, who had murdered his family for their wealth, he now engaged in an amiable discussion with the short, rubicund Anthony Palmer, QC (equally well known for his successful prosecution of the M50 killer, Eddie Browning, and winning protagonist against Arlidge in the case of the Redditch car-park killer, Stuart Hopkins) who was leading for the prosecution.

While the jury was sent out, it was agreed that nothing of the fraud case would be mentioned during the murder trial. The Crown giving its support for two reasons: there could be grounds for an appeal due to prejudice; and prejudice would apply to the defendant in both trials.

The judge was Sir John Owen, a small, dark-haired Welshman referred to in court as Mr Justice Owen. Subsequently, in 1990, he earned his place in the history of English law by residing over the first case in the land where a husband was found guilty of raping his wife. Throughout the trial he took as many notes as the visiting journalists crammed in the small press gallery. A small number of privileged guests sat in the seats reserved for friends of the Judge or High Sheriff, and elicited comment from other spectators: 'See that blonde woman sitting in the special seats? That's the wife of Viscount Portman – seventeenth richest man in England.' The woman in question, a very beautiful Catherine Deneuve type, looked up amused as she caught the press's excited whispering and then looked coolly away. But cool as she was, she could not rival the straight-backed, dark-haired woman sitting in the dock with her spectacle case and notebook laid out tidily before her.

On the second day the Baroness did not shift as Anthony Palmer outlined the case that many had already heard at the committal proceedings. She had changed her outfit and wore the dark jacket and floral skirt – her daughter's mix-and-match policy was working well.

Palmer told the court that Marcus and Sophia had been taught to snoop on their father – to listen to his telephone calls (easy with that fruity booming voice) and intercept his mail. At times they would also remove items from the house, which was perfectly easy for them since they could get in and out at will.

By day three, 20 July, the trial was well into its stride with the chief witness that day, Dr Norman Weston, the forensic scientist. In his slow, pedantic way, holding in front of him a huge file of notes, he gave his opinion that Dale, although a man of considerable bulk, had been pushed from the lobby into the kitchen. Dr Weston said that, after carrying out a series of tests, he could find nothing that linked the Baroness with the murder scene at Heath House.

Previously, Anthony Palmer had dealt skilfully with the question of the five sherry glasses that had caused such a furore of speculation at the committal proceedings. Of the five glasses, one was cracked and three were of the same pattern. They were the three used by Dale and his two guests, Susan Evans and Ben Scott. He implied to the jury, in a voice that often resembled the tones of a kindly schoolmaster, that they need worry their heads no more over the matter.

Linda Williams, Simon Dale's home help, a plump, motherly figure with gleaming, hennaed red hair, revealed under cross-examination from Anthony Arlidge that she thought someone other than herself was cleaning the house. She had found a tin of Mansion polish in one room and a tin of Brasso in another. She had also found a pair of ladies' high-heeled shoes in Simon Dale's bedroom. Again, the court had something to wonder over and whisper about into their neighbours' ears. Dale, she knew, was working on a book about the Civil War. And he believed that the ancient capital of Powys lay beneath the house.

But even more dramatic, though not for public viewing, was the police video revealed to judge, jury, press – and the defendant. The video was shown on a large television screen in a room above the number-one courtroom. According to *The Times* report of the event: 'The victim was seen lying on his back on the blue and white tiled kitchen floor, with a pool of dried blood around spread a yard from his head. His fingers were clutching the jumper he was wearing. On the table there was more blood. Five sherry glasses could be seen on a worktop. In the lobby outside the kitchen, what was described as blood was seen splattered on a white door.'

The Baroness, the same report added, watched 'impassively'. Later she was to say under cross-examination that she felt not impassive but sick; however, as she had explained her behaviour when Detective Inspector Matthews first informed her of Simon Dale's death, she had been brought up to sit still and not show any emotion. She was to follow the dictates of her upbringing even more dramatically at the end of the fraud trial.

The tanned, self-consciously debonair figure of Ben Scott, with his white handlebar moustache complementing his white hair and blue and white striped shirt and designer jeans, was recalled by the prosecution to clarify whether Dale was expecting another visitor on the night of the murder. He said that Dale *was* expecting another guest, but not that night. Whereupon the authoritative figure of Anthony Arlidge sprang out of his seat to suggest, on behalf of the defence, that Mr Scott was merely 'jumping to conclusions'. Mr Scott disagreed rather angrily, but admitted that Dale had not specifically said his guest was *not* coming that night. It was a tiny victory for the defence, and it added to those points gained from the valuable evidence given by Dr Norman Weston that there was no forensic evidence linking her with the murder.

The neat, blazered figure of Ian Peill, a local chartered surveyor, said that the Baroness had asked his company, Cook & Arkwright, to put Heath House up for auction early in 1985; but because of Dale's attitude in refusing entry to prospective buyers the house had been put up for sale instead. The only way the house could be viewed was from the road, as Dale would not allow prospective buyers closer access. Matters, he disclosed, were left unresolved.

Simon Dale's sexual demands were revealed in the matter-of-fact tones of Detective Constable Michael O'Keefe, who read from one of the Baroness's statements in which she claimed that Dale wanted her to participate in anal sex, for which purpose he bought baby oil. He also wanted her to rub him with face cream. 'When I refused, he said I was inhibiting.' On many occasions she had seen him wear ladies' high-heeled shoes. 'He was very sexually active and aggressive, but it was certainly not loving. He simply needed sex to satisfy himself.' On one occasion, the Baroness said, after the end of their marriage, she had seen a woman knock on the door and shout: 'Let me in, you bastard!' After the woman had gone she noticed Dale 'wearing lipstick, tatty trousers and socks and a pair of ladies' high-heeled shoes. He was making faces at himself in the mirror, imitating how the woman had shouted at him.'

Dale, the written statement continued, used to smack their four sons 'but he could never catch our daughter. He showed the children no affection at all. He displayed sullen moods and made violent attacks on me and the children. We had no social life because he was boring and mean.' She also said that Dale dug a grave for her and threatened to throw her body down a lead mine between Bishop's Castle and Shrewsbury. She had sent a note of the location of the lead mine to her solicitor, for the record. 'It would be difficult to find,' she explained.

Almost a week to the day after the trial started Susan de Stempel entered the witness box. It was Wednesday, 26 July. Earlier the same day Anthony Arlidge, opening for the defence, explained why the Baroness's two children had not been called. She had not wanted them to give evidence on her behalf, he said. He caused a small but welcome titter of amusement when he referred to the Friday evening of the murder and said that the Baroness had gone home to watch the Agatha Christie character, Miss Marples, on television in *Murder at the Vicarage*. 'Perhaps we could do with Miss Marple's assistance now,' he said light-heartedly.

By this stage of the trial the bad acoustics of the courtroom were causing everyone to listen as carefully as possible. It was only the professional tones of the various lawyers that carried through the room easily, and when Susan de Stempel took the oath it was immediately apparent that she could not be heard properly. Accordingly she was moved nearer the jury, but this proved unsuccessful and she was moved back again, with a direction to make her remarks straight to the jury.

Wearing her usual high white collar above the seersucker jacket, she told the court almost in a whisper of the unhappy life at Heath House. Replying to Arlidge's questions, she was, she said, five foot eight inches tall and weighed nine stone six. For the first time in a week of hot, humid weather she sipped occasionally from a glass of water, as she related that, such was Dale's violence towards her, she now had an injury to her spine that could not be operated on. She had paid for all the work on the house. She had hoped that her children would have an amicable relationship with their father, but he 'just wasn't interested' and eventually they resented him living alone in the house. In the end no estate agent would handle the house and Dale's refusal to co-operate continued for many years.

Anthony Palmer was braced for a tough cross-examination. At times resembling a bewigged Jack Russell terrier shaking a small rat from side to side, he pitched straight into the Baroness and suggested that she was cunning and clever when it suited her. The reason she had gone back on the Saturday was to replace the murder weapon, the jemmy. 'You can suggest that until you are blue in the face – that is not true,' she replied, adding to a rather red-faced barrister, 'It doesn't make sense for me to have killed that man. The court was going to get him out cleanly and legally.' But when asked if Marcus had anything to do with it she replied firmly 'Certainly not' – he had

160

undergone hours of grilling by the police and they had laid no charges.

During one heated exchange, when Anthony Palmer accused her of becoming angry, frustrated and pent-up by the obduracy of her ex-husband, she placed her hands on the side of the witness box and said, in just audible tones, 'Bollocks!' Journalists queried it with their colleagues, while the public gallery almost cheered. Anything for the underdog. But this was as nothing to the prosecutor's own surprise. 'I beg your pardon?' he said, his voice several notes higher than his usual mellifluous tones. The judge made one of his many notes and the Baroness replied in more suitable vocabulary, 'Nonsense.' Exasperation getting the better of her, she leaned forward a few minutes later and said, 'This is a case against a woman made up by men.'

Another surprise was waiting for the court as Anthony Palmer, in his closing speech for the prosecution, invited the jury to bring in a lesser verdict of manslaughter if they were undecided on murder. He said, 'This was not a planned and premeditated murder; this is a matter that started, as so many domestic matters do, with a build-up of events and then a sudden explosion.' There was a valuable house involved, he added, and this became the battleground for the war – a war in which someone was likely to be injured or killed. 'You may think she was a witty, clever, very, very determined and spirited woman. But in the end Simon Dale was not going to get the better of her.'

The main thrust of Anthony Arlidge's defence speech, couched in gentle, reasonable tones, was that this was a case where a 'skilful attempt had been made to present white as black'. The case depended entirely on circumstantial evidence, and the prosecution had tried to draw a greater inference than was merited. There was a problem, he added, right at the heart of the case which the prosecution had never solved – that Simon Dale would never have opened the door to his wife. At this point Sebastian Wilberforce, who was sitting in the public gallery along with Marcus and Sophia, held up two crossed fingers in a gesture of good luck for his mother to see.

Arlidge continued his fluent discourse, referring to Simon Dale as the 'most difficult man in three counties'. He pointed out that the jemmy was not an *exact* match for the wounds inflicted on the dead man – 'any firm, blunt, angular instrument could have done it, yet the jemmy is the high point in the Crown's case'. Most of the evidence that the police had accumulated had come from Susan de Stempel herself in the form of statements, he said. 'Almost anything you look at can be looked at in other ways.' Furthermore, if it had been a spur-of-the-moment killing would there not have been something to give her away – even a fibre of her clothing? 'For all their exhaustive inquiries, the prosecution has been unable to link her with the crime other than by pointing to the surrounding circumstances.'

In an equally beautiful voice (at a high level the law seems to specialize in if not demand) Mr Justice Owen, addressing the eight men and four women jury members, said they had to be satisfied on four counts if they were to find the murder charge proved. They had to be certain that the Baroness was the killer, that the act was deliberate, that it was unlawful and that at the time of the attack she had the intention of killing Dale or causing him serious bodily harm. But if they felt she had been provoked in a manner that would have made any reasonable person lose their self-control, they could find her not guilty of murder but guilty of manslaughter. The prosecution had relied on circumstantial evidence to prove its case and said it was open for the jury to draw inferences; but, the judge stressed carefully, 'You may draw inferences if they may be safely, surely and properly drawn – but not otherwise.' He told the jury to ignore the fact that the defendant had used the word 'Bollocks' while under cross-examination. 'Words which our grandfathers would not have used are today used in mixed company.'

In what seemed to many a rather peculiar addendum, but which was anyway struck from the summing up, the judge referred to the Baroness's lack of tenderness in revealing before a court and her children their father's odd sexual proclivities. Arlidge, however, objected that the Baroness had been asked by the police to mention anything that might have a bearing on the murder. Had the judge forgotten the high-heeled shoes under the bed? The judge said he had, and instructed members of the jury to erase the incident from their minds.

At eleven o'clock on Tuesday, 1 August, the jury retired to consider its verdict. Outside the heavy old court-house the sun shone powerfully as it had all through the trial. A few journalists sloped off to the pub, leaving a posse on the steps to warn them if the jury came back quicker than expected. Did she, didn't she? Opinion was against her – that coolness of hers was not found charming by many – yet all had to agree that the evidence was flimsy, to say the least. As the late morning turned into the lunch hour, more reporters deserted the sun-warmed steps of the portico to find a sandwich.

At 2.45 there was a bustle, a commotion and the report came that the jury had a verdict. Hastily the court reassembled, the jury filed in, the judge took his place and the defendant was led up the steps to the dock. As the clock read 2.53 Susan de Stempel heard that she was found not guilty of murder and not guilty of manslaughter. She didn't flicker, but up in the gallery her children cheered and a friend threw a small posy of orchids that, fortunately for dramatic effect, fell neatly at her feet. Quickly she stooped to collect it before disappearing below to talk to solicitors, barristers and her children.

Outside the court-house the children, most naturally, smiled happily and Sebastian, in a surprisingly vulgar gesture for a person of his anguished refinement, waved a clenched fist in the air. Loving every minute of it, Susan de Stempel waved to press photographers and friends as she was driven away from Worcester Crown Court in a white taxi, still holding the little posy of flowers. Through her solicitors she issued a statement: 'I am delighted with the outcome. I am relieved it is over.' But of course it was not over, as she was to experience nearly six months later.

11

H·I·G·H S·O·C·I·E·T·Y
A·N·D L·O·W D·E·E·D·S

THE blazing summer had burnt itself out before I saw Susan de Stempel again. This time it was at Risley Remand Centre, outside Warrington in Cheshire, to which she had been transferred from Pucklechurch. If Pucklechurch is bad, Risley is appalling – well deserving its sour reputation as 'Grizzly Risley'.

Visitors are shown first to a shabby waiting room with two sets of lavatories and a small cafeteria. In this bleak, unwelcoming atmosphere I waited until one of the group of prison officers milling outside appeared and called the name of the inmate I was visiting.

The women's section is set apart from the main block, which meant a bitter, rain-drenched walk – it always seemed to be raining at Risley – past municipal-looking flower beds that appear as drained of colour and vitality as the humans that inhabit the place. Then, led by one of the officers, I was taken up a short flight of stairs to another door and into a chamber off the visiting hall. Here I was asked to fill in a form, and the flowers I had brought were taken away to be given to the Baroness later.

On this occasion Susan seemed her normal pale self, buoyed up with distaste and bitter amusement for the life that fate had dealt her. The food was disgusting, she complained, and there was just as much lesbianism and drug-taking as at Pucklechurch. She had been denied her daily copy of *The Times* and was appalled at the tabloids that were available. And, no, she did not have a wireless, which would anyway be useless against the background of loud pop music preferred by other inmates. Visitors were not allowed to bring in scent or soap, since they could contain alcohol or drugs. She shrugged off the disadvantages.

Near us a young man was engaged in a long-drawn-out kiss with his girlfriend. 'That's the way they get drugs in,' she whispered, 'mouth to mouth.' Startled, I looked at the warders to check their reaction, but they appeared sublimely indifferent either to the moment of passion or to the possibility that it might be a cynical exchange of 'substances'. Susan was amused.

I asked if she was relieved now that the murder business was out of the way, and she shrugged that off too. She laughed, however, when I told her what support she had gained by using the word 'Bollocks' in court. To my surprise she said that she had checked first if she could use such a word, found that she would not be the first person in a law court to do so, and gone ahead with confidence. Not for the first time I found myself faced with the extraordinary contradictions of the woman. How on earth could she have checked it? How could she have known that Anthony Palmer would so enrage her that she would want to respond in this way? It seemed, however, entirely symptomatic of her need to be in 'control'. *She* must make the decisions. It was a remark which in its unlikeliness also showed her lack of contact with reality, which I was to become aware of more and more in talking to her.

Just before I went she whispered that she had something brilliant up her sleeve. Absolutely brilliant. She smiled with a vitality rare to her. But she wouldn't tell me what it was. She wasn't ready yet.

I left her in good spirits. How much she loved the dimensions of conspiracy. First there had been the suggestion of dressing as a nun, now there she was preparing something unexpected. At the end of one of her letters to me she wrote, 'Do you think I would make a good spy?' It came out of the blue and had been added as an afterthought, and I wondered at the time what on earth she meant. But, thinking it over later, I decided that she would indeed make a good spy. I had read it before the fraud case revealed just how devious she could be.

Styal, near Manchester, is a semi-open prison and, as such, infinitely more relaxed than the dreadful Risley. It is arranged in streets of red-brick housing along Victorian philanthropic lines, with large gardens around each house. Susan had been transferred there at the end of December 1989, for reasons never explained. Perhaps she complained too much or they felt she justified a change to a more relaxed prison. I went to see her on a cold and frosty day in February when she had already been held there for several weeks. The visiting area appeared to have been an ex-school hall, with a stage and, at one end, a little place for buying tea and coffee which one could actually share with the inmate. Moreover, visitors and inmates had separate tables distanced from each other, so that there was some degree of privacy.

I had been intrigued to see amongst the visitors a huge West Indian who, despite the winter cold, was wearing a straw boater and a blazer and carrying a vast bouquet of flowers for whoever he was seeing. It was an extraordinarily inappropriate outfit, but he cheered up the entire surroundings.

A young girl in her early twenties with a mutinous toddler waited at the next table for her sister. The baby, encumbered with nappies and thick clothes, wobbled over to where Susan and I were sitting. She picked at Susan's skirt and for once I detected a warmth in Susan's reactions that surprised me. It was not an attractive child, yet the so-called Ice Queen bent over from her seat and fielded her back to her mother with tenderness. I wondered if babies played no part in the world this woman felt had cheated her that she could respond to them with the normal female affection for tiny, helpless beings. The mother, who had come from Oldham, was abruptly informed that her sister had been transferred to another prison the day before, and back we were inveighing against a prison system that can be so unthinkingly callous.

The big surprise turned out to be that she was pleading Guilty in the fraud case. Much as she herself wished to plead Not Guilty, she had been persuaded by her lawyers that it was a good idea. If she did it, her children would be arraigned on the lesser charge of Conspiracy to Defraud, rather than actively defrauding someone. Once again I was reminded of Sidney Carton with his 'far far better thing' – his noble self-sacrifice. There was no point in striving for true understanding of the Lady Illingworth case, she intimated; the police simply did not speak her language. How could she explain that 'our sort of people don't have money, they have *things*'. And things like furniture, for instance, were regularly switched from one house to another. They were never mentioned in wills because then they would be liable to tax – and tax, for heaven's sake, was what people of standing spent a good part of their lives avoiding. She was resolute, she was pale, she was noble. She would plead Guilty and save her children's lives.

Cynical it may be, but I felt she was highly pleased at this interpretation of her behaviour towards a feeble old aunt.

But the question raises its head: if she really wished to save her children, why did she not exonerate them completely? All she had to do was swear on oath that they had had nothing to do with the machinations leading to the forged will and theft of Lady Illing-worth's estate. All she had to say was that they were completely innocent and had been totally manipulated by her. Admittedly, she would have had to take the witness stand and undergo cross-

166

examination, but by doing so she might have saved Marcus and Sophia a prison sentence and the consequent blackening of their characters.

All very well such self-sacrifice, all very Sidney Carton, but consider what that cross-examination would have revealed: the lies, the cunning, the deviousness with which she had acted. What effect on her vanity would the prosecution's ruthless, probing questions have had? Could she have withstood this stripping of her character in public and still kept her famous ice-cold equanimity? And is there not, on reflection, an inherent contradiction in her view that her children had minds of their own, that she was not a 'mastermind'? If that is so, given the undoubted facts of the fraud and forgeries, then her children do stand as guilty as the jury found them. Yet I was told by someone who has no wish to be named that, once she had agreed to plead Guilty, they detected obvious signs of relief in her. This was one pretence she no longer had to keep up.

Anyone dealing with Susan de Stempel has ultimately found that the aspects of her personality which do not integrate – in psychiatrists' jargon 'splitting' – made a sound relationship impossible. Her letters are as peculiar as herself. Furthermore, her handwriting is so execrable that it takes much effort to decipher them. A friend of hers laughingly commented, 'You need to read each Susan letter fifty times before you know what the actual words are.' No wonder she appeared indifferent to the censorship maintained by the prison staff; she had invented a method of her own. The most secretive woman in England had the most secretive handwriting. But once mastered, it opened fresh doors to her character.

Early in 1990 she wrote to me, 'Now we are near the end of the beginning. I did some fast talking to the Governor [of Risley] and got myself transferred to Styal. It is so much better than the dreaded Risley.' She had been amused by an American magazine that wanted to feature her using a picture taken by the famous photographer David Bailey. The Governor, she joked, was dying to be photographed as well, but the Home Office had put a stop to it: 'All prisons seem paranoid about the press, with reason.' In another letter, written shortly before the fraud trial started, she said, 'I am so sick of being accused of doing things I haven't done.' She also mentioned in passing that she could not stand 'unpleasantness especially on the doorstep'. The great storms of January had devastated homes and many trees throughout the country, but she was glad that at Heath House only two trees had fallen and nothing had happened to the chimneys. 'I'm always expecting those towering chimneys to fall down one day.'

Still at Styal, her next letter was written after the fraud trial had commenced at Birmingham. This time *The Independent* newspaper, she wrote, having watched her in the witness box during the murder trial, wanted to do a profile. So did another American journalist. Her 'tormentor' in the dormitory, an aging hippy American with 'thunder thighs and an immensely complicated thought process mind' had been replaced by a member of the Spiritualist Church who she thought might initiate a seance. They used to dabble in table turning when she lived in Paris, she said, and on one occasion the message had been that she would be famous.

By the third week of March, and with the trial still to run another four weeks, she was back at Risley. As with all her previous letters, she had written at the top of the first page the number of days she had been in custody. This one read '837'. 'Now we are approaching the end of the beginning I can't wait to get to the beginning of the end. Anything to get out of this place. Can you tell me what the Mongolian Bog-Rat's [Baron de Stempel] activities are?' She had a penchant for bestowing nicknames of an ironic or dismissive nature on people; Alexander, her de Stempel stepson, was called 'The Rat', Simon Dale 'Birdbrain', Jane Mackay 'Sandwich Carrot' and her counsel 'The Cardinal'.

When I visited her at this time she still professed absolute innocence and, interestingly, she denied being the mastermind that the prosecution had called her. Her children, she stated, had minds of their own. There were volumes and volumes still to be revealed about the whole case, she said. When I told her I was going to write a book she said she would rather write her own. And, if they made a film of her life – the idea pleased her immensely – she wanted to play herself.

Her last letter, dated before the end of the trial, told of a visit by her counsel, during which 'I didn't discover anything I didn't know already although the same can't be said of them.' Life was hectic in the dorm – she thought she had learnt all she ever wanted to know about drugs, she added – and finally she wrote, 'If this trial isn't finished soon my clothes are going to fall apart. Still, better than me, I suppose.' This was the letter that ended, 'Do you think I would make a good spy?'

Interested in the link between handwriting and personality, I showed a completely anonymous sample – with no indication, either, of where it was written – to a couple of graphologists. Their reactions were interesting. One said: 'An imaginative woman, full of flair and whimsical ideas. She has great cerebral sensitivity. Her perceptions excite her imagination and vice-versa to the point of illusion.' The report went on to say that the writer had a strongly impulsive nature which, unchecked, encouraged her to satisfy 'unrealistic perceptions without ever recognizing the unreality of the situations'. There was great difficulty retaining contact with reality: for her, reality is 'only what she feels through her senses and instincts . . . she is unaware that there is a difference between her fantastic concepts and true reality'. Surprisingly, this report concludes with the opinion that the writer has a weak character and is devoid of any 'malignant calculation, cunning or slyness'. The West Mercia Fraud Squad would find that interesting.

The second graphologist's report is more in keeping with the personality of Susan de Stempel as revealed through the murder trial and, more significantly, the fraud trial. It immediately recognizes the secretive nature she has developed over the years. 'The writer is used to space and plenty. She is a collector, hoarder. A habit to hide things away. Secretive.' Furthermore, the graphologist believed that the writer was 'malicious and critical' while also verbally aggressive, with much studied charm and sharpness. 'She is enterprising, quick-thinking, impatient. She is ambitious, bossy, has a longing to be at the top. Has been taught to be diplomatic, smile beautifully and be socially discriminate.'

In the second graphologist's view Susan de Stempel had an inner emotional poverty which she always saw expressed in terms of financial poverty. In other words Susan de Stempel, alone and lacking a husband, would more than ever need the reassurance of money about her. Maybe that is why, although comfortably off, she always professed great poverty.

This expert also felt: 'She has so much self-confidence that it could sometimes lead to a kind of foolhardiness.' Isn't that precisely what happened in the forgeries? For, as Dr David Baxendale, the Home Office handwriting expert, said, the early forgeries were exceedingly well done while the later ones were sloppy and careless. Interestingly, the second report mentions 'low backache and leg ache and this could have come from an accident at some time which could have been to the lumbar spine'. Or could have been, as Susan de Stempel claimed, from repeated blows to her lower back inflicted by Simon Dale.

*

Eventually, after months of investigation on both sides, it was asserted that the prosecution and defence cases for the fraud trial were complete. The opening day was set for 19 February at court 12 in Birmingham's new red-brick Crown Court. As Detective Inspector Mike Cowley, head of the West Mercia Fraud Squad, freely admitted, the case was the most extensive fraud inquiry his team had ever undertaken.

Two of its members, Detective Constables Mick O'Keeffe and Kevin Baylis, had had the difficult job of locating and identifying valuable paintings, objets d'art and furniture that had been sold off via auction houses. Since both were untrained in this field they took advice from a local antiques expert, Philip Baldwin. With his help, and armed with a number of books on antiques, they began their long, slow, painstaking search for Lady Illingworth's possessions.

Giltspurs provided them with a 200-page inventory of the items she had stored with them. Lady Illingworth's former staff furnished further details. According to O'Keeffe, butlers, chauffeurs, domestic staff, anyone who might have had memories of the furnishings of 44 Grosvenor Square, were traced and then quizzed over the contents of the house. They were helped by the discovery that *Country Life* magazine had featured the house in a 1961 issue, with a prolific spread of photographs of the most valuable items. Then, as Baylis recalled in an interview with the *Hereford Times*, 'what the butler saw' provided a vital clue. In this case the butler concerned was an aging, retired member of the Illingworth staff. 'We were showing him around the items stored at Docklow and, out of the blue, he said "Hello, Julie – haven't seen you for a while" to a marble statue of a nude woman that once stood at the foot of the stairs in the Grosvenor Square house. He told us that each morning Sir Albert would come down the stairs, slap the statue on the backside and say "Mornin' Julie". It was one of our first sure identifications.'

After London, the inquiry moved to salerooms in Bath, Leominster and Jersey, where items were identified from pictures in several sales catalogues. One hidden haul, including 194 solid silver plates, was eventually traced to the barn that Marcus had rented at Wickton Court, near Docklow. These investigations took the police over six months. The frequency with which the jury was asked to check an item in one of the blue, black, yellow, green or red box files containing photographs and illustrated material became a feature of the trial. No wonder they had to make so many notes. One of the women sitting on the front bench was observed to fill notebook after notebook – as many as the journalists covering the trial and the judge hearing it.

A surprising feature was the extent of legal aid in the case. The general rule of thumb is that nobody with assets worth more than £3000 receives legal aid. Since this caveat covered all four defendants, all were eligible for legal aid. Any existing monies had been legally frozen as soon as they were charged. So interesting was the case that barristers formidable both in reputation and for the fees they normally commanded were lining up to be engaged. 'Think in terms of telephone numbers and you get an idea of what the combined fees might be in this case,' said a court-hardened reporter. It was a popular game to speculate on how much the entire murder and fraud cases cost the state and therefore the taxpayer – certainly more than the amount by which Lady Illingworth was defrauded, was the general verdict. Justice is a costly business.

Leading for the Baron was Richard du Cann, QC, past chairman of the Bar Association and a participant in the famous obscenity case concerning the publication of D. H. Lawrence's *Lady Chatterley's Lover*. Appearing for Sophia was Richard Wakerly, QC, a notable barrister in the Midlands, as was Conrad Seagrott, QC, who represented Marcus. Stephen Coward, QC, made a late appearance on behalf of the Baroness. The prosecution was in the long, bony hands of the cadaverous Timothy Barnes, QC. Two years earlier he had acted in a black magic murder case heard at Shrewsbury. Never again would he get a case like this he told one journalist, and revealed that his small son had given him a lucky nine of spades playing card which he always carried with him. He had a way of dotting his i's and crossing his t's orally when addressing the jury that much infuriated the defendants. But then, in the light of his success, it would, wouldn't it?

Contrasted with Worcester's semi-stately old pile, Birmingham's new Queen Elizabeth II Building looks more like an hotel or airport than a dignified place for the administration of Her Majesty's laws. Inside, the atmosphere is even more that of an airport lounge or upmarket health club – all potted plants set in stone beds round a central atrium. It is for some the worst kind of modern architecture – tasteless, remote, its integral lack of design masked by what is called in the trade 'architectural ivy'. The lighting is discreet, with plenty of curved sofas set in curved bays for private conversations. There is a closed-circuit television surveillance system and a refectory with a separate glass-walled area for barristers and solicitors. At the main entrance visitors split into two queues for the rigorous security

171

check of themselves and their hand luggage normally endured at airports.

Confusion reigned as the trial started – to the onlookers, anyway. It was *Hamlet* without the Ghost. Where was Susan de Stempel? Although referred to in a semi-abstract way as the 'alleged ringleader', she was conspicuous by her absence. Indeed, for almost the entire nine-week period in court 12, Susan de Stempel did not appear in the dock alongside her second husband, Michael, or her two children, Marcus and Sophia. And never was a ghost felt more strongly as the case against the other three was laid out.

The reason was a purely technical one: because she had already pleaded Guilty to five charges of theft and two of forgery, there was no requirement for her to be in court. Moreover, reference to her guilt might conceivably prejudice the jury against the defendants, or so it was argued in the early stages of the trial. This was later withdrawn as on the tenth day Richard du Cann, on behalf of the Baron, told the jury that evidence would be put before it 'establishing beyond doubt' that the Baroness stole money, silver, jewellery, share certificates and furniture from Lady Illingworth. Du Cann also revealed that the Baroness had forged Lady Illingworth's will and the warrants to obtain the release of property and documents from the National Westminster Bank in Kensington. Judge Richard Curtis, QC, Recorder for Birmingham, explained to the jury, 'You may have asked yourself why on earth Susan de Stempel was not in the dock – you now know.'

Three days previously, on 5 March, he had addressed the jury on the subject of the murder of Simon Dale. This had inadvertently been revealed the previous Friday, 2 March by William Wilberforce, son of Susan's brother John, while testifying to Lady Illingworth's generosity. 'In the course of his evidence,' said Judge Curtis, a pale-faced man with a suitably noncommittal expression that hung firmly between two rather protuberant ears, 'and I stress, not in answer to any question put by counsel, William Wilberforce made reference to the murder of Simon Dale. No previous reference has been made to the murder for the simple reason that it has got absolutely nothing to do with the case you and I are trying. Susan Wilberforce, or Susan de Stempel, as we know her, was arrested for that offence and stood trial on her own at Worcester Assizes.' He told them in no uncertain terms that she had been acquitted and that they must concentrate on the case before them.

Although both the murder and plea of Guilty had nothing to do with the trial of the defendants, their admission in court at least

172

helped to clear away some of the undergrowth in such a complicated story. In fact, Judge Curtis made a point of noting down a chronology of events to help the jury when the time came for them to retire and consider their verdicts.

And so in a modern courtroom, with four lines of lawyers taking up the main space in the centre, with the dock almost touching some of the seats in the public area, and with the Baron standing slightly away and with his back half-turned to Sophia and Marcus Wilberforce, Timothy Barnes got to his feet, stretched to his full length, looked at the jury and said in a voice that carried through the court: 'The case for the Crown is that Susan Wilberforce, her two children Marcus and Sophia, and Michael de Stempel stole Lady Illingworth's property on a massive scale and on a continual basis, from the moment she arrived in Docklow, in February 1984. They stole her money, stocks and shares, jewellery, valuable paintings and objets d'art. Everything that they could lay their hands on was taken and stolen. The case for the Crown is that Lady Illingworth knew nothing of what was going on.' They were, he added, 'virtually complete strangers' to Lady Illingworth before she was brought in a state of senility to Docklow.

It has to be admitted that much of the evidence that followed over the next nine weeks was dreary stuff – necessary, of course and a tribute to the exhaustive investigation by the West Mercia Fraud Squad – but to onlookers minute details of this bank account and that bank account quickly became repetitious, abstract stuff compared with the vivid detail of the murder trial. But there were odd moments of drama and colour, even vitality, when human beings spoke of Lady Illingworth as opposed to the necessary but dull cash dispenser accounts.

On the third day John Wilberforce, the diplomat said by friends to have retired early due to the scandal of his sister's behaviour, was called. He was a handsome man, tall, slim, dressed in a well-cut grey flannel suit. But through the reserve and poise of the practised diplomat, embarrassment spoke. It was obvious that he hated revealing what, under oath, he had to reveal: that in November 1983, when he had last seen Lady Illingworth while on a flying visit from Cyprus, she had appeared 'very senile'; that, knowing her previous wealth, he had been very surprised at the paucity of his aunt's will, and that, in his view, she would have been perfectly looked after by Kathy Whelan at York House. Any extra help could well have been paid for out of the large annual income she enjoyed. He had not been informed by his sister of Lady Illingworth's move to Docklow or her removal to Langford House. All in all, he painted a picture of a family split down the centre, with little rapport between brother and sister.

During his evidence he was closely watched by Sophia, wearing a dark sweater and a high-necked blouse similar to her mother's outfits, Marcus, in one of his two suits (grey), striped shirt and red paisley tie, and the Baron, dressed in his seedy best of grey pin-striped suit with a pale double-cuffed (naturally) shirt and regimental tie. As on many an occasion the afternoon found him looking half asleep with eyelids drooping, head on one side. In fairness, the fact that every day he was forced to take an early train from London to be there in time for the court to rise may have made him genuinely tired – although he was heard to bleat one day that the waiters had 'kept his luncheon wine waiting an unreasonable time'. He did not make notes, confident in the prowess of his counsel, Richard du Cann, but the two young adults, Marcus and Sophia, were frequently as busy as examinees (which they sometimes resembled), heads poised over notepads, pens busy.

The next family member to appear in court was the elderly but very spry figure of Lord Wilberforce, cousin to Lady Illingworth, who had also been left money in the forged will. Thin as a bird, and just as alert, he told the court how the Illingworths had entertained 'with affection and generosity'. Referring to the late Lord Illingworth, he described him as a rich man, a typical Yorkshire businessman. No, he had not expected to inherit any money, but he too had been surprised at the inability of Lady Illingworth's estate to honour her bequests. 'I was frankly very shocked and distressed,' he said on receiving the letter from Susan which had stated that her aunt had no wish to be buried alongside her husband. Following him on the witness stand was his wife, a comfortable, cheerful, vivacious woman, who spoke tenderly of Lady Illingworth and of her own shame at not having kept a closer eye on her. 'It was always a labour of love to go and see her at York House,' she added.

Neither she nor Lord Wilberforce looked in Sophia and Marcus's direction, and the two young Wilberforces retained the expression of impassive reserve that they carried throughout most of the trial. Sometimes, though, the strain would show through and their faces would look too bony and thin for their years. At times they gave the impression of hiding behind the bones of their faces, determined that the world should not see any emotions they might have. On one occasion Sophia spilt some water and they mopped it up together, smiling like little children. They had a curiously remote air, ageless, even sexless, as they sat day after day listening to the history of the woman they called Aunt Puss.

Unlike Sophia, who had found her bossy and domineering, Lady Wilberforce spoke affectionately of Kathy Whelan, describing her as both 'a friend and a help'. According to her, not only was Lady Illingworth well looked after, but she had the best room in the large mansion block flat. Kathy was a woman of 'great dignity and intelligence' who was, she repeated, a friend but not bossy – 'she was respectful'. Through her the court learned that Lady Illingworth loved shopping, visiting local restaurants and feeding the pigeons in Kensington Gardens; as in earlier years, she had loved party-going and party-giving. The court heard of the old hedonistic days, the trips to Ascot and Windsor, the holidays in Monte Carlo and Switzerland, the embassy parties, the luxury hotels that made Claridges sound like their equivalent of 'the little bistro round the corner'. Unhappily for the defendants, whose plea was that their great-aunt was perfectly capable of making a new will, Lady Wilberforce led the many in whose opinion she was not.

From the bright Grosvenor Square days, the court turned now to Lady Illingworth's advancing years. Elizabeth Gregg-Smith, her part-time secretary, took her place on the stand. Taken on in 1981, she had walked into an unholy mess of old papers, bills and visiting cards. 'I threw hundreds of receipts and bills away and filed stock and share certificates,' she said. It was obvious that the old lady had liked this new and bustling charge of energy that had now entered her life, for, far from treating her as strictly an employee, Lady Illingworth would often voyage out with her into the hustle and bustle of Kensington High Street, sometimes for lunch, or for a coffee at Barkers, and sometimes for a walk in Kensington Gardens. Never mind the paperwork – off they would go arm in arm for an outing. If Susan de Stempel was one ghost in court, her much-loved aunt was an equally powerful second apparition.

The sad days of her old age, however, became increasingly apparent as the ex-secretary recounted how her employer had started to wear odd stockings and shabby coats. It was she who told the court of the finding of Lady Illingworth's favourite bag, containing £160 and a brooch, under the bed in Sophia's room. Sophia did not thank her for that detail, as was evident in the slight tightening and distancing of her face while it was recounted.

But the saddest recollection of all came from the social worker Monica Wilberforce-Makra, whose parents actually owned the York House apartment which had been leased to 'cousin Irene' – Lady

Illingworth's equally aged companion. It was she who recounted the terrible loss of dignity when, walking past a lavatory in the flat, she had observed Lady Illingworth sitting on the seat 'with her pants round her ankles' and the door open for anyone to see. When questioned as to whether the two old ladies got along, she said cheerfully, 'They used to scrap in a childish way but they got on well together.' Her evidence was to offer no support to the defence's case.

Gradually, as the days went along, the court and the long carpeted corridors leading from it became a tiny, enclosed world. Witnesses who had been called for such and such a day sat on the curved sofas near the door to court 12. Barristers flapped to and fro, gowns trailing, the police stood stolid yet alert, while the key people – Michael de Stempel, Marcus and Sophia Wilberforce – chatted with friends, relatives, even journalists.

The Baron was always asking everybody, journalists included, how the previous day had gone, and remained eternally optimistic that the whole farce would end so that he could get back to the real world of London. Birmingham, he said (and many would agree), was a terrible place that was only suitable to get drunk in. But he, too, appeared to enjoy the coverage in the press. 'Good show in the qualities,' he would say. Nor did he seem in the slightest discountenanced when his old friend from Oxford, Lord Coleraine, gave evidence that he had originally been asked to draw up a new will, but that the matter had been dropped and that he had refused to telephone Kathy Whelan when the Baron had requested the release of all Lady Illingworth's papers from York House. He had, he said, recommended a stockbroker who might assist in the sale of 'substantial holdings', but he had not, as again and again he had been quoted as doing by the 'Catholic con man', suggested various bank officials who might help in the transfer of money and stock; nor had he given his consent for the Baron to use his name.

Lord Coleraine said that in about 1984 he had received instructions from Michael de Stempel with regard to the purchase of a house at Talybont-on-Usk on the Welsh borders which was being bought in the Baron's name; but again, like the house in Alderney, the matter was dropped. This was the result of a suggestion from Susan and Sophia that all three should live in the country together, but the Baron, it transpired, had got cold feet – and no wonder. Lord Coleraine did not say so, but several in the court felt that he took the Baron's waterfalls of emotion with a decided pinch of salt and some amusement; it was evident, for example, when he had been telephoned from Leominster jail in July 1985, by the Baron, 'in a frightful state', on the famous day when Susan de Stempel had attempted to have him committed.

One of the highlights of the trial was the arrival of Dr David Baxendale, the Home Office expert on handwriting. So bulky were his numerous accompanying files that the judge, noting his obvious difficulties in moving from one to another as the prosecution's questions continued (at one moment the whole lot looked about to cascade over the floor), offered him space on his table, which greatly assisted the poor man. Here was the stuff of the true thriller, as Dr Baxendale told how he had compared early examples of Lady Illingworth's signature with later ones, how he had also compared the typeface on three typewriters that were being used, and come to the conclusion that they were all the typewriters at Docklow, and that his conclusion was that the letters 'were not written by Lady Illingworth. They were written by somebody else who deliberately attempted to copy the design of the signature.' He was not sure about the first request for a cash card, which had been ordered less than a fortnight after Lady Illingworth arrived at Docklow, so he had given the defence the benefit of the doubt. But, one felt, he was speaking here as a very cautious expert. In private, he might have had different conclusions.

Eventually, the court arrived at the fateful forged will day. Father Dooley from Stonyhurst, the Catholic public school, was called. The public gallery was full. In loud, confident tones that frequently echoed the way in which he might have addressed the boys, he outlined Michael de Stempel's visit and his own subsequent stay at Docklow. He had no idea who the beneficiaries to the will were, he said, and when asked by the Baroness had dutifully signed his name on the bottom of each page. Importantly, he divulged that he had never witnessed a will before, and when asked if he had read the will he drew himself up slightly and said that he certainly had not.

Equally ignorant of the legal requirements of witnessing a will was Ann Devey-Smith, who for days previously had sat with her husband in the public section, listening to the evidence unroll about her erstwhile friend Susan de Stempel. Surprisingly – for she seemed a diffident woman outside the court – she was steadfast and remarkably calm when cross-examined by Richard du Cann on behalf of the Baron. When asked if she had had any suspicion about the will, she replied, 'I trusted her [Susan]. I did not think there was anything wrong or unusual about it. One doesn't suspect one's friends of doing something like this.' Unlike Father Dooley, who gave it as his opinion that the bottom of each page of the will was blank when he signed it, she believed that Lady Illingworth's signature was already on at least one page of the will. Referring to the old lady, she said, 'I did think she was vague and not with it, I don't think she knew what was going on.' She was amazed at the sheer opulence of Docklow, with its carpets and paintings. 'It was,' she said 'bulging with antiques.' And so was the barn at Wickton Court, which she had also been shown.

Although the financial details made tedious listening, they too had their highlights. On 13 March, the sixteenth day of the trial, a London solicitor, Michael Fenton, told the court that after Lady Illingworth's death in 1986 the executors of the 1984 (forged) will, the National Westminster Bank, were worried about the property not mentioned in it. In one reply the Baroness answered the bank's queries by saying that there had been little left of her aunt's possessions – her jewellery had been sold to pay off old gambling debts. The only reason, the Baroness explained, that she had left bequests of £60,000 to three people in the 1984 will was because 'My aunt lived in the hope of winning the pools.'

In all, six letters were written by the bank requesting information about Lady Illingworth's personal effects. Being in possession of an inventory from Giltspur Bullens which detailed a considerable amount of furniture, they were naturally curious. In October 1987 they received a reply from the Baroness which must go down in their own personal history as the most bizarre letter a bank could receive in the circumstances. It read (and one can almost see Susan de Stempel smiling as she wrote it), 'My first husband was found murdered recently and this has had a disruptive effect on our family.' Even Richard Sax, her long-suffering solicitor and the recipient of many eccentric missives, couldn't match a remark like that.

The Baron was the first of the three defendants to stand in the witness box. Someone, it seemed, had told him to end every sentence with the word 'sir', and this he did relentlessly – spitting it out with increasing venom when the going got tough for him under Timothy Barnes's keen cross-examination. He had peculiar but damaging remarks to make about his ex-wife. 'Susan liked cash,' he said. He had never been 'romantically linked with her' and their marriage was a 'technical one'. Before their marriage Susan had been in 'terrible financial straits. She and her first husband had been living on money left by her father. They were starving. They had no fire or heating and were five miles away from the nearest shop.'

Of Susan's relationship with Lady Illingworth he said, 'I would say that Susan treated her kindly but severely. I wouldn't say that she was a very loving person.' Twiddling the largest signet ring in the world, he got very testy when the prosecution taxed him on the dealings with Channel Island banks and with auction houses. He said he was just trying to put Lady Illingworth's affairs in order. As for Phillips and Jollys of Bath, he had never heard of them. At another point he burst out childishly: 'It wasn't *my* house, it wasn't *my* aunt.' In a similarly childish boast he attempted a long discourse on the grandeur of *his* grandmother's house that was so infinitely better than anything Lady Illingworth possessed. Why, she had a ring worth £75,000 alone, he said, and was prepared to go on until told, politely but firmly, simply to answer the questions.

As for the forged will, he maintained complete innocence, saying he was a mere 'messenger boy' in its creation. Asked about Susan's payments to him of £40,000 when she had been known to be as 'poor as a church mouse', he replied that he thought some trust funds had 'fallen in. I know some people who have been as poor as Susan and then suddenly become quite rich because of estate changes.' He wound up his evidence: 'I did not conspire with anybody over Lady Illingworth's affairs. I did not think the police were on to me because there was no reason why they should be on to me. I had been in Spain before my arrest and if I had these criminal intentions I would have just stayed out of the country.' And with that a tired old man stepped down from the witness box.

A friend of the Baron's, no doubt irritated by the man's pretensions, disclosed that there had been much amusement in certain London circles when it was learnt that the Baron had been arrested wearing silk pyjamas while staying with Jane Mackay who, furious with embarrassment, promptly 'hopped it abroad' until the case was over.

For all her young years and soft looks, Sophia Wilberforce conveyed an underlying toughness of character in the box. She was calmer than the Baron and as cool as her mother, whom many think she strongly resembles. In fact she has a distinctly different bone construction – rounder and less angular. Her mother, she said, had loved her Aunt Puss because she had been much more of a mother than her own. 'But my great-aunt was disappointed when my mother married. My father was not what was considered suitable.' The rift was healed, however, when she went to stay at York House in 1982. 'Aunt Puss and my mother seemed to be a team. My mother spent a great deal of time with her.' Asked if she knew anything about the forged will, she said she had been on holiday in Japan with her brother, Alexander, before it was signed and had no knowledge of it. 'I thought the police were mad, off their rockers. I was very angry when it was alleged that someone had forged the will. I was told by my mother that my great-aunt had made a will and that Father Dooley and Mrs Ann Devey-Smith were coming to the house to witness the will. I was told to exit myself and not clutter up the place.'

Richard Wakerly, her defending counsel, who much resembled a bewigged, begowned and bespectacled Mr Toad, with a tiresome habit of addressing the jury in a manner that suggested they might be slow-witted and needed much time to consider even the simplest of statements, asked her, 'Did you know that payments were being made into a bank account from the sales of furniture at auction houses?'

'No, I didn't,' replied Sophia. She said that she thought Aunt Puss had wanted her mother to have her possessions. She still thought that. She had never suspected her mother of behaving dishonestly. She thought that family silver brought from Lady Illingworth's London home had been sold to pay off a £14,000 tax bill owed by her great-aunt. That is what her mother had told her.

But Sophia lost her cool in a dramatic way when asked about police interviews. In fact she turned to face Detective Constable Robin Longmore, who was sitting near her, and accused him of a vicious style of interrogation. 'I think that DC Longmore was very vicious. He was very vicious,' she spat at him. 'When I was interviewed by the police all the accusations came thick and fast. It was difficult to think straight.' What she did not inform the jury was that during all the interviews (and this was true of all the defendants) her own solicitor had been present, and he had been at liberty to intercede if he felt the interviewing was improper.

All the children – including Alexander, Sebastian and Simon – have maintained that the police behaved abominably throughout both cases. However, no one outside the family, whom I questioned and who had been interviewed by the same investigating teams believed that the police had either been heavy-handed or had acted on the basis of prior conviction of guilt. Not one had found them so. Yet to this day all the Wilberforces think they have had a bad deal. Ask them if they think Lady Illingworth had a bad deal, and they are curiously silent.

By contrast with his sister, Marcus presented an angry, even insultingly off-hand manner in the box, totally unlike his normal persona. He admitted that he often had to remind Lady Illingworth where she was, telling her that she was staying in Herefordshire with her niece. 'I thought there quite a few occasions when she didn't know who your mother was,' suggested Timothy Barnes.

In an oddly snappy way Marcus replied, 'I am not a psychologist, but I think that at times my great-aunt was perfectly lucid.' He told the court that his mother had revealed to him what an unhappy marriage Lady Illingworth had had with her husband. There was a letter from Lady Illingworth's mother among the personal possessions that indicated she was unhappy about her daughter's marriage to a divorcee. Lord Illingworth was a womanizer, Susan de Stempel had told her son. But he hadn't read any other letters because 'it was none of my business'.

Conrad Seagrott, for the defence, asked his client, 'Did you know during that period of time that your mother was thieving your aunt's possessions and turning them into money?'

'No,' said Marcus.

'Would you have had anything to do with it if you had known?'

Again Marcus said, 'No.' But he agreed with Timothy Barnes that he had not told other members of the family of Lady Illingworth's whereabouts when she was moved to Langford House, and that she had never been invited back home to Docklow – 'not even for a cup of tea'. To that assertion Marcus replied that it had never occurred to him.

The prosecution was beginning to get under his skin, and it showed minutes later when Timothy Barnes put it to him: 'Is it not the truth that you wanted to get rid of Lady Illingworth?'

With anger Marcus replied, 'It is a despicable assertion.' It was a pompous way of talking, which was clearly meant to make him seem older and more confident in dealing with this line of attack, but it didn't work. When he replied 'So what' to other assertions, the court listened but it was doubtful if it was on his side.

Just before he stepped down, the judge leaned forward and asked him quietly if he had attended Lady Illingworth's funeral. He said he had, and the judge made yet another of his notes.

Finally, after what seemed an inordinate amount of time – nine weeks in all – the case reached its conclusion. Prosecution and defence had made their final speeches, which contained no surprises. Still Susan de Stempel had not made an appearance in court. Easter was on the horizon when the judge began his summing up. He told the jury they had to decide the true state of Lady Illingworth's health.

181

'Not just her physical health but also her mental health.' Resuming his address on Tuesday, after the Easter break, he told the jury to bear in mind the criminal offences of the 'missing lady' and the way she interacted with the defendants. 'You have to decide this case in so far as it may be affected by the ideas, actions and effect Susan Wilberforce had on other people in the light of the evidence. . . . You may put a tick against Susan Wilberforce's name, but the question is did Michael de Stempel or Miss Sophia Wilberforce or Mr Marcus Wilberforce know that this [forged will] was part of a dishonest enterprise to steal Lady Illingworth's property?'

On Wednesday, 18 April, the jury retired to consider their verdicts. Unknown to them, Susan de Stempel had been brought from Risley to Winson Green Prison pending sentence. The 'missing lady', the ghost, the Ice Queen was about to be seen in court. For the whole of Thursday the jury was out while the Baron, accompanied by his daughter Tatiana, chain-smoking and holding him closely and supportively by the arm, walked up and down, up and down the corridors of law. The Ice Queen sat alone in the dock, making notes on a large pad, while Timothy Barnes swiftly went through the Crown's case against her. Since she had already pleaded Guilty on several counts, the presence of the jury was unnecessary; but it was obligatory for the judge to hear the case in view of his sentencing.

At just before 5.30 there was a stir among the court officials: the jury had a verdict. The court swiftly took its various places, the jury filed in, the judge appeared through his own door and the court was 'upstanding' for him. Then the foreman of the jury revealed that they had but one verdict: they had not yet reached a unanimous finding on Marcus or Sophia. The Baron stood as he and the court heard him found guilty of conspiring to steal from Lady Illingworth. It was not the verdict he expected as his liver-spotted hands gripped the dock, and he bowed his head. More than ever he looked like a beaten old man in a frayed good suit. He was allowed further bail until the jury should settle their differences on the other defendants. To journalists he claimed he was innocent, saying: 'What can you expect of a working-class jury?' before his daughter hustled him away.

All day Friday the jury went on debating. 'The children', as they were still being referred to – despite their ages of twenty-eight and twenty-seven respectively – had a 'cordon sanitaire' around them made up of solicitors' assistants and friends. Once again the jury retired to an hotel for the night (another night of smoked salmon, was the joke amongst the cynical). Saturday morning arrived, and still no verdict. The judge ordered them back into court and

182

reminded them with infinite courtesy that he would accept a majority verdict, but that that must not hurry them.

The press were debating what would happen if they could not reach one – 'Not another retrial' was a common groan. In one of the alcoves, attended by a few friends, Alexander, Sebastian, Marcus, Sophia and Simon Wilberforce played word games and charades. There was a burst of laughter as the youngest and tallest, Simon, revealed that his word had been 'Porridge'. It was gallows humour without the gallows. The Baron, a sad, crestfallen man, walked apart, again supported by his daughter.

In mid-afternoon, just as a rather desperate boredom was making itself felt, there was that rustle of excitement – 'We have a verdict' – and everyone crowded back into court. This time all four stood together in the dock – Susan de Stempel next to her ex-husband Michael, then Sophia, then Marcus. The jury foreman recorded the verdicts: Sophia Wilberforce found guilty on an 11–1 majority; Marcus Wilberforce found guilty on a 10–2 majority. An extraordinary example of the Ice Queen's coldness was about to reveal itself. . . .

Coming first of all to Marcus, the judge told him sternly that, while he recognized that the young man had been 'under the malign influence of his mother', yet he had played an important role in the conspiracy; he was, therefore, sentencing him to eighteen months. He next moved to Sophia, and was about to address her when Marcus suddenly and most dramatically collapsed on the bench behind him. Consternation in court – consternation, that is, from all but his mother, who, though less than six feet away, remained standing still and looking straight in front of her, arms folded across her chest. Would that the nanny or nun who had trained her in self-control could have seen her now, in her finest hour!

The judge ruled that Marcus be taken away, and continued his sentencing. To Sophia he said that he was certain she had helped to plan and execute the fraud for which she had been rewarded by holidays and a flat in Spain. He sentenced her to thirty months. A true daughter of her mother, she betrayed no obvious emotion.

'Stripped of your airs and flowery language, you are undoubtedly a con man,' Judge Curtis said to the Baron. Michael de Stempel was sentenced to four years.

Finally he turned to the mastermind, Susan de Stempel, who stood before him in a pose of studied, heightened indifference. Looking sternly at her, the judge said, 'Your treatment of Lady Illingworth was absolutely barbarous. . . . Having taken all her money you cast her off. . . . She went to an old people's home, but you allowed her to go there as a pauper. It was a truly wicked thing to do.' What had also concerned the judge was the way 'the chief architect', as he called her, had involved her children. It was a heartless and wicked plot. He sentenced Susan de Stempel to seven years' imprisonment.

At 3.30 on Saturday, 21 April 1990, approximately five and a half years since she had abandoned Lady Illingworth to the care of Hereford General Hospital, Susan de Stempel paid the official price for cheating Aunt Puss. In the public gallery Sebastian Wilberforce wept as his family was taken away.

12

U·N·F·I·N·I·S·H·E·D B·U·S·I·N·E·S·S

I N the long run-up to the trials the police have probably had more
to do with Susan de Stempel than anyone apart from her
children. How did she strike them? Chief Superintendent David
Cole, head of the whole twin investigation, said of her in a television
programme: 'She is an extremely intelligent and articulate person.
She's also, no doubt, a very cunning person and she very cleverly
manipulated affairs to her own ends. She is also quite a domineering
person and she was able to, I think, manipulate those closest to her
to become her lieutenants in the whole affair. . . . She can be witty
and charming and considerate and on the other hand there's another
side to her – she can be patronizing, dismissive, haughty and she can
show an unpleasant side to her character – there's no doubt about
that.'

Solicitors working for her have found her 'very, very amusing'. But
the most common word to describe her is 'extraordinary'. David
Cole found her the most extraordinary woman he'd met, as did Mike
Cowley of the Fraud Squad, but Cowley added that what she did
was 'totally and utterly ruthless and very, very evil'. Even the
barristers concerned, much accustomed as they are to 'extraordinary'
clients, voted her *the* most extraordinary woman they had encountered. A minor court official who had watched her carefully gave
another viewpoint: 'She is not sad,' he said, 'she is not mad, she is
that rare being – a *bad* person.' Ann Devey-Smith, who had been so
exploited by her friend over the years, commented sadly, 'She is not
the person I used to know. She has become devious and cunning.'

What made her do it? And what made her leave her aunt in such
callous fashion after she had gained much of her fortune? Timothy
Barnes, QC, in his closing address for the prosecution, maintained
that Susan and her immediate family bitterly resented the other half
of the Wilberforce family who lived at Markington Hall. He even

185

conjectured whether or not the fraud might have stemmed from a desire for revenge. Certainly, Sophia and her mother did resent John's fortune and success in the world. During one of the visits I made to Susan in custody I remember her saying that her brother had done nothing for her, and that he only went to see her once in Pucklechurch because he happened to be in that area visiting his son's wife's family and did not want to attend some function with them.

The woman who employed Sophia at Oxford received the impression that she, too, resented her Markington cousins. Susan had fed her children with the idea that 'John's lot' had already benefited to a large extent from Lady Illingworth's generosity. It is easy to see her brooding over her conspicuous lack of similar fortune. Wasn't it her turn? Even when her mother died, it was rich brother John who had inherited the house. To know that he was to inherit even more on the death of her aunt must have been a bitter pill to swallow.

There she was, divorced from a shambling, blind architect; owner of a crumbling house that, though valuable, needed much spent on it and, moreover, was taking her considerable time and money to repossess; and in love with a man whom she knew she could not tie down satisfactorily without the wherewithal to support them both. She had never been trained to work. Furthermore, why should she? Did John's wife, the hated Laura, work? Of course not. If an American like Laura could play lady of the manor why not Susan, who had been born to it? How much she resented having to borrow money from her friends. Kind they might be – but the humiliation of having to ask them! The shame of having to exist on hand-outs from Aunt Marion, the knowledge that all the family knew of her distress but had turned their backs on her.

What a rich field of resentment all this was. How much she must have brooded on it in the solitary hours she had inflicted on herself. How much she must, with all nanny's training, have longed to cast off the mould of indifference, of stoicism. And who was Lady Illingworth to cheat anyway? She was gaga, didn't know where she was or who she was with. Would it hurt taking the money from her? She wouldn't even know, for heaven's sake. Wouldn't it have been Susan's money anyway – in a manner of thinking – if the family monies had been fairly divided?

Once the plan was launched, once Lady Illingworth had arrived at Docklow and that first request for a cash card had been posted, there was no going back. To quote from *Julius Caesar*: 'On such a full sea are we now afloat and we must take the current when it serves or lose our ventures.' They had had enough of the 'shallows and miseries'. All of this is, I maintain, highly understandable.

Why then the squalor of Lady Illingworth's last two years, the pretence that she was a pauper, the cheap cremation, even the non-payment of the £389 cremation bill? Could not Susan de Stempel have allowed her aunt a dignified end? Could she not, out of the old lady's large annual income, have paid for a luxurious nursing home in the country? Very expensive, admittedly, but surely possible without leaving themselves short. Ah, but there was a chance that, if Lady Illingworth had been allowed into the sort of home where old aristocrats spend their last days, someone might have found out. A family visiting another inmate might have passed on the word to an Illingworth or to another branch of the Wilberforce family. The world is a small one – even smaller if restricted to *Burke's Landed Gentry*. Better by far the anonymity of a state home. Nobody they knew went to such places. And the cheap cremation afterwards? For the same reason – the anonymity.

But there may also be a psychological reason for Susan's behaviour. Might not the knowledge of how much she had cheated her aunt have caused Susan de Stempel deliberately to avoid thinking of it, to stow it away at the back of her mind and refuse to admit it? In which case, the less she had to do with the old lady the better. The state would do these things, not Susan de Stempel. Is it not part of the schizoid tendencies so evident in her letters to Lord Wilberforce and others, written after Lady Illingworth's death?

What is so surprising is that no psychiatrist has been called in to compile a report on Susan de Stempel, and none of her misfortunes were quoted by her counsel, Stephen Coward, QC, when he asked for mitigating circumstances to be taken into account before she was sentenced. He might not have been aided by her snobbish indifference to him – at one stage she told me he used the word 'Pardon' to her and said he was 'Pleased to meet you' – both solecisms unforgivable in her eyes. In a decidedly lame speech, however, he merely drew attention to the desperate financial state she would be in when released from prison.

And desperate all four could well be, for the Illingworth case has not ended yet. On 12 May 1990 writs were served on them, as well as on Simon Wilberforce, on behalf of the administrators of Lady Illingworth's estate, asking for the return of 'chattels and property converted by the family, and exemplary and aggravated damages for

187

wrongful interference'. It is a civil case that will take months of preparation and is not likely to be heard until well into 1991 or even 1992. It is being contested by the Baroness, her former husband and the three children. But what makes it even more intriguing is that in August 1990, three months after the original writ, the solicitors for the administrators were granted an injunction in the High Court to freeze further assets of the five defendants to the value of £12 million; this is part of the same action to recover further property that they claim is unaccounted for. Ten million pounds of that claim is the value of gold bars allegedly missing from the estate. None of this was mentioned in the fraud trial. Even now Theodore Goddard, the solicitors concerned, will not make any statements about the gold but, it is argued, they would have to have more knowledge than just rumour to proceed with such a claim. Not that it is a claim that worried Simon Wilberforce. 'Oh that old myth,' he laughed over the telephone one day while I was writing this book. 'The police have gone into that and there isn't a shred of evidence about it. It's just one of those stories that gets about.'

So now there is the mystery of the missing gold bars. Where did they come from? Where were they hidden? Were they in the Kensington bank vaults or, as one story goes, hidden in a crate under a pile of papers? And, if so, where are they now? The story of the defrauding of Lady Illingworth continues. . . .

In the same week that the writs were issued, a memorial service for Simon Dale was held on 19 May at the little church of St Edward, sited so sweetly in the fields near Hopton Castle. Veronica Bowater who, with her husband Geoffrey, had been such a trusty friend of Simon Dale and his two sons, Sebastian and Marcus, said of the event: 'We thought we must get all the things out of the way – there was the murder trial first and then the [fraud] trial of his ex-wife – and we all felt, all Simon's friends round here, that when everything was over and we couldn't prejudice anything or upset anything we would have this service to remember him. We felt we wanted to say goodbye properly to Simon, to wave him away. We felt much better afterwards for having done so.'

The service was attended by Sebastian and Alexander Wilberforce. According to a report in the *Shropshire Star*, Sebastian gave a moving address in which he stated that, nearly three years after his father's murder, time had not yet healed family wounds. His brother Marcus and sister Sophia were unable to attend, he added, but wished to. Significantly, he did not mention his mother; nor was she mentioned

188

during the service, which was attended by some fifty people. 'With tears in his eyes', went the report, 'he thanked all those who had offered the family support during the traumas that followed his father's killing.'

What the report did not add was that a small tea party was held afterwards at Heath House, to which a number of local people who had given much help to his father were not invited. Sebastian's thanks, it seemed, went no further than the pulpit from which he spoke. And, despite the local wish that the money from the collection plate should go to the Royal National Institute for the Blind, Sebastian decided arbitrarily that it should go to a new charity, of which he was a member, called Victims of Crime. The disaffection for this act still rumbles on.

Outside the church, the new leader of the 'Docklow faction' (as Judge Curtis referred to them) said to the television cameras, 'My father's killer has not been found, and until he is we still have that hanging over us. It is very sad indeed that the police concentrated so much on our mother. She was the obvious choice because so many murders are domestic events, but they went down a blind alley and they should have known better.'

Brother Alexander added in that peculiar, almost foetal voice of his, 'He loved us but still, as Sebastian says, somebody out there is walking around free. . . .'

Why, I ask myself, do I retrace my steps to Heath House so often? Why do I keep coming back? The reasons are not always rational. As the main character in Daphne du Maurier's *Rebecca* is fascinated by the house called Manderley, so too do I find myself fascinated by Heath House. Granted, there have been two legitimate reasons when I have called to see Marcus and Sophia. The atmosphere was as calm and relaxed as it could be in the circumstances – the children bright and optimistic, laughing a little too readily, a little too rapidly for complete ease. Other times I have come alone just to absorb the atmosphere – hoping to extract some clue to the events of that September evening by the very fact of sharing for a time the same surroundings.

Does this house, beautiful as it is, *invite* dark and dreadful crimes? For, strangely, the murder of Simon Dale is not the only blood to have been shed within the orbit of Heath House. On the evening of 9 November 1968 the local doctor, Alan Beach, was found in a white three-litre Austin car dying of gunshot wounds. The car was parked at the opening of the drive to Heath House. The murderer was the village hairdresser, Arthur Prime. Deranged with grief over the death of his wife, he blamed the doctor for it and sought revenge. 'An eye for an eye, a tooth for a tooth, a life for a life' he is claimed to have said before emptying the contents of a 12-bore from a distance of three feet into the unfortunate man's chest. Arthur Prime was found guilty and sentenced to life imprisonment; subsequently he was proved insane and moved to a psychiatric unit.

His other odd claim to fame is that he is currently in the *Guinness Book of Records* for gaining the largest number of O-levels ever achieved – over thirty. He has now been released and is living in another part of the country. The police questioned him, but could find no link to Dale's murder. But that crime, sad and pathetic as it was, cannot rival the grim brutality of the murder that was committed here more recently.

So two mysteries still occupy the Wilberforce family. The missing gold bars, supposing they exist, and far greater – in human terms – the identity of the murderer of Simon Dale. Who would have wanted to kill him? There was no forced entry, there was no robbery – £25 in cash was found in his wallet. He still wore his gold cufflinks. The case, the police state, is still open. . . .

Index